D1179425

Romantic Genius and the Literary Magazine

In early nineteenth-century Britain, there was unprecedented interest in the subject of genius, as well as in the personalities and private lives of creative artists. This was also a period in which literary magazines were powerful arbiters of taste, helping to shape the ideological consciousness of their middle-class readers. *Romantic Genius and the Literary Magazine* considers how these magazines debated the nature of genius and how and why they constructed particular creative artists as geniuses.

Romantic writers often imagined genius to be a force that transcended the realms of politics and economics. David Higgins, however, shows in this text that representations of genius played an important role in ideological and commercial conflicts within early nineteenth-century literary culture. *Romantic Genius and the Literary Magazine* also bridges the gap between Romantic and Victorian literary history by considering the ways in which Romanticism was understood and sometimes challenged by writers in the 1830s. It not only discusses a wide range of canonical and non-canonical authors, but also examines the various structures in which these authors had to operate, making it an interesting and important book for anyone working on Romantic literature.

David Higgins is a Lecturer in English at the University of Chester, and has published articles on Wordsworth, Hazlitt and nineteenth-century constructions of race.

Routledge Studies in Romanticism

Romantic Genius and the Literary Magazine

Biography, celebrity and politics

David Higgins

Routledge
Taylor & Francis Group

LONDON AND NEW YORK

First published 2005
by Routledge
2 Park Square, Milton Park, Abingdon, Oxon, OX14 4RN

Simultaneously published in the USA and Canada
by Routledge
270 Madison Ave, New York NY 10016

Routledge is an imprint of the Taylor & Francis Group

Transferred to Digital Printing 2007

Typeset in Garamond by
Newgen Imaging Systems (P) Ltd, Chennai, India

British Library Cataloguing in Publication Data
A catalogue record for this book is available
from the British Library

Library of Congress Cataloging in Publication Data
A catalog record for this book has been requested

ISBN 0–415–33556–6

To my family: Alex, Deidre, John and Julia

Contents

Plates

Acknowledgements

This book is based on a doctoral thesis written at the University of York and I owe much to my two supervisors. It would never have been conceived or produced without the ideas, inspiration and guidance provided by Gregory Dart. I am also very grateful to John Barrell for much good advice and for commenting on my work with exemplary care and insight. Thanks also to Kiera Chapman, Jack Donovan, Robert Lapp, David Latané, Nigel Leask, Robert Morrison, Becky Edwards Newman, Ve-Yin Tee, Kim Wheatley and Simon White. I am particularly indebted to Kiera Chapman: not only has she given me sterling intellectual and moral support over the last few years but she also cheerfully took on the onerous task of reading the final draft of this book. The three anonymous readers for Routledge all produced acute and useful reports and I have done my best to respond to their suggestions and criticisms. The editorial staff at Routledge – Amrit Bangard, Katherine Carpenter, Terry Clague and Joe Whiting – have been notably efficient and helpful. Responsibility for any errors or omissions remains, of course, my own.

I gratefully acknowledge the financial support of the Arts and Humanities Research Board, which funded three years of doctoral study. I have received invaluable assistance from the staff of the British Library, the Brotherton Library at the University of Leeds, the University of Cambridge Library, the J. B. Morrell Library at the University of York and the National Art Library. I would also like to thank Derek Alsop for arranging that the Department of English at University College Chester would pay for the cost of the illustrations.

My family, especially my mother, have been very supportive throughout, as have a number of friends, most notably Laurence Kiddle, Bronwen Richards and Nic Smith. The late John Wynne Williams gave me, as with so many others, cheery encouragement when it was much needed. Special thanks must go to Neil Ehrenzweig and Clare Farnell for their kind hospitality during my research trips to London.

An earlier version of Chapter 4 was published as '*Blackwood's Edinburgh Magazine* and the Construction of Wordsworth's Genius', *Prose Studies* 25, 2002, pp. 122–36 (published by Frank Cass). This number of *Prose Studies*, edited by Kim Wheatley, was also published as *Romantic Periodicals and Print Culture*, London: Frank Cass, 2003. A few paragraphs of Chapter 6 appear in my article 'Art, Genius, and Racial Theory in the Early Nineteenth Century: Benjamin Robert Haydon', *History Workshop Journal* 58, 2004, pp. 17–40 (published by Oxford University Press).

Abbreviations

AFA	*Annals of the Fine Arts*
BEM	*Blackwood's Edinburgh Magazine*
BLM	Alvin Sullivan (ed.) *British Literary Magazines: The Romantic Age, 1789–1836*, Westport, CT: Greenwood Press, 1983
CWH	William Hazlitt, *The Complete Works of William Hazlitt*, ed. P. P. Howe, 21 vols, London: J. M. Dent & Sons, 1930–3
CWS	Percy Bysshe Shelley, *The Complete Works of Percy Bysshe Shelley*, ed. Roger Ingpen and Walter E. Peck, 10 vols, London: Ernest Benn, 1965
ER	*Edinburgh Review*
FM	*Fraser's Magazine*
LM	*London Magazine (Baldwin's)*
MR	*Monthly Repository*
NMM	*New Monthly Magazine*
OED	*Oxford English Dictionary*
PL	John Milton, *Paradise Lost*, ed. Christopher Ricks, Harmondsworth: Penguin, 1989
PWW	William Wordsworth, *Prose Works*, ed. W. J. B. Owen and Jane Worthington Smyser, 3 vols, Oxford: Clarendon Press, 1974
QR	*Quarterly Review*
SMA	*The Spirit and Manners of the Age*
TEM	*Tait's Edinburgh Magazine*
VPR	*Victorian Periodicals Review*
WDQ	Thomas De Quincey, *The Works of Thomas De Quincey*, ed. Grevel Lindop, 21 vols, London: Pickering & Chatto, 2000–3
WTC	Thomas Carlyle, *The Works of Thomas Carlyle*, ed. H. D. Traill, 30 vols, London: Chapman and Hall, 1896–9

Introduction

In early nineteenth-century Britain, there was an unprecedented interest among writers and readers in the subject of genius and, in particular, in examining and discussing the personal characteristics and life histories of 'great men'. This was also a period in which magazines played a uniquely important role within literary culture, acting not only as powerful arbiters of taste but also as coherent entities that helped to shape the ideological consciousness of their middle-class readers. This book is about the relationship between these two phenomena. It considers how debates about the nature of genius, and the relationship between genius and society, were conducted in Romantic-period magazines, and how and why they constructed particular individuals (mainly, but not exclusively, poets) as geniuses.

It has long been recognized that an emphasis on originality and individuality in artistic creation was an important aspect of Romanticism and in recent years there has been increasing scholarly interest in relating this emphasis to cultural change in the period from 1750 to 1850. However, little attention has been paid to writing in the periodical press, which had far more influence on how genius was understood in the early nineteenth century than the types of works – philosophical treatises, or passages in poets' letters – to which literary historians and critics have usually turned, in their attempts to comprehend the contemporary meanings of the term. This, therefore, is the first study to consider the role of literary magazines in the Romantic construction of genius, and the importance of representations of genius in terms of the self-fashioning of those magazines. These representations were crucial for the formulation and dissemination of 'Romantic ideology' but they were riven by tension and contradiction. Although genius was often put forward as a force that transcended the political and commercial conflicts of the early nineteenth-century public sphere, representations of it actually served to articulate the ideological positions of particular journals and therefore helped to distinguish them from their competitors. Furthermore, the prestigious forms of literature associated with genius – poetry and drama – were often imagined, sometimes by journalists themselves, to be under threat from more populist genres such as periodical writing. Magazine accounts of genius, then, were caught between the supposedly debased literary culture in which they were produced and read, and the supposedly pure realm of autonomous creativity that they often sought to describe.

The principal modern usage of the word 'genius' – 'native intellectual power of an exalted type . . . instinctive and extraordinary capacity for imaginative creation, original thought, invention, or discovery' (*Oxford English Dictionary* (*OED*)) – emerged at the beginning of the eighteenth century and had become widespread a hundred years later. Previously, the term had been used mainly in its Latin sense, meaning an attendant spirit attached to a person or place, or to refer to a person's characteristic disposition or inclination. The new meaning of 'genius' arose as the result of developments in European thought, which saw an increasing emphasis on the creative powers of the human mind and made individual expression and originality the *sine qua non* of important art and literature.[1] During the second half of the eighteenth century, a number of treatises on the subject were published in Britain, including William Duff's *Essay on Original Genius* (1767), Alexander Gerard's *Essay on Genius* (1774), William Sharpe's *Dissertation on Genius* (1755) and Edward Young's *Conjectures on Original Composition* (1759). These works, especially Young's *Conjectures*, were influential in Germany, and it was there – during the *Sturm und Drang* period (1760s and 1770s) – that writing on the subject appeared in its most extreme form.[2] Authors like Hamann and Lavater exalted the creative genius as an unstoppable, godlike force: 'Genius is not learned, not acquired...It is our unique property, inimitable, divine, it is inspired...Gods in human form! Creators! Destroyers!'[3] This level of hyperbole is exceptional, but by the end of the eighteenth century, genius had become a key term across Europe in aesthetics, literary criticism, and accounts of subjectivity. In particular, its valorization of originality and self-expression – and its concomitant downgrading of the virtues of emulation and education – gave writers the courage to experiment with literary form and content. Genius was one of the concepts fuelling the cultural revolution that we now call Romanticism.

Zeynep Tenger and Paul Trolander have suggested that eighteenth-century British theories of genius were not primarily aesthetic, but constituted a discourse which 'argued that the productive forces of society were, or ought to be, organized according to the distribution of natural or acquired intellectual powers'. This discourse existed in competition with the emerging discourse of political economy, but the latter's success led to the marginalization of the discourse of genius; in the Romantic period, they claim, it became mainly limited to discussions of art and literature.[4] It is certainly the case that in early nineteenth-century writing, the term 'genius' often means, in effect, 'great creative artist(s)' or, even more specifically, 'great poet(s)'. This book focuses mainly on representations of literary genius as, unsurprisingly, this is what most interested Romantic journalists and critics.[5] I do, however, consider the career of the historical painter Benjamin Robert Haydon in my final chapter, as he was deeply involved with the magazine culture of the period.

If discussions of genius may, from a modern perspective, seem to have become marginalized, the Romantic creative artist was at the same time granted a great deal more cultural authority than had been the case during the eighteenth century. One reason for this was the increasing influence of German Idealism, which began to filter into Britain after 1800 through various authors, most notably Samuel Taylor Coleridge, but also periodical writers such as Thomas De Quincey, John Gibson Lockhart, Thomas Carlyle and John Abraham Heraud.[6] Coleridge's famous distinction between the primary and secondary imagination in the *Biographia Literaria* (1817) was inspired mainly by the writings of Schelling and Tetens.[7] Consciousness, he claimed, was fundamentally and automatically (re)creative: 'the primary IMAGINATION I hold to be the living Power and prime Agent of all human Perception, and as a repetition in the finite mind of the eternal act of creation in the infinite I AM'. But the secondary imagination, the equivalent of Schelling's *Dichtungsvermögen* and the distinguishing characteristic of creative genius, is

> an echo of the former, co-existing with the conscious will, yet still as identical with the primary in the *kind* of its agency, and differing only in *degree* and in the *mode* of its operation. It dissolves, diffuses, dissipates, in order to re-create; or where this process is rendered impossible yet still at all events it struggles to idealize and to unify.[8]

That is to say, the possessor of the secondary imagination *wilfully* dissolves, alters and remoulds the images of nature formed by the primary imagination, and thus consciously participates in the creative power of God. As James Engell has noted, Coleridge's metaphysics of the imagination 'renovated' the 'age-old saying that the poet . . . is divinely inspired'.[9]

Although philosophical aesthetics were discussed in the literary magazines, arguments about genius were generally conducted at a less rarefied level because they were meant to appeal to a relatively large middle-class readership. In the late eighteenth century, accounts of genius generally took the form of theories of how the mind worked, or how society should be organized, or arguments about the importance of artistic originality. But in early nineteenth-century writing, these considerations were often secondary to debates on topics such as how the possession of genius affected a person's character and life history (whether 'men of genius' were generally virtuous or vicious, sane or mad, celebrated or neglected); the relationship between genius and normal society; and the distinction between different types of genius. A great deal of writing on genius in the 1820s and 1830s was biographical, for the Romantic emphasis on the individual consciousness behind artistic creation – and on the exceptional nature of genius – contributed to an increasing fascination with the personalities and private lives of creative artists.

This fascination was part of a wider obsession with personal fame across Europe and America, which, as Leo Braudy has shown in his classic study *The Frenzy of Renown*, was encouraged by a range of 'political and economic factors': 'the unprecedented growth of urban population, the expansion of literacy, the introduction of cheap methods of printing and engraving, the extension of the political franchise, and the revolutionary overthrow of monarchical authority'.[10] From the late eighteenth century, the public was much more actively involved in the construction of 'great men' than had hitherto been the case. Men like Byron, Napoleon and Washington were presented (and presented themselves) as exceptional individuals, but their 'self-stagings implied that buried in each spectator was a greatness that could be exposed for public display and fascination'. Byron, for example, was

> celebrated not for his position or his poetic ability so much as for his literary display of 'himself' – a swirling whirlpool of almost sexual allure in which his audience might glimpse an image not of their public selves so much as those desires and aspirations that had seemed socially unfit or irrelevant, now writ large and grand.[11]

The case of Byron exemplifies a widespread tendency in the treatment of literary figures during the Romantic period. Authors such as Burns, Coleridge, Scott, Shelley and Wordsworth were often portrayed as fundamentally different from normal people, but also functioned as sites of desire for readers and critics who felt that they too were somehow different from the norm. The fact that, in the case of writers associated with social transgression, this desire existed alongside a degree of fear or repulsion probably only added to its power.

As Braudy argues, the increasing possibilities for individual fame in the Romantic period, particularly that associated with the notion of genius, were accompanied by a degree of suspicion towards new audiences and strenuous attempts to distinguish true fame from false: 'an increasingly fame-choked world was beginning to reach out for solace and value to anonymity and neglect as emblems of true worth'.[12] The popular theme of neglected genius, with its focus on posthumous reputation over debased contemporary celebrity, was not only a means for artists to understand alienation or commercial failure, but could also be invoked by the relatively successful to avoid being associated too strongly with such celebrity – the appearance of reticence and neglect itself became part of the mechanism of fame. Literary journals acted as vital conduits between authors and readers because they were able simultaneously to publicize the genius of particular individuals whilst claiming, implicitly or explicitly, that *only their readers* were capable of truly appreciating that genius. The journal's audience was thus constructed as *avant-garde*: avatars of the more enlightened general audience of the future. This book applies the term 'celebrity' to this process, rather than 'fame', in order to challenge the Romantic distinction between true and false fame. The genius figures that were partly created by literary magazines, particularly those like Wordsworth that were most strongly based on 'the sanction of neglect', were, we shall see, utterly caught up in the commercial and ideological conflicts of literary culture.

***

A number of modern scholars have linked the rise of the idea of genius with changes in the ways in which literature was produced and consumed in the long eighteenth century. Raymond Williams famously argued in *Culture and Society* that Romanticism's 'emphasis on the special nature of art-activity as a means to "imaginative truth", and . . . on the artist as a special kind of person' was in part a compensatory response to the decline of patronage and the growth of the commercial market for literature. However, he also stressed that it represented a broader reaction to the threat to 'certain human values, capacities, [and] energies' which the development of 'industrial civilisation' seemed to hold.[13] Pierre Bourdieu has criticized this account for failing to acknowledge that it was only the growth of a reading public that enabled the formation of a literary field that was relatively autonomous from political and religious authority, itself 'the condition of the appearance of the independent intellectual, who does not recognise nor wish to recognise any obligations other than the intrinsic demands of his creative project'.[14] For Bourdieu, the development of the literary marketplace was a double-edged sword that alienated writers from their readers, but which gave them, for the first time, status as 'independent intellectual[s]', or, less anachronistically, 'men of genius'.[15]

Recently, our knowledge of the relationship between developments in aesthetics and changes in literary production has been enriched by work that has linked the emergence of the idea of original genius in the eighteenth century to the needs of writers to establish legal ownership of their works in order to protect their livelihoods.[16] This emphasis on the economic function of genius does not necessarily contradict Williams's or Bourdieu's notions of it as, in part, an attempt to escape from economic realities. It was only in the early nineteenth century – after the idea of genius had helped to constitute modern notions of authorship and intellectual property – that it became widely used in a more restricted, 'elitist' sense to refer to a small group of special individuals whose creativity was supposedly unbound by material considerations. At the same time, it retained vestiges of its wider eighteenth-century application – thus although in the Romantic period, the plural 'genius' sometimes refers only to the 'master spirits' (or even simply the great poets) of the time, it can also be used to denote a much larger group comprising the more able writers, artists, scientists and so forth. We will see in Chapter 1 that there were complaints in the 1820s and 1830s that the power of the term was being weakened by its indiscriminate application to mediocre individuals.

The Romantic separation of art and life – the claim that 'only a poet and his works can transcend a corrupting appropriation by "the world" of politics and money' – has been identified by Jerome McGann as one of the 'basic illusions of Romantic Ideology'.[17] He is describing a powerful type of writing on genius and literature in the early nineteenth century, which presents the male poet as a highly spiritual being who is completely separate from the debased everyday world. That this is often a politically reactionary account is evinced by its utilization by Tory journals like *Blackwood's Edinburgh Magazine* (*BEM*) and *Fraser's Magazine* (*FM*). And recently Robert Lapp has described the similar ideological implications of Coleridge's articulation of 'a Romanticism of withdrawal into visionary idealism that locates cultural authority in the attractive figure of the poet-prophet' and that draws on 'the emergent tradition of bardolatry and its celebration of autonomous "Poetic Genius"'.[18] However, we must not forget Williams's insight that, as well as 'simplification', there was also 'high courage and actual utility' in Romantic claims about art and genius.[19] Romantic idealism was often articulated in response to the equally extreme claims of other discourses, particularly utilitarianism.[20] Furthermore, genius was certainly not a monolithic concept in the early nineteenth century. If one account constructed its possessors as superior beings who cut themselves off from the world in order to meditate on higher things, then another represented them as rebellious transgressors who questioned the very foundations of contemporary society. And although the meritocratic implications of genius were often lost in the way in which the term was used, it was still capable of carrying a radical political charge by offering a theory of human value based on mental aptitude rather than rank or wealth.[21]

If the political resonances of genius were complex, so was its relationship to religion. In France, as Paul Bénichou has shown, counter-revolutionary and liberal conceptions of literature had fused together by the 1820s to create a romanticism that replaced the priest of the *ancien regime* and the *philosophe* of the revolutionary period with the figure of the inspired poet.[22] It is clear that British Romanticism saw a similar consecration of the poetic genius, but it is important to note that this took place in a very different context: a period of 'national religious revival...which brought about a remarkable transformation in British society'.[23] Although there were, certainly, tensions between literature and religion at this time – witness the outraged Evangelical response to Byron – the challenge to the authority of religion that the valorization of genius *could* represent tended to be muted by writers in the late Romantic and early Victorian periods. The critical emphasis on the contribution to the nation's spirituality made by figures like Wordsworth, Coleridge, and even Shelley, made genius seem likely to support Christianity, rather than to supplant it.[24]

One more aspect of McGann's statement needs consideration: the claim that Romantic ideology focused on 'the poet and *his* works' [my italics]. Although the Romantic genius was supposed to have qualities such as sensibility and intuition, which were traditionally associated with femininity, he was almost always imagined as a virile, masculine figure. As Marlon B. Ross has argued, the reliance on 'masculinist metaphors of power' in the writings of the Romantic poets and their supporters was a defensive response to perceived challenges to the poetic vocation, perhaps most crucially the increasing prominence of women writers and readers in the period.[25] Critics sometimes applied the term 'genius' to successful women writers like Joanna Baillie, Maria Edgeworth, Madame de Staël and Letitia Landon, but it generally seems to have been assumed by male writers that female genius, if it existed, was both less powerful and less extensive than male genius and that women wrote best when they confined themselves to sentimental subjects.[26] When magazine writers discuss genius in the abstract, they almost always mean the male version and, although there is something of a debate in the Romantic period about the intellectual faculties of women, I have found relatively few considerations of this issue in literary magazines. Furthermore, there are very few biographical accounts of female genius in Romantic magazines: this is not simply because such genius was often believed to be relatively unimportant, but because the publicizing of private life, always controversial, was thought to be particularly indelicate in the case of female subjects.

***

This book focuses on the period from *c.*1815 to *c.*1835, not only because it saw a cultural fascination with genius, but also because during this time magazines were the predominant literary form.[27] They were so widely read that it would not be an exaggeration to state that most middle-class readers would have been exposed to many of the writers and works which were later to become canonical *solely* through the reviews, surveys and biographical articles to be found in the periodical press. In his recent work *Literary Magazines and British Romanticism*, Mark Parker argues for the study of magazine literature in its own right, rather than as an adjunct to more 'creative' forms of writing.[28] It is not just that much of the best and most interesting literature of the 1820s and 1830s was in the form of the periodical essay, but that individual magazines constituted themselves as coherent, powerful entities with particular ideologies and rhetorical styles. As Parker puts it, 'the periodical does not simply stand in secondary relation to the literary work it contains; a dynamic relation among contributions informs and creates meaning'.[29] Thus throughout this book, I have considered the position of each article I discuss within its host magazine, and the place of that magazine within literary culture. I focus principally on the literary magazines that came into being in the period after the end of the Napoleonic wars, especially the *New Monthly Magazine* (NMM), *BEM*, *FM* and *Tait's Edinburgh Magazine* (TEM). These journals, which both produced and reflected their readers' interest in genius, were considerably less ponderous and more accessible than those of late eighteenth century, and even compared to the two powerful Reviews of the Romantic period, the *Edinburgh* and the *Quarterly*. At the same time, they can also be distinguished from the more 'mass market' publications that began to dominate the literary marketplace during the 1830s. I see them as occupying something of a middle ground between 'elite' culture and 'mass' culture, 'genius' and 'the public', 'Romantic' and 'Victorian'.

The interstitial nature of the literary magazines meant that they played an important role in helping the middle classes, as David Hogsette puts it, 'to culturally legitimate their growing economic and political power and aided them in creating a unified national identity'.[30] In the 1830s, he claims, critics represented Coleridge as 'the English consummation of poetic genius, a secular messiah whose creative power redeems the middle classes and provides a cohesive structure to the universal middle-class Mind'.[31] This draws on Jon Klancher's influential argument that through the 'great public journals' of the early nineteenth century, a nascent middle-class audience learnt to define itself:

> What will finally distinguish the new middle-class audience of the nineteenth century from its radical antagonists and the mass public's fascination with commodities is the activated interpretative mind in its power to reincarnate everyday life: to form a 'philosophy' of one's encounter with the street and the city, with fashion, with social class, with intellectual systems and the mind's own unpredictable acts.[32]

Klancher argues that this project of 'generalizing the philosophic, interpreting mind' is particularly apparent in the 'tireless promotion of "intellect"' by *BEM* — not only in the content of its articles, but through an elaborate style which invited its readers to exercise their own mental powers in the act of reading.[33] There is no doubt that in its early years, *Blackwood's* evinces a strong interest in exploring and defining 'genius', or 'the power of mind itself', as Klancher puts it. However, although his work is enormously suggestive, it sometimes exaggerates the coherence of particular periodicals: I am not convinced that *Blackwood's* most characteristic project is to transmit 'an ideology of mind', or for that matter that the *New Monthly's* aim is to educate its readership in cultural semiotics, or that Carlyle's *Edinburgh Review* (ER) essay 'Signs of the Times' typifies the Reviews' searches for 'master keys' to the 1820s.[34] If critical accounts of Romantic prose have often been impoverished by wrenching texts from their original locations, Klancher goes too far the other way by overemphasizing the unity of particular periodicals and, indeed, the function of middle-class periodicals as a whole through presenting a handful of articles as exemplary.

There is no doubt that literary magazines had a powerful impact on the construction of middle-class identity in the early nineteenth century. Although some people read more than one magazine regularly and therefore would have been encouraged to make connections between different readerships, generally speaking, it may be useful to consider journals in terms of the middle *classes*, rather to imagine them as creating a unified class consciousness. Writing on genius – in both its abstract and specific forms – often sought to create or emphasize distinctions within the middle-class public. *Blackwood's*, for example, by celebrating genius and 'Mind', also celebrates and elevates its readers as exceptionally able individuals who are capable of appreciating and sympathizing with great writers like Wordsworth. Around 1820, the literary marketplace was saturated with products: the poetry market was at its peak and about to decline, while the periodical market was burgeoning rapidly.[35] Thus while it is no doubt true that, as so many critics have argued, the 'romantic myth of the Genius Author...rose to obscure the reality of the literary marketplace', representations of genius also played an important role in the way in which that marketplace operated.[36] The essence of genius is its claim to distinctiveness – it stands out from the crowd – and it was offered to consumers by publishers, critics, and authors as a mark of quality at a time of increased literary production. Magazines sought to define and expand their readerships by recourse to particular pantheons of genius represented in reviews and biographical articles. The promise of all such texts is that they give their readers a *connection* with 'men of genius', which distinguishes them from other readers of the same or similar social background. So if at times genius was represented as a unifying cultural force – a site of aspiration and desire for all middle-class readers – it could also be used as a way of carving out smaller audiences within a larger public.

Periodical writing on genius was not only partisan, but was also often marked by anxiety and tension. Authors like John Wilson, Thomas De Quincey and Thomas Carlyle began writing for magazines because they could not subsist by producing more prestigious forms of literature; this sometimes lent a certain bitterness to their accounts of more fortunate and famous creative artists. And for many writers in the 1820s and 1830s, the rise of newspapers and magazines was the reason for the apparent dearth of poets, dramatists and novelists of the first rank. Original genius, it was claimed, was being swallowed up or stifled by the anonymous, teeming mass of periodical writing.[37] Like the urban crowd, the periodical press was imagined as being both dangerously various and fragmented, and disturbingly amorphous and uniform. David Latané has suggested that celebrations of genius in periodicals were undercut and ironized by their position as anonymous texts within a realm of apparently authorless discourse, which placed the idea of the 'transcendent author' firmly in the past.[38] There is no doubt that there was a tension in the way in which unsigned biographical or critical articles effaced the identity of their own authors whilst simultaneously exploring and celebrating that of their subjects. However, Latané's claim is surely overstated. Although accounts of genius were sometimes retrospective (because they were posthumous), in the 1830s it was still frequently put forward as an immensely powerful force, which would overcome the temporary impediments of political or cultural change. The idea of 'genius' was clearly put under pressure in the late Romantic period because its association with social transgression or alienation jarred with attempts to constitute writing as a respectable profession, but Victorian models of authorship were still dependent on notions of autonomy and originality, even if not taken to the extreme that we find in Romantic writing on genius. Once the idea of the 'transcendent author' had taken hold, it was to prove impossible to get rid of.[39]

Modern criticism, however, has subjected this idea to sustained critique as a Romantic construction, which hides the fact that writing is at least partly created by social and/or linguistic forces. The 'transcendent author' is, no doubt, a fantasy but it is not one that we can easily analyse out of existence. Not only has this construction irrevocably shaped how readers, writers, and critics think about literature over the last two centuries, but it has also irrevocably shaped the production of that literature. Whether or not there is such a thing as 'genius' is perhaps less important than the fact the most people involved in the cultural field have believed (and probably still believe) in its existence and value. Having said that, early nineteenth-century periodical writing, by virtue of its anonymous and collaborative nature, tends to draw attention to the limitations of this notion of authorship, and this, perhaps, is one reason why there was such anxiety about the growth of the periodical press in the early nineteenth century. This book, I hope, supports the view that genius, rather than being an innate gift that can be discovered in certain individuals, is *always* socially constructed. There is nothing inevitable about the process which leads a person to be described as a genius: this depends on a large number of factors which are extrinsic to his or her mental abilities, and what appear as the 'signs' of genius at a certain time and place may not be considered as such in other contexts.[40] I am not suggesting that those writers and artists who have been described as geniuses owe their success entirely to luck or good publicity but it is certainly the case that the word 'genius' tends to work against investigation into the operations of cultural production. The constructivist approach to genius falls in with modern critical attempts to open up the literary canon, or even to deconstruct the very notion of canonicity. The Romantic 'discourse of posterity' claims, as it were, that the cream always rises to the top (albeit posthumously),[41] but studying the social construction of genius makes us aware of the complex set of mechanisms – particularly the valorizing activities of critics, academics, publishers and so on – by which long-term literary reputation is secured. This, in turn, sheds light on the ways in which it has been denied to certain groups of authors (e.g. female or working-class poets).

To argue that genius is socially constructed is not to deny that authors and other cultural producers are also agents, and it is the interaction between agents and structures that I focus on in this book. Here I am influenced by Pierre Bourdieu's work on the sociology of literature, which seeks to avoid the polarities of (idealist/Romantic) 'subjectivism' and (Marxist/structuralist) 'objectivism'.[42] Bourdieu argues that the literary world, at any given time and place, is a field of forces, 'a network of objective relations' between agents. Any literary work places the writer in a certain position within this field – areas of which correspond to genres, sub-genres and particular audiences – and these 'position-takings' tend to result from the writer's 'disposition' (which Bourdieu relates to class background), and ownership of different forms of capital (economic, cultural and symbolic). The literary field is a constantly shifting site of struggle between agents for economic and symbolic capital (prestige). Like all fields of 'cultural production', it is dominated by the field of power, that is, the site of struggle for political power and economic capital among the ruling elite.

The degree of autonomy that the literary field has from the field of power can be assessed by looking at the extent to which it has its own rules governing the distribution of symbolic capital. Bourdieu argues that the idea of 'the pure aesthetic' becomes more prevalent as the literary field (or any other artistic field) becomes more autonomous. This helps to explain why the interest in genius, and the celebrity accorded to artists, is different in different periods: 'the interest in the personage of the writer or artist grows in parallel with the autonomization of the field of production and with the correlative elevation of the status of producers'.[43] Bourdieu critiques the notion that aesthetic creation or perception is unmediated and a matter of the emanations or responses of individual consciousness, independent of socio-cultural context. He shows that a number of different consecrative agents (publishers, reviewers and so on) work together to create the symbolic value of the work of art, and argues that in order to understand a work historically, one must analyse the way in which the entire field of production acts in order to give the work its contemporaneous meaning.

There are two main problems with Bourdieu's theory. First, it is based on an analysis of the peculiarly polarized literary culture of late nineteenth-century France, and it seems likely that more fluid cultural fields will be much harder to map out. Second, his method requires an enormous amount of research – if the historical 'meaning' of a work is the function of the operation of the entire cultural field at a given time, then, ideally, one would want to have a sophisticated schematic model of this field before embarking on any substantial analysis of that work.[44] There is no such model available of British literary culture in the Romantic period and I suspect that such a model may be impossible to produce. This book, then, is not a fully fledged Bourdieuvian study, but it shares his focus on cultural production and cultural prestige as the result of subjective agency working within the lines of force created by institutional, generic and social structures.

Chapter 1 examines magazine discussions of the nature of genius and its relationship to modernity. Journalistic accounts of the subject were often troubled by the fear that the growth of the periodical press threatened the success of true genius by swamping the reading public with a tidal wave of inferior productions. But this anxiety about the modern neglect of genius existed alongside a discourse that associated genius – or at least writing on genius – with an excessive and pernicious individualism. By the 1830s, a gap had developed between an emergent model of the professional man of letters – meant to be a productive member of civil society – and an account of literary genius – focused mainly on poets – which emphasized the inevitable separation, perhaps even antagonism, between great writers and normal people. Reformist journals, such as the *NMM* and the *Monthly Repository* (*MR*), tended to try to normalize the figure of the writer, whereas conservative journals, such as *BEM* and *FM*, tended to celebrate the transcendence of genius, but at the same time attempted to disassociate it from transgression or alienation.

Chapter 2 focuses on Romantic debates about the validity of literary biography. If the early nineteenth century saw a strong interest among readers and journalists in the personal lives of authors, this interest was resisted by writers – most notably Wordsworth and Coleridge – who claimed that this was an unwarranted intrusion into the private sphere. The problem faced by literary biographers was how to distinguish a legitimate and elevated interest in the private characteristics of genius from vulgar and pernicious gossip. Following on from this, my third chapter is a set of case studies of some of the most interesting and significant biographical accounts of writers in late Romantic literary magazines. I look at literary galleries by William Hazlitt and William Maginn, and literary reminiscences by Leigh Hunt, Thomas Jefferson Hogg, Richard Pearse Gillies and Thomas De Quincey, focusing throughout on the relationship between these texts and the magazines in which they first appeared.

The other three chapters are extended case studies. The fourth considers how and why *BEM* represented Wordsworth as a great genius in the period from 1818 to 1822. I show that its celebration of the poet was informed by a range of commercial and ideological factors: for example, its opposition to the *ER*, and its desire to put forward an account of poetic genius as, ideally, a locus of timeless, orthodox values, rather than a dangerous, transgressive force that threatened the socio-political *status quo*. I focus in particular on John Wilson's 'Letters from the Lakes' and argue that these articles were intended both to improve Wordsworth's cultural status and to offend him by publicizing his private life, thus making him part of the culture of 'personality' which the poet so deplored.

My fifth chapter is on William Hazlitt, who argued throughout his literary career that contemporary genius was 'degraded' by the influence that political power had over the literary world. Writing for the *Examiner* in the mid-1810s, he violently attacked the 'apostasy' of the Lake Poets and claimed, famously, that the poetic imagination had an innate sympathy with power; by the 1820s, he was declaiming against literary reviewing as utterly corrupted by political partisanship and class prejudice. But I argue that Hazlitt's association with the *Liberal*, the short-lived quarterly journal founded by Byron, Shelley and Leigh Hunt, helped to modify his jaundiced view of literary culture. Read in the context of its original publication in the *Liberal*, his famous and influential essay 'My First Acquaintance with Poets', which describes meeting Wordsworth and Coleridge in 1798, suggests that literary genius can resist political oppression.

In the final chapter, I consider the career of the historical painter Benjamin Robert Haydon, who, at the peak of his fame, was often represented as an artist capable of achieving true greatness. The self-defeating nature of the Romantic attempt to distinguish between transcendent genius and debased celebrity is nowhere more apparent than in his case. Aided by a number of journalists, he attempted to promote himself as a disinterested artistic hero but this threatened to undermine the cause it was meant to support by so obviously imbricating him within a magazine culture that based itself around the commercialized construction and consumption of genius. By the time of his death in 1846, not only was he a marginalized figure, but, I would suggest, the ideal of autonomous genius that informed his career was itself under considerable pressure from a culture that was increasingly suspicious of Romantic individualism.

1 Literary genius, transgression and society in the early nineteenth century

'The LITERARY CHARACTER', announced Isaac D'Israeli in 1795, 'has, in the present day, singularly degenerated in the public mind. The finest compositions appear without exciting any alarm of admiration'.[1] The reason for this, he argued, was that the massive amount of literature produced in the eighteenth century and its wide availability, even to 'the lowest of artisans', meant that authors were no longer viewed as exceptional individuals worthy of veneration.[2] And yet D'Israeli was writing at the beginning of a period in which the figure of creative artist, particularly the writer, was celebrated as never before, largely through the valorization of genius as the highest form of human subjectivity.[3] His popular works contributed to this phenomenon but, like many other Romantic writings on genius, they were written as a defensive response to the perceived degradation of literary production in contemporary Britain. In particular, the increasing popularity and cultural power of the periodical press was the cause of much anxiety. Was the reading public's obsession with magazines and newspapers, it was frequently asked, responsible for the neglect suffered by poets and dramatists? This anxiety contributed to the growth of literature based on the theme of 'neglected genius', which used figures like Chatterton and Burns in order to argue that the sufferings that so often seemed to afflict men of genius were caused by the failure of their contemporaries to recognize and reward their achievements.[4] However, this was frequently countered by the claim that such men reaped the harvest of their own improvidence and eccentric behaviour. This in turn gave rise to a further important question, which was whether or not such behaviour was the natural concomitant of the possession of genius. Although the notion of the 'artistic temperament' had classical antecedents, it was given new force by the rise of the idea of original genius during the eighteenth century. In the Romantic period, it was frequently argued that the aesthetic rule-breaking associated with genius was reflected in the transgressive conduct of its possessors in private life.

This chapter examines debates on genius in literary magazines during the early nineteenth century, and the relationship between these debates and changing representations of the literary marketplace. Attempts to describe the (male) genius author as a figure who, ideally, stood apart from the literary and political maelstrom were put under pressure by a developing model of literary professionalism, which claimed that writers should be fully engaged with contemporary society. But the attempt to constitute writing as a respectable profession was itself vitiated by contemporary accounts of the 'man of genius' as an eccentric Bohemian, or even a transgressive hero, who did not respect middle-class mores. The results of this clash of different models of authorship can be seen in the extreme positions taken up by writers in the 1830s, ranging from the elevation of the genius author – particularly the poet – into a morally perfect, Christ-like figure, to a suspicion that 'genius' was little more than a code word for vice and madness.

Samuel Taylor Coleridge and the Reviews

Although the aim of the *Essay on the Manners and Genius of the Literary Character* was to improve the status of writers, D'Israeli himself argued that genius was peculiarly antisocial and often subject to 'infirmities and defects': 'degrading vices and singular follies have dishonoured men of the highest genius. Than others, their passions are more effervescent and their relish for enjoyment more keen. It is a perilous gift of Nature'.[5] This was a common claim in the Romantic period, but it was resisted by some writers who believed that literature was threatened by society's maltreatment or neglect of the most able authors, and who thought that to associate genius with vice was to suggest that society was not responsible for its sufferings. Samuel Taylor Coleridge seems to have taken this view in the second chapter of the *Biographia Literaria* (1817), which is on 'the supposed irritability of men of genius'.[6] His discussion is typically free-wheeling and digressive, but can be summarized as follows: the mass of readers, taking the side of critics, believe geniuses to be innately 'irritable', by which Coleridge means 'readily excited to anger and impatience' and also, though with less emphasis, 'excessively or morbidly excitable or sensitive' (*Oxford English Dictionary* (*OED*)). There are some men who have something more than talent, but something less than 'absolute Genius', and although 'in tranquil times' these men of '*commanding* genius' can greatly benefit mankind, in 'times of tumult' they are ruinous and disruptive – Napoleon is the obvious example. However, men of the greatest genius are of 'a calm and tranquil temper', at least in what relates to their own interests.[7] The 'prejudice' that genius is irritable is caused by: (a) the irritability of talented men who are not geniuses (and who are jealous of those who are); (b) the excesses of men without talent or genius (periodical writers in particular); and (c) the false distinction popularly made between literature and other forms of property, because if other manufacturers were attacked in the same way, geniuses would not appear particularly irritable.[8] Coleridge's argument is typical of Romantic writing on the nature of genius in that it quickly becomes an account of the degraded nature of modern literature. Furthermore, and this is also typical, although the discussion implies the link between genius and virtue that he puts forward elsewhere in the *Biographia*,[9] he is more concerned here with contemporary *representations* of genius, than he is with genius itself. Men of genius are imagined as being under threat from literary manufacturers like the ex-shoemaker William Gifford, the editor of the powerful *Quarterly Review* (*QR*), who supposedly misrepresents them in his writings, and also through his own 'ungenial' nature.

The *Quarterly*, and its main rival, the *Edinburgh Review* (*ER*), dominated British literary culture in the first two decades of the nineteenth century.[10] The *Edinburgh* was founded in 1802 by a small group of Whiggish Scottish lawyers; sceptical, highly trained professionals, with a great interest in new learning. This was reflected in the subjects covered by the new journal, which also quickly differentiated itself from the Reviews of the late eighteenth century by its selective approach to the works it dealt with and the long length of its review articles. Its editor and main critic, Francis Jeffrey, is best known now for his attacks on the 'Lake School': in general, he tended to treat authors as the accused, who had to be judged against what he saw as fixed standards of polite taste and social decorum.[11] The *Quarterly* was founded in 1808 by a group of Tories – including Walter Scott, George Canning, and the publisher John Murray – who were concerned by the *Edinburgh's* increasingly reformist stance. As Marilyn Butler puts it, the *Quarterly* 'conducted a comprehensive campaign on behalf of conservative, Christian and family values ... [it] hunted down "infidel", irreligious, or sexually explicit subject-matter in texts of all kinds'.[12] It is not surprising, therefore, that it strongly attacked 'second generation' Romantics such as Shelley, Hazlitt and Keats.[13]

Although it is no doubt true that the two Reviews took a punitive attitude to what they saw as the excesses of genius, some of the attitudes they expressed were much closer to Coleridge's than he might have liked to imagine. Consider, for example, Jeffrey's controversial 1809 review of R. H. Cromek's *Reliques of Burns*. Although he describes Burns as 'a great and original genius',[14] he spends some time discussing the unfortunate 'peculiarities' of the poet's works, by which Jeffrey means anything that reminds the reader of 'the lowness of [Burns's] origin'.[15] In particular, he states that

> the leading vice in Burns's character, and the cardinal deformity indeed of all his productions, was his contempt, or affectation of contempt, for prudence, decency and regularity; and his admiration of thoughtlessness, oddity, and vehement sensibility;- his belief, in short, in *the dispensing power* of genius and social feeling, in all matters of morality and common sense. This is the very slang of the worst German plays, and the lowest of our town-made novels; nor can any thing be more lamentable, than that it should have found a patron in such a man as Burns, and communicated to a great part of his productions a character of immorality, at once contemptible and hateful.[16]

Burns's belief in '*the dispensing power* of genius and social feeling' is, Jeffrey goes on to argue, a form of cant which seeks to disguise or validate selfishness and criminal behaviour, but which has fortunately 'never found much favour in the eyes of English sense and morality'. He then refers to a group of German students who were inspired by the noble character of the bandit leader Charles Moor in Schiller's play *Die Räuber* (1782) to 'rob on the highway', but states that in England 'a predilection for that honourable profession must have preceded this admiration of the character', and thus that 'the style we have been speaking of, accordingly, is now the heroics only of the hulks and the house of correction'.[17]

Jeffrey was not the first critic to attack Burns for seeking to palliate moral transgression by claiming that genius was naturally eccentric. A stanza in 'The Vision', first published in the Kilmarnock edition of *Poems, Chiefly in the Scottish Dialect* (1786), was often seen as particularly offensive. The speaker is Burns's Muse:

> I saw thy pulse's maddening play
> Wild-send thee Pleasure's devious way
> Misled by Fancy's *meteor-ray*
> By Passion driven;
> But yet the *light* that led astray
> Was *light* from Heaven.[18]

Jeffrey was probably unconcerned about the arguably blasphemous content of the stanza, but saw Burns's argument about the transgressive nature of genius as an example of the latent Jacobinism that he had also identified in the work of the Lake Poets.[19] His reference to 'the worst German plays', and specifically to Schiller's *Die Räuber*, harks back to the anti-Jacobin rhetoric of the 1790s.[20] We should also note that he associates Burns's argument with the 'lowness of his origins', 'slang' and the 'lowest of our town-made novels'. Thus it is represented as essentially *vulgar*.

Now it may seem that Coleridge and Jeffrey are talking about very different things. Coleridge describes the claim that genius tends to be irritable as an unfair calumny provoked by ignorant critics, whereas Jeffrey suggests that the claim that 'genius and social feeling' are a justification for defying 'morality and common sense' is normally to be found in low-quality literature but, unfortunately, has also been used by a man of genius. There are, however, two crucial links between these descriptions. First, both men are disagreeing with characterizations of genius that emphasize its incompatibility with normal society.[21] And second, both link the claim that genius is naturally eccentric or 'irritable' to the degradation of the modern literary marketplace, and in particular, to the increased diffusion of literature. Significantly, both displace this claim to a readership which they believe to be below their own – in Coleridge's case, the audience for periodical criticism, and in Jeffrey's, the consumers of the 'worst' plays and the 'lowest' novels.

Jeffrey's antagonistic attitude towards Burns (and many other poets) and the *Quarterly's* attacks on Shelley and Keats support Coleridge's assertions about the oppositional stance that the Reviews took towards authors. In both the *Edinburgh* and *Quarterly*, critics represented themselves as mediators between authors and the public, mediators whose main task was to control the excesses of genius in order to make it fit in with prevailing social and artistic norms. But the years surrounding 1820 saw the emergence of a counter-discourse in magazine literature, which sought, at least ostensibly, to emphasize the autonomy of the aesthetic from the socio-political realm. New magazines such as *Blackwood's Edinburgh Magazine* (BEM) (1817), the *London Magazine* (LM) (1820), and the *New Monthly Magazine* (NMM) (1814; 'relaunched' in 1820) emphasized their difference from the Reviews by claiming that they took a non-partisan attitude to criticism and that they celebrated and supported genius. In the process of making these claims, the reviewing practices of the *Edinburgh* and the *Quarterly* were often caricatured, but this second generation of Romantic journals certainly tended to give genius much more emphasis and importance than did the

Reviews, and in some cases, represented it as a reason or alibi for an author's personal and/or textual flouting of the rules that govern polite society. These new journals proved Jeffrey's judgement that the belief in '*the dispensing power* of genius' had not found favour in England to have been premature.

Blackwood's Edinburgh Magazine

In *The Economy of Literary Form*, Lee Erickson argues that the 'poetry boom' of the first two decades of the nineteenth century ended due to developments in printing technology and a decrease in the price of paper. This made possible economies of scale, which meant that 'diffuse prose was no longer at a comparative economic disadvantage with compressed poetry'.[22] Erickson's argument is open to the charge of economic determinism, but it seems to me to be a good, if partial, explanation for the large increase in the numbers of periodicals published after the end of the Napoleonic wars, although the poetry market itself did not peak until 1820. During this period, a number of monthly miscellanies appeared in direct competition with the older quarterlies. The relatively high rates of pay offered by these magazines offered new opportunities for writers who were unable to subsist by writing in other genres. For example, towards the end of his life, John Keats, in severe financial difficulties, which could not be alleviated by the very poor sales of his poetry, was seriously considering becoming a magazine writer and planned to consult William Hazlitt for advice: 'I will write, on the liberal side of the question, for whoever will pay me'. Although some writers may have felt that they had little choice other than to turn to periodical writing, they did of course have a measure of autonomy in which journals they wrote for; Keats was determined to do 'any thing but Mortgage my Brain to Blackwood'.[23]

This was a reference to William Blackwood, proprietor of *BEM*, which had recently contained a series of articles entitled 'The Cockney School of Poetry' attacking London writers such as Leigh Hunt, Hazlitt and Keats himself. Blackwood had founded the periodical early in 1817 in order to counteract the commercial success of his local rival, Archibald Constable, proprietor of the *ER* and the *Scots Magazine*, who had taken on Walter Scott after Blackwood had fallen out with the author during the publication of *Tales of my Landlord*.[24] Blackwood was also politically motivated, a staunch Tory who was concerned by what he saw as the Whig dominance of Edinburgh's cultural life. Unfortunately, under the editorship of Thomas Pringle and James Cleghorn, his magazine was not only dull – it even praised the *ER*. So Blackwood got rid of his editors, enlisted John Wilson and John Gibson Lockhart – both young, briefless barristers – to help him, and relaunched the periodical in October 1817. This edition contained the 'Chaldee Manuscript', a parody of the Edinburgh literary scene couched in mock-Biblical language, the first of the 'Cockney School of Poetry' articles, and a vicious review of Coleridge's *Biographia Literaria*. As a result of these attacks, *Blackwood's* quickly became infamous; that it was able to maintain its early success and rapidly increase its sales was due to the ability of its writers, who delighted in formal experimentation and parody.[25] The magazine also came to be regarded, and to an extent still is seen by modern critics, as an extreme example of the political partisanship of the periodical press during the early nineteenth century.

However, one of the extraordinary things about *Blackwood's* is that even while it attacked Keats and Leigh Hunt as lower-class interlopers and 'Cockney' radicals, it claimed that it was free of the political bias of the quarterly Reviews and that it supported literary genius regardless of its social origins or political affiliations. For example, Lockhart's article 'On the Periodical Criticism of England', purportedly by the 'Baron von Lauerwinkel', appeared in March 1818, during the same period as the 'Cockney School' attacks. The article presents the Reviews as despots ruling the republic of letters and preventing literary freedom. 'Lauerwinkel' contends that periodical criticism is becoming hijacked by political discussion and claims that a critic will often use a review

> as an excuse for writing, what he thinks the author might have been better employed in doing, a dissertation, *in favour* of the minister if the Review be the property of a Pittite; *against* him and all his measures if it be the property of a Foxite, bookseller. It is no matter although the poor author be a man who cares nothing at all about politics, and has never once thought either of Pitt or Fox, Castlereagh or Napoleon, during the whole time of composing his book. The English Reviewers are of the opinion of Pericles, that politics are, or should be, in some way or other, the subject of every man's writings.[26]

'Lauerwinkel' goes on to attack the editors of the *Quarterly* and the *Edinburgh*. Despite his talents, Gifford's political bigotry makes him a bad critic and insensible to genius. His Review is right to oppose Napoleon, but wrong to denigrate his abilities: 'it is an insult upon common understanding to tell London in the nineteenth century, that Buonoparte is an ordinary man'. The *Quarterly's* 'rancour' against the defeated Emperor reveals an endemic lack of sympathy with greatness, for

> there is something dignified and sacred in human genius, even although it be misapplied. The reverence which we feel for it is an instinct of nature, and cannot be laid aside without a sin. He who is insensible to its influence, has committed sacrilege against his own spirit, and degraded himself from the height of his original elevation.[27]

This extraordinary 'sanctification' of genius, in which it becomes a sacred duty to reverence 'great men' regardless of their crimes, is surprising in a magazine that professes Tory values. It is, however, an attitude that one repeatedly finds in the pages of *Blackwood's*.

After accusing the *ER* of failing to appreciate geniuses like Byron, Wordsworth and Goethe, and, more seriously, of acting as a treasonous 'apologist for Napoleon' and 'a covert champion of infidelity', 'Lauerwinkel' considers the question of whether the growth of criticism means the decline of literature. He fears that talented writers with 'gentle and elegant minds' who are not in the first rank suffer from the taunts of the reviewers, but states that the greatest writers will always be immune to the effects of contemporary criticism, for 'these go on in their destined way, rejoicing in the consciousness of their own strength, and having their eyes fixed upon the sure prospect of immortality – far above the reign, either of calumniating wit or ignorant approbation'.[28] This recourse to what has been described as 'the discourse of posterity' is a common strategy of Romantic writers.[29] Lockhart's article is typical of this discourse in that it laments the state of contemporary literature, whilst simultaneously asserting that genius will ultimately always succeed in overcoming any obstacles to its eventual fame. That this argument appears in *Blackwood's* is meant to suggest that the journal itself transcends the 'debased' literary culture to which magazines supposedly belonged, and that unlike its competitors in the periodical marketplace, it is capable of recognizing and supporting genius as it appears.

One of the foundations of *Blackwood's'* success was its self-promotion and Lockhart's article was the first of a number of attempts by its writers to suggest that it was a new type of journal. It was important for the magazine to differentiate itself from the *Quarterly* as well as the *Edinburgh*, even though *Blackwood's* was on the same side as the former in terms of politics.[30] In 1826, William Maginn would claim, with a degree of ironic hyperbole, that before *Blackwood's* appeared, 'men of genius were insulted by tenth-rate scribblers, without head or heart'. But, due to the journal's example,

> the whole periodical criticism of Britain underwent a revolution. Principles were laid down and applied to passages from our living poets. People were encouraged to indulge their emotions, that they might be brought to know their nature. That long icy chill was shook off their fancies and imaginations, and here, too, in Criticism as in Politics, they began to feel, think, and speak, like free men.

As a result of this liberation, the 'Critic-king' Francis Jeffrey was 'deposed': 'so fared it with many an anointed head ... This universal dethronement is accomplished and there is once more a Republic of Letters'.[31]

The political language of this extract is fascinating. Maginn, an extreme Tory, celebrates a 'revolution' in sensibility prompted by *Blackwood's*, which has resulted in the dethronement and humiliation of literary despots. But although Maginn claims that there is a similarity here with the journal's encouragement of, as he puts it a few lines above this passage, 'that latitude of opinion which is the Englishman's birthright', it would certainly not have wanted a 'universal dethronement' outside the literary sphere. There was a tension between *Blackwood's'* staunch monarchism, and its desire to be seen, in literary terms, as a republican force that supported a meritocracy of genius. For remarks like Maginn's must have seemed laughable to the victims of its attacks. How could a journal that told Keats 'back to the shop Mr John, back to "plasters, pills, and ointment boxes," ' and vilified Hazlitt as a 'quack', 'scribbler' and 'charlatan' be ending the 'daggers-drawing' between author and critic?[32]

It is clear that some of the criticism produced by *Blackwood's* was founded on political partisanship and class prejudice. But its treatment of authors *was* very different from that of the Reviews. Those whom the magazine supported were generally praised in a concerted and eulogistic fashion that had not been seen in periodical criticism before. For example, as I will show in Chapter 4, *Blackwood's* not only extolled the merits of Wordsworth's poetry in a sustained critical campaign, but constructed an image of the poet as a virtuous poet–priest which was highly influential on his reception later in the nineteenth century. It is not surprising that *Blackwood's* would support someone like Wordsworth, but during 1819 and 1820 it also contained several generous reviews of Shelley, whose atheism and radicalism were anathema to its political ethos. These reviews, I think, constitute strong evidence that the magazine's claims to be revolutionary were not merely empty propaganda; they reveal that, as Robert Morrison puts it, 'throughout its early years, *Blackwood's* literary criticism repeatedly flew in the face of its own political and literary dogma'.[33]

Blackwood's and Percy Bysshe Shelley

Blackwood's first Shelley review (of *The Revolt of Islam*) begins ominously, attacking 'the sophistical and phantastical enemies of religion and good order among mankind' who have always eventually secured the 'contempt and disgust' of their fellow men: 'they had no part in the just spirit of respectfulness which makes men to contemplate, with an unwilling and unsteady eye, the aberrations of genius'. It seems to be limbering up for a savage assault, but then describes Shelley as different from other radical writers:

> Mr Shelly [*sic*] is devoting his mind to the same pernicious purposes which have recoiled in vengeance upon so many of his contemporaries; but he possesses the qualities of a powerful and vigorous intellect, and therefore his fate cannot be sealed so speedily as theirs. He also is of the 'COCKNEY SCHOOL', so far as his opinions are concerned; but the base opinions of the sect have not as yet been able entirely to obscure in him the character, or take away from him the privileges of the genius born within him.[34]

Throughout, the review distinguishes Shelley's political opinions and associations from his intellectual abilities. The 'privileges' of genius are that its possessor can be forgiven sins, which would damn his less brilliant fellows. Shelley's poetical powers became the key to his possible redemption from what is represented as an inchoate and vicious philosophy, for 'the native splendour of [his] faculties has been his safeguard from universal degradation, and a part, at least, of his genius, has been consecrated to themes worthy of it and of him'.[35]

This argument is reiterated in the next three reviews of Shelley. The beauties of his poetry are contrasted with the errors of his morality: his genius acts as an alibi for his political transgressions; prevents him from being irrevocably damned for his erroneous principles; and, the review hopes, will eventually lead him to embrace religion and respect for authority. Although it was a typical reviewer's rhetorical trick to launch an attack under the pretext of attempting to educate misguided ability, this is not the case with these reviews. Shelley is exhorted to change his opinions, but this subordinate to a generous appreciation of the merits of his poetry. However, I cannot agree with Morrison that '*Blackwood's* did not de-politicise or aestheticise Shelley' and that it 'fully understood the radical nature of [his] vision'.[36] For while the magazine admitted the radical sentiments in his verse, it also made this philosophy extrinsic to his poetic genius. By positing an *absolute* separation between the political content of his poetry and its merits, the magazine not only attempts to make Shelley palatable for its readers, but seeks to aid its construction of a version of genius that is fundamentally conservative. Like the wayward son of a nobleman, it is Shelley's privilege to be allowed certain youthful transgressions, with the understanding that he will eventually return to the fold.

We can get a better sense of the relationship between *Blackwood's* Toryism and its account of genius by examining two articles by John Wilson. In 'On Literary Censorship' (November 1818) he attacks literary critics as gratuitously cruel to youthful writers, and probably unnecessary to 'the literature of a country', the 'excellence' of which 'does not depend on tribunals of criticism: it depends on the spirit of the people. It is the state of the mind of the whole nation that must determine the character of its literature'.[37] He goes on to state that

> we must desire to see writers of genius and power perfectly bold and free – submissive, indeed, where all minds should submit – but within that circumscription, uncontrolled, impetuous, trusting to their own spirit, and by that light fearlessly exploring and fearlessly creating. A literature generous and aspiring – yet guarded alike by wisdom and reverence from all transgression – is alone worthy of England.[38]

This is, in a nutshell, the dilemma of the *Blackwood's* approach to writers of genius. They must be allowed to be 'perfectly bold and free', but also 'submissive' to Church and State; 'uncontrolled', yet 'guarded'; literary republicans, but political monarchists. This balancing act makes necessary the construction of a sharp division between the aesthetic and the political, manifested in the Shelley reviews as a distinction between form and content.

Just over a year later, Wilson developed his argument about the relationship between the creative artist and the nation in 'On the Analogy Between the Growth of Individual and National Genius'. He argues that its development must be a balance between the forces of what Coleridge would later call, in *On the Constitution of Church and State* (1830), 'Permanence' and 'Progression':

> It is to be desired that the living generation should derive as much as possible of good from those which have preceded, without being so far subjected to them as to lose the good which is open to it to acquire. But it ought not, in eagerness for acquisition of its own, to forego the good which may be inherited ... Among ourselves, the tendency of deviation seems to be towards too great relaxation of the subjection of our minds to the great generations from which we spring.[39]

By 'analogy', Wilson does not just mean that the developments of individual and national genius are similar. He is also relying on a more archaic usage of the word – 'adaptation of one thing to another' (*OED*) – to suggest that the two processes are linked. Although individual genius is a progressive force, it has to recognize that, as an emanation of the national spirit, it must be restrained by an adherence to custom and history. 'The human intellect', Wilson argues,

> is not an unfettered intelligence, ranging through absolute existence, and creating ideal form. It is the power of a being who in all parts of his nature is subjected to conditions of life, who, in his sensibilities, his knowledge, his productions, is under restraint and limitation of his individual nature, and of his place among mankind... He who, in the pride of his own age, believes himself independent of the ages to which he succeeds, shuts out from himself the highest influences under which it was given to his mind to live.[40]

Shelley's errors, for his *Blackwood's* critics, are because he does not recognize the responsibilities that individual genius has to 'the ages to which he succeeds', he is not 'submissive... where all minds should submit'. But because these errors are, as Lockhart emphasizes in the review of *Rosalind and Helen*, 'devoid of any essential or fundamental alliance with his masterly genius', they may be overcome in the future.[41]

It is instructive to compare the *Blackwood's* reviews of Shelley with John Taylor Coleridge's review of the *Revolt of Islam* in the *QR*. Although Coleridge grudgingly admits Shelley's gifts, he spends the bulk of his review attacking the poet's 'system' and ends by claiming that he has personal knowledge that reveals the hollowness of Shelley's philosophical professions:

> if we might withdraw the veil of private life, and tell what we *now* know about him, it would be indeed a disgusting picture that we should exhibit, but it would be an unanswerable comment on our text; it is not easy for those who *read only*, to conceive how much low pride, how much cold selfishness, how much unmanly cruelty are consistent with the laws of this 'universal' and 'lawless love'.[42]

Coleridge evinces little interest in Shelley's poetry and certainly no desire to give it wide circulation: in a twelve-page article, he quotes one passage of four stanzas, one individual stanza, and eight fragments. This contrasts with Lockhart's seven pages on the *Revolt of Islam*, which quotes a total of well over thirty stanzas. Later *Blackwood's* reviews of Shelley contain an even greater proportion of quotation than this, for the journal sought to mediate the poet to a large audience in order, Lockhart claimed, 'to support the cause of genius and of imagination'.[43]

Lockhart responded to the *Quarterly's* article in his review of *Alastor* in November 1819. He launched a scathing attack on Shelley's reviewer, describing him as 'a dunce rating a man of genius', and stating that:

> nor will any man who loves and honours genius, even though that genius may have occasionally suffered itself to be both stained and led astray, think but with contempt and indignation and scorn of a critic who, while he pretends to wield the weapons of honour, virtue, and truth, yet clothes himself in the armour of deceit, hypocrisy, and falsehood. He *exults* to calumniate Mr Shelley's moral character, but he *fears* to acknowledge his genius.[44]

As in the other reviews, Lockhart emphasizes here that Shelley's genius is the key to the poet's possible redemption. He also argues that Coleridge's inability to recognize this truth disqualifies him from being Shelley's critic. This is akin to the criticisms of the *Quarterly* that Lockhart made in 1818 for failing to sympathize with Napoleon's 'misapplied' genius. Coleridge is criticized for his underhand and hypocritical reference to Shelley's personal character, although such 'personality' and 'deceit' was of course the stock-in-trade of Lockhart himself. Finally, he argues that there is a generosity and love among the British people towards genius which will aid Shelley's redemption, for 'they are willing to pardon to [*sic*] its possessor much extravagance and error – nay, even more serious transgressions'. This should encourage the poet to 'walk onwards to his bright destiny', while his critic should feel his own 'insignificance', and be ashamed of having gloated 'with a sinful satisfaction on the real or imaginary debasement of genius and intellect'.[45] It is telling that it does not seem to matter to Lockhart whether Shelley's 'debasement' is 'real' or 'imaginary'.

Thus here we have the strange spectacle of a Tory reviewer, in a virulently Tory periodical, defending a radical atheist from the attacks of another Tory reviewer during a period of intense political unrest and partisanship, when one would expect political allegiances to be at their strongest. These reviews do not square with modern critical representations of the 'fractured' public sphere of the early nineteenth century, in which criticism was 'unabashedly political'.[46] However, they are totally consistent with the various comments on contemporary periodical criticism to be found in *Blackwood's*. The sanctified nature of genius allows 'its possessor' to be forgiven even 'serious transgressions' – and those who fail to understand this reveal their own deficiencies. Lockhart forgives Shelley on an epistemological level, through the construction of the aesthetic category of 'genius', separate from the poet's 'moral character' or political beliefs. By placing Shelley's poetic gifts in this category, he redeems him for a Tory readership by divesting his work of the radical political themes that, for modern critics, are so integral to it. But this begs the question of why *Blackwood's* treated Shelley in this way, and yet strongly attacked 'Cockney' writers. If the Shelley reviews bear out the magazine's claims to be carrying out, at least at times, a new sort of criticism that respects and celebrates creative endeavour, regardless of its source – even if this is at the cost of 'cleansing' it of unfortunate associations – then why are Keats and Hunt not subject to a similar process?

The *Blackwood's* treatment of Shelley was noticed by contemporaries, in some cases with a degree of cynicism. In June 1820, William Hazlitt, who by this time had been warring with the magazine for nearly two years, claimed that its support of the poet was due entirely to his social background: 'it is name, it is wealth, it is title and influence that mollifies the tender-hearted Cerberus of criticism . . . This is the reason why a certain Magazine praises Percy Bysshe Shelley, and villifies [*sic*] "Johnny Keats" '.[47] In his review of *Prometheus Unbound*, Lockhart angrily denied this accusation and defended *Blackwood's'* conduct towards Hunt, Keats and Shelley.[48] But there is no doubt that *Blackwood's* writers tended to have an elevated respect for rank and, as recent critics have shown, the 'Cockney School' articles are riven with class prejudice.[49] Such prejudice may well have influenced the Shelley reviews; for unlike the Cockneys, he is seen as 'a scholar, a gentleman, and a poet'.[50]

Another reason was mooted by the poet himself in a letter to Charles Ollier; pleasantly surprised by the review of *The Revolt of Islam*, Shelley states that 'the article in *Blackwood* could not have been written by a favourer of the Government and a religionist', and asks his publisher, 'is it not some friend in disguise and don't you know who wrote it?'[51] Writing nine months later, in August 1820, an anonymous reviewer in the *Honeycomb* gave a similar explanation for this strange anomaly, arguing that there must be 'some secret machinery' in operation, 'some friend behind the scenes, or some working of personal interest, which thus induces that magazine for once to throw aside the trammels of party prejudice, and to do justice to a man who even advocates the French Revolution'.[52] When *this* passage was written, there was indeed a 'secret machinery'. Charles E. Robinson has shown that towards the end of 1819 William Blackwood made contact with Charles Ollier, Shelley's publisher. They began corresponding and Blackwood became Ollier's Scottish agent. Thus in 1820, Blackwood 'was not only advertising, selling, and reviewing Shelley's works (and those of Ollier's other authors) but also announcing in the Edinburgh advertisements that he was co-publishing Shelley with the Olliers'.[53] It is possible that the reviewer quoted above may have known something about this arrangement.

Clearly, the *Blackwood's* treatment of Shelley was overdetermined, a function of a number of different factors including his social class, the relationship with Ollier, his distance from the cut and thrust of British literary culture, and, no doubt, a genuine pleasure in his poetic gifts. But the motivation behind the reviews is not as important as the language in which they are written and thus the discursive possibilities that are present. What matters is that *Blackwood's* was consistently willing to distinguish Shelley's artistic abilities from his political philosophy, and his personal morality. These distinctions were impossible for Coleridge in the *QR*. The Shelley articles see *Blackwood's* actively trying to break free from the dominance of contemporary literary culture by party politics, a project which it made one of its major selling points. However, as we have seen, the only way in which 'a favourer of the Government and a religionist' *could* criticize Shelley favourably was by arguing that his politics and poetry should be viewed entirely separately. Thus in the hands of *Blackwood's*, the apparent emancipation of literary criticism from politics was ultimately a conservative strategy. Literary genius was only allowed freedom in so far as it did not transgress against the respect for Church and State that the journal argued was fundamental to British culture.

Evangelicalism and the dangers of genius

Although 'genius' was a key term in the literary criticism of the Romantic period, some writers, like Francis Jeffrey, viewed it with suspicion. Indeed, pressure on the idea of genius actually *increased* during the first few decades of the nineteenth century. This is apparent even in the pages of *Blackwood's*, for which 'genius' (denuded of its less respectable associations) was so important. Shortly before becoming editor of the *QR* in 1825, Lockhart reviewed Sir Samuel Egerton Brydges's *Recollections*, which he claimed was 'extremely dangerous to young minds'. First, because Brydges argued that genius 'incapacitates a man for mixing in the ordinary society and business of the world', and second, because he encouraged the view that the only thing of value in literature is self-expression regardless of 'art' and 'arrangement'. As a result, Brydges was likely to encourage young people without ability to attempt to become writers:

> That one word *genius* has done more harm than anything in the vocabulary. It has been prostituted until it has lost all meaning. Not a beardless driveller in the land who does not expect, if he produces a sonnet on a rose-leaf, that we shall see *genius* in his bauble. Genius, so help us, inspires the leading articles of our newspapers – the small print of our Magazines is redolent of *genius*![54]

Lockhart's problem is that genius has been debased, not only through overuse, but also through its association with weakness, eccentricity and unpopularity. His dislike of what he terms 'THE MOPING SCHOOL' is not primarily political; in fact, he admires Brydges as a thoroughbred Tory. But the *Blackwood's* notion of genius as a conduit of national power is vitiated by the term being linked with antisociality and 'beardless driveller[s]'.

A more moralistic reaction can be found in the magazine four years later. In one of John Wilson's *Noctes Ambrosianae*, a series of conversations between *Blackwood's* imaginary contributors, Christopher North (the fictional editor of the magazine) states that, 'we idolize Genius, to the neglect of the worship of Virtue'.[55] He lambasts the idea that genius is an excuse for transgression: 'it makes my very soul sick within me to hear the puny whinings poured by philosophical sentimentalists over the failings – the errors – the vices of genius'. And he particularly focuses on Burns; speaking of the poet's 'aberrations', he attacks those critics who 'dared to declare that we were bound to forgive and forget them on the score of the poet's genius – as if genius, the guardian of virtue, could ever be regarded as the pandar to vice, and the slave of sin'.[56] The crucial difference between Wilson's argument, and that of Jeffrey in his 1809 review of Burns, is that Wilson wants to give an alternative account of genius to the one that presents it as 'the slave of sin'. For, as we saw in the reviews for Shelley, genius is not generally represented as a transgressive force in *Blackwood's*, but as, in essence, 'the guardian of virtue'.

One of the main forces behind the reaction against genius was the rise of Evangelical morality and the concomitant development of what has been termed 'domestic ideology'.[57] In 1812, Barbara Hofland published the first of many editions of her popular conduct novel, *The Son of a Genius*.[58] This attempted to teach young people that intellectual gifts were useless without self-control, humility and religious feeling. The genius of the title, a gifted painter called Mr Lewis, eventually drags his family into penury because of his belief that the 'super-excellence of possessing Genius' means that he does not need to work hard, or conduct his affairs with prudence.[59] His wife, however, is determined to prevent her son from following in his father's footsteps:

> [she] had some portion of that finer perception of beauty and excellence, which, in whatever path it walks, may be designated *genius*: but she had an aversion to the *word*, amounting almost to horror, from having observed its application tend

to injure either nearly, or remotely, every one to whom it had been her lot to see it applied; and as it was ever in *her* mind associated with imprudence, imbecility, folly, or vice, was made the excuse for one man's eccentricities, another man's errors, and not unfrequently the crimes of a third; it was no wonder that she shrunk from its application to a son . . . We flatter ourselves every young person who like him has been praised for this rare, indefinite, and often blameably extolled quality so much the subject of attention in the present day, will see the folly of depending upon it either for happiness, or respectability, in *this* world, and the sin of making it an excuse for neglecting *that* 'which is to come'.[60]

Hofland's main target is similar to Jeffrey's – contemporary belief in '*the dispensing power* of genius' – but her emphasis is very different. The belief is represented as threatening middle-class family life and religious sentiment by encouraging fathers and sons into 'imprudence, imbecility, folly or vice'.[61] The novel is interestingly inconsistent on the question of whether or not 'genius' is a 'real' quality bestowed only on an elite few. At one point in the story, Mrs Lewis tells her son that the attainments of great men are the result of 'a decided preference for a particular art or science', combined with hard work: 'this preference is called *taste*, and united with perseverance, it produced that superiority which became *genius*'.[62] But at other times, Hofland clearly suggests that people *do* have high mental abilities without having worked for them, and, furthermore, that

in proportion as the mind is endued with higher powers, and acuter sensibilities, it is annoyed with stronger passions, and more dangerous propensities, and calls in a more peculiar manner for the controul of reason, and the aids and restrictions of religion.[63]

The danger she identifies, then, is actually twofold. First, that the word 'genius' is too often used as an excuse for immoral or imprudent behaviour, and second, that genius, or something very like it, has in itself 'dangerous propensities' which need to be controlled. Thus both contemporary representations of genius, *and genius itself*, are a threat to social stability.

A similar account can be found throughout *The Spirit and Manners of the Age* (*SMA*), an Evangelical journal, published in London, which appeared weekly from 1826 to 1829 before becoming the short-lived *British Magazine* (1830). In the preface to the first volume, its purpose is described as being 'to impart just views of men and manners; to form a correct taste for literary pursuits; to advocate the cause of humanity, virtue, and, above all, to give prominency to the sublime proofs and principles of genuine Christianity'.[64] There is very little information available about the journal; all that I have been able to discover is that in 1829 it was edited by Samuel Carter Hall, who continued in this role when it changed into the *British Magazine*, and later became editor of the *New Monthly*.[65] It was a miscellany that contained a variety of mostly anonymous articles: didactic moral tales, reviews, poems, disquisitions on the evils of slavery, attacks on irreligion and so on. One of its constant themes was the personal and literary transgressions of men of genius. An early series of five articles discussed Sheridan, Byron, Burns, Cowper and Bloomfield, and drew moral lessons from their unfortunate histories: for example, that Sheridan's life 'should teach us, that genius without virtue is but a fire which consumes its possessor'.[66] The article on Burns prompted a lament on his sufferings:

> Genius, alas! alas! what are the varieties of thy history? – melancholy, disease, poverty, insanity, and premature dissolution! Warm-hearted Burns! thou wert too genuine a son of the Muse to run thy brief career unscathed by the ills which are allotted to her children... Thine errors we can neither excuse or palliate... But thou hadst virtues as well as vices, and these thy verses have embalmed – would that they were not also the record of thy follies.[67]

This is a fairly typical account of Burns in the 'calamities of authors' tradition, but with an added emphasis that his pains and passions – even though they may have been 'allotted' to him by his Muse – do not excuse his behaviour. However, the tone here is sympathetic in comparison with later articles in the magazine, which took a more punitive approach to the errors of genius. Byron was a particularly useful hook on which the magazine's writers could hang moral disquisitions. An article entitled 'The Cant of Lord Byron' attacked the poet for ridiculing everything 'esteemed fundamental, sacred, and indisputable by Englishmen' and predicted that his fame would prove transitory.[68] This assertion was answered the following week by a writer who claimed that Byron 'will descend to posterity as a poetical genius of a very high order' – however, this was anything but a defence of the poet, for the writer added that this 'only increases his moral delinquency'.[69] Byron is represented as a terrible corrupting influence on the age whose genius has prevented critics from chastising him, and the article concludes that 'the meanest follower of Christ, with an intellect but a few removes from idiotcy' is 'a far more distinguished and glorious being than this infidel and licentious man of genius'.[70]

It is hardly surprising that a writer in an Evangelical magazine would value Christian feeling over mental ability, but it is interesting that the writers of the *SMA* felt obliged to keep up an unremitting assault against misapplied genius. The most notable example of this is an article strikingly entitled 'Literary Men often the Patrons and Apologists of Vice', which claims that 'the master spirits in the republic of genius are generally among the most sceptical and depraved of their species' who are 'endeavouring to hasten on a universal corruption of social manners' by attacking Christianity.[71] This is because they are 'generally men of strong and ardent passions, impatient of restraint', and 'too lofty in their imaginative conceptions to yield to the government of those common-place maxims, on which the virtue and happiness of society depend'.[72] This rhetoric seems to accept that genius cannot be reconciled with normal society and therefore, despite the writer's moral outrage, in effect *supports* the sort of extreme claims surrounding genius that, as I argued in the introduction, were most often associated with German writers of the *Stürm und Drang* period.

The article goes on to describe geniuses as 'alternately the apologists and the defenders of each other's conduct', which leads the writer to quote the stanza from Burns's 'The Vision' that I discussed at the beginning of this chapter. He or she is

even more appalled by the poet's special pleading than Jeffrey or Wilson and fears
that it is becoming 'a popular opinion' which is

> so dangerous in its moral influence and consequences, [that] I cannot let it pass
> without offering some remarks on it. If that great Being who created the intel-
> lectual powers of man created his vicious propensities, than man becomes *an
> object of pity, but not of blame.* To what a frightful extent will this doctrine carry
> us. We see the fell murderer embruing his hand in the blood of his brother's life!
> We see the spoiler of domestic happiness coming up, and laying waste every safe-
> guard which has been thrown around our virtue and our honour! We see the
> midnight plunderer bearing off our property, after he had abused and insulted
> our persons. But when arraigned and accused of these crimes, would an honest
> jury acquit them, if they were to offer as an apology, the apology which a
> depraved genius, and his impassioned admirers, think admissable.[73]

We recall that Jeffrey initially identified the idea of eccentric genius as a threat to
society, but argued that it had not taken hold in England and implied that it was
unlikely to do so. In contrast, this writer describes, somewhat hysterically, its possible effects as a total breakdown in law and order. This is because the claim that 'the
light that led astray/ Was *light* from heaven' threatens the idea that we have full
responsibility for our actions. However, the writer asserts that 'the tribunal of public
opinion' will share the opinion of the *SMA*, which is that

> such men, by being entrusted with superior abilities, ought to have employed
> them for the *moral* benefit of mankind ... but having, like the author of all evil,
> failed to maintain the high elevation of their dignity, and prostituted their tal-
> ents to offend God and corrupt man, our admiration for their genius is lost amidst
> those more righteous emotions which a recollection of their sad history excites
> within us; and while we cannot forbear to pity, we cannot forbear to condemn.[74]

The problem with the argument of this article is that the writer states initially that
the mental constitutions of men of genius cause them to transgress socially beneficial
'common-place maxims', but later tries to separate the 'intellectual powers of man'
from his 'vicious propensities' in order to show that a divine gift could never have
immoral or antisocial effects. His or her opening remarks thus comes perilously close
to the argument that he or she is seeking to attack, for if 'men of genius' are bound
by their 'lofty imaginative conceptions' to offend against society, then it is hard to see
how this cannot be, in all justice, at least a partial palliation of their crimes. This
contradiction occurs throughout the *SMA*; its writers, unlike Lockhart and Wilson
in *Blackwood's*, or, as we shall see, Heraud and Brydges in *Fraser's Magazine (FM)*, do
not tend to argue that genius is *essentially* virtuous and socially conservative; rather,
they seem to believe that they have found something rotten and rebellious in it which
is their duty to reveal to their readers. This extreme stance may have been a result of
the magazine's anomalous position as a self-styled 'Christian and Literary Miscellany';
perhaps it was only possible for an Evangelical magazine to evince literary interests

by constantly reminding its readers that it had no time for the moral errors of 'men of genius'. We should also recall that the magazine – due to its relatively low price and denominational stance – would have been aimed at a different audience from the cultured, middle-class readers who were the main consumers of the literary periodicals that I deal with in this book. Genius was one of the means by which these latter readers constituted themselves as a public – and they would have been unreceptive to articles that sought to denigrate its importance as a source of value. On the other hand, those who felt themselves excluded from literary culture by education or social class are likely to have been more receptive to articles that constantly emphasized that religious faith was far more important than literary ability. In the following section, we will examine how John Abraham Heraud, in *FM*, tried to reconcile these two things by representing genius as the highest form of Christian spirituality.

Fraser's Magazine

Fraser's, founded in 1830, has been caricatured by Terry Eagleton as 'an insulting rag', but was arguably the best and most vibrant magazine of the 1830s, with similar sales to the *Edinburgh* and the *Quarterly*.[75] It continued the spirit of *Blackwood's*, which was by now relatively respectable, into a new decade, packed full of squibs, doggerel, invective, personal attacks, and some fine writing, which generally adhered to a strongly Tory ethos. The character of its editor, William Maginn, a strange mixture of childish vindictiveness, deep erudition, emotional volatility and brilliant creativity, pervades its pages. In its early years, *Fraser's* positioned itself against its competitors by accusing them (with some justification) of being dominated by commercial interests, especially in their reviewing.[76] Its other major literary target was the fashionable novel and in particular the work of Edward Lytton Bulwer (later Bulwer-Lytton), writer of 'silver fork' and 'Newgate' fiction, editor of the *NMM* during the early 1830s, dandified man about town, and Radical politician.[77] The novels of such an author, it was argued, were necessarily showy and superficial: 'Man cannot serve God and Mammon. It is denied him to be a labourer in the field of fashion and the field of intellect'.[78] And his fiction lacked any sort of improving qualities: 'What noble faculties are addressed in such works? Are they calculated to make readers in general better or worse? – to brace up manly energy and promote heroic virtue?'[79] *Fraser's* represented Bulwer as an effeminate purveyor of fashionable luxuries for a debased public, whose writings lacked the organic sensibility to be found in works of lasting value.[80]

The *Fraser's* attacks on the shallowness of contemporary literature existed alongside a powerful interest in the subject of literary genius. This was a topic of particular concern in the late Romantic period because Britain seemed to be so lacking in great writers. For most contemporary critics, the collapse of the market for poetry proved that they were living in a literary 'age of Bronze', and the chorus of lamentation grew louder during the early 1830s, when, it was often claimed, the Reform Bill agitation resulted in 'Literature' being ignored by the public.[81] It was also felt that the increasingly powerful discourse of Benthamite utilitarianism threatened literature and the fine arts by representing them as no more than amusing luxuries.[82] At the same time, the continuing expansion of the periodical press saw the emergence of a new class of professional journalists, the existence of which, as Nigel Cross has pointed out, problematized earlier models of authorship because they were perceived neither as 'men of genius' nor as booksellers' hacks.[83] Considering these pressures, it is not surprising that in the late Romantic period, discussions of genius, particularly poetic genius, were more urgent and polemical than earlier in the nineteenth century. Patrick Leary has written that in its early years, *Fraser's* 'stands astride a fault line of conceptions of what constitutes the literary life' between 'the Romantic ideal of the literary man as heroic genius' and 'the mid-Victorian author-businessman as a respectable literary professional'.[84] This is true up to a point, although I would add that another possible conception of 'the literary life', which was sometimes important to the magazine, was the author as hard-living Bohemian. And Leary's claim that *Fraser's* position entailed a 'distaste for the pretensions of the Romantic ideal' is entirely inaccurate, for one can find articles in the magazine in the 1830s that discuss genius in highly elevated terms.[85]

However, the magazine was not entirely consistent in its approach to genius. For example, in July 1833, in the first part of his historical biography 'Count Cagliostro', Thomas Carlyle says of his subject's youth, 'we hear that Beppo was "often punished": painful experiences of the fate of genius; – for all genius, by its nature, comes to disturb *somebody* in his ease, and your thief-genius more so than most!'[86] Yet for other Fraserians, such as John Abraham Heraud and Sir Samuel Egerton Brydges, who gave genius a semi-divine status and emphasized its virtuousness, the very yoking of the words 'thief' and 'genius' would have been little short of blasphemous.

The transgressive nature of genius had become a particular issue in the early 1830s due to the spate of biographies of Byron that had appeared after the poet's death in 1824, in particular Leigh Hunt's *Lord Byron and Some of his Contemporaries* (1828), and Thomas Moore's 'authorized' *Life of Byron* (1830–1). Moore's biography took a much more generous approach to its subject than Hunt's hatchet-job, but contained some lengthy and controversial remarks on the relationship between the artist and society, particularly on the 'unmarriageability' of genius. In the first volume Moore states baldly that 'the truth is, I fear, that rarely, if ever, have men of the highest order of genius shown themselves fitted for the calm affections and comforts that form the cement of domestic life.' He goes on to argue that if a man of genius wishes to achieve greatness, he must avoid being 'tamed and domesticated in society', as social affections disturb the 'power of self-concentration', which is essential to genius.[87] These comments were defended by the physician R. R. Madden in his book *The Infirmities of Genius* (1833), an interesting adumbration of scientific accounts of the pathology of genius later in the nineteenth century.[88] Madden argues that the studious habits of literary men are injurious to their physical health, and therefore cause mental 'irritability'. He places some weight on the idea of the 'poetic temperament', but concentrates mainly on the physical causes that he believes lie behind the errors and improvidence of men like Byron. This led one reviewer to remark that 'every true son of genius' was indebted to Madden 'for the kind-hearted "apology" which he makes for their many-sided perversenesses'.[89] Such discussions, as well as the explicit association of Byron with various forms of transgression in more lurid, if less prestigious, publications, made him a locus for debates about the relationship between the creative artist and society.[90]

Dealing with Byron was a severe problem for conservative writers such as Heraud, poet, disciple of Coleridge and follower of German transcendentalism. Heraud was Maginn's editorial assistant and wrote many articles on literature and aesthetics for *Fraser's*. In an article for the opening number of the magazine, he attacks the idea that the exercise of genius is a matter of the association of ideas, and argues that it has the 'power of creation in the most extended sense; not only in the combination of ideas, but ideas themselves, primarily and underived, as its own absolute and independent production'.[91] He emphasizes that this power is a divine gift, a 'vital spark of heavenly flame', which cannot be acquired by education; the creations of the genius, and those of God, are different only in degree.[92] This elevation of the creative artist – for Heraud is most interested in poetic genius – to an individual with literally divine abilities has some basis in the Classical tradition of poetic frenzy, however, its main source is the philosophical idealism that Heraud had imbued from Coleridge.

In order to maintain his argument that genius was a divine gift, and that men of genius had God-like power, Heraud had to divest it of its newly resurgent associations with insanity and other forms of transgression. Thus in the following issue of *Fraser's* he argues that it is a priori impossible that such a gift, which gives its possessor 'a participation in the rights, privileges, and attributes of beatified saints' can have anything to do with sickness:

> By abstraction from the world, and self-reflection, and self-improvement, and self-regeneration, genius will ultimately make man a partaker of the joys of heaven...But that this blessed consummation should be induced through the means of imbecility and disease, we doubt altogether...By the thorough cultivation of genius, man partakes of a portion of the essence of the Divinity. How can this state be akin to madness – the most lamentable infirmity to which humanity has been made subject?[93]

Heraud is an heir to the Romantic elevation of the poetic genius to a man of great moral virtue which we find in Wordsworth, Shelley and Coleridge, but he pushes this to an extreme by strongly linking genius with Christian spirituality.[94] This argument is expressed even more strongly in a short pamphlet he published in 1837 entitled *Substance of a Lecture on Poetic Genius as a Moral Power*, a transcendentalist farrago in which he argues that genius is a manifestation of 'the divine WORD',[95] and that only the 'moral poet' is capable of original creation, because his possession by 'the universal Spirit' allows him to escape from the influence of his forebears.[96]

Heraud deals with Byron in a review of John Galt's biography of the poet.[97] He dismisses Galt's account of genius as unintelligible and gives an alternative: 'it may be simply described as the communicative intellect between God and man, the power of self-intuition...It is the primary imagination, which is set forth in the following passage from Mr. Coleridge's *Biographia Literaria*'. He then quotes the apposite passage from chapter 13 of the *Biographia*. I will take Heraud's definition of genius as 'the primary imagination' to be either a typographical error or a surprising misreading of Coleridge, for if that was what he meant to say he would effectively be claiming that all individuals had genius, which is certainly not his argument. Assuming him to mean the *secondary* imagination, then, as in the previous article, genius is represented not only as a rare gift, but one that elevates its possessor to partake of the divine. And as one might expect, this sanctified representation of genius does not really fit Byron: 'The question is, had Byron that inappreciable gift which we denominate genius? We think, undoubtedly not. Was he the truly great and lofty poet which his admirers would make him? By the same rule, we think not'.[98] Heraud has to deny Byron's greatness in order to maintain his argument that genius is the highest form of Christian spirituality, rather than relying on more usual definitions such as high mental abilities or artistic originality. For the problem with Byron is not his abilities as a versifier, but the fact that his pride and misanthropy lead him to write about the 'baser passions of the soul'.[99] The themes of his poetry degrade rather than elevate mankind.

Heraud's criticisms of Byron were not particularly original, but his use of them to deny that the poet had genius was strikingly novel – as we have seen, even the morally outraged writers of the *SMA* did not normally go so far. His argument is one of the early stirrings of the moralistic reaction against Byronism that was to lead to a decline in the poet's reputation in the late 1830s and the 1840s.[100] Predictably enough, the contemporary poet who most seemed to cohere with that period's – and Heraud's – governing representation of poetic genius was Wordsworth.[101] In the pages of *Fraser's*, we see a continuation of the idealization of the poet which began in the early volumes of *Blackwood's Magazine* and was to become much more prevalent in the Victorian period. In his review of the Wordsworth's *Poetical Works* in November 1832, Heraud is keen to emphasize the 'moral purity' of his writings.[102] Three years later, in a review of *Yarrow Revisited*, the writer, probably Heraud, narrates the transformation of the poet into a priestly figure: 'Wordsworth is no longer the poet of nature altogether or mainly – no longer the natural theologian in chief, but the druid of a purer faith – the minstrel of a holier shrine. His religion is now of heaven'.[103] Wordsworth is the perfect exemplar of Heraud's theory of genius because he seems to exhibit the reconciliation of the poetic imagination with moral and religious duty, both as natural theologian in his youth and a 'heavenly' poet in his maturity. This can be understood as another way in which the 'high Romantic' emphasis on the power of genius was becoming vitiated at this time; in this case, by being transformed into moral authority and distanced from innovation and transgression.

Sir Samuel Egerton Brydges and Edward Lytton Bulwer

Wordsworth was useful to Heraud because his growing reputation could be adduced as proof that true genius would rise above neglect and calumny, thus revealing that it had divine sanction. But *Fraser's* also had its very own 'neglected genius', Sir Samuel Egerton Brydges, who published eight articles and a few sonnets in the magazine during the period from 1833 to 1837 (he died in September that year).[104] Born in 1762, he was a prolific poet, genealogist, editor of Elizabethan literature, *soi-disant* aristocrat and had been Member of Parliament for Maidstone during the 1810s. He was obsessed with the negative attitude society took to men of genius and, in particular, the way it had treated him. All of the articles contain disquisition on genius and four are mainly on this topic: 'On Intellectual Endowments' (September 1833); 'Sir Egerton Brydges' Reply to the "Edinburgh Review" ' (December 1834); 'On the Charge that Men of Genius and High Talents Want Judgment and Practical Sense' (June 1836) and 'An Essay on Originality of Mind' (May 1837).

In 'On Intellectual Endowments', Brydges constructs a familiar, if extreme, formulation of the relationship between the artist and society. He begins by asserting that 'every one is really great in proportion to the greatness of his intellectual powers, provided they are accompanied by virtue', and he describes genius as 'an intuitive power, in which sagacity and sensibility operate on imagination'.[105] Like Heraud, he emphasizes its divine nature, though without recourse to the former's idealism:

> It must be something that approaches to the axiomatic wisdom of the moral part of the sacred writings. God has sent us into the world with spiritual powers to operate upon matter; it is the act of associating those spiritual powers with matter, and bringing them thus into view, that constitutes the great duty of genius.
>
> (1833, p. 292)

Because genius is so morally pure, its possessor needs to seclude himself from the rest of mankind who are engaged 'in an unprincipled struggle for selfish advantages' (p. 292). And the intellectual faculties are weakened by social intercourse: 'when the ardour of genius endeavours to keep down its impetuosities, it loses its strength and its zest. The collision of society forces us to smooth down our roughnesses, and, with our roughnesses, all our characteristics' (p. 293).

This description of the relationship between genius and society contrasts strongly with that found in the *Edinburgh* and *Quarterly* earlier in the century, which emphasized that the excesses of genius needed to be curbed by reference to the standards of polite culture. We have also seen that Brydges's claim in his *Recollections* of 1825 that genius was alienated from ordinary life was offensive to Lockhart, because it weakened the *Blackwood's* account of genius as emerging from and contributing to national history and custom. For Brydges, however, modern society is utterly debased, comprising individuals pursuing their own private interests, whereas genius seeks to benefit the public interest at whatever cost to itself. This configuration clearly owes much to eighteenth-century representations of the gentleman as a disinterested figure who stands above the division of labour.[106] In Brydges's writings, these representations are combined with a Romantic valorization of authorship, and emphasis on its neglect, to produce his despairing vision of the disinterested genius who is continually preyed upon by the mass of people whom he is trying to help. At the same time, Brydges seeks to avoid representing the genius as a marginal figure. First, by asserting a 'providential' view of literary fame; ultimately it is the best authors who will be known to posterity (p. 291). Second, he argues that despite this seclusion, the 'fruits of the workings of lonely inspiration' will gradually affect the community 'like a subterraneous spring' (p. 292); this is interestingly similar to Shelley's characterization of the poet as an 'unacknowledged legislator'.[107]

Halfway through 'On Intellectual Endowments', Brydges mentions the discourse which is his implicit target throughout: 'the devil is always at the cauldron that brews evil, and spreads its smoke over the world...At this crisis, radical falsehoods in political economy are in full operation; are they to be left to detect themselves?' (p. 294). Like Shelley, Brydges is suggesting that only the original truths produced by the imagination can save England from the crisis brought on by an adherence to political economy. However, unlike Shelley, Brydges's distrust of political economy was in part due to its association with Reform and anti-aristocratic principles, for his views on social organization were conservative:

> We have a strong opinion of the variety of our destinies, and of the uses of it; and therefore we are advocates for the distinction of ranks and the demarcations of society. It contributes to the energies of our social state, and the nutriment of hope...There is nothing more stupid nor more odious than to try all men's duties by one test of excellence. He who executes the necessary business of life, is not more useful than he who executes the ornamental...There is a strange theory of dull men, which applies measure and value to everything; and there are two classes of politicians who do this – fools and Radicals.
>
> (p. 299)

In Brydges's hands, genius becomes an anti-democratic principle because it is conflated with the eighteenth-century claim that society could only be properly run by gentlemen whose lack of a specific occupation allowed them to see society as a whole. Brydges's argument about the necessity for an intellectual division of labour – an argument that he represents as alien to Radicals – thus requires that the 'distinction of ranks' is maintained. There is no intrinsic reason why an account of genius as public-spirited *should* support 'the distinction of ranks', but Brydges uses this account in order to assert the value of an aristocratic model of government. Genius, divested of any transgressive or pathological qualities, is allied with rank and pitched against political economy, Reform and the 'mob'.

Brydges continues his attack on 'self-interested' society in 'On the Charge that Men of Genius and High Talents want Judgment and Practical Sense'. Men of genius, he states, need to be protected from 'the false stigmas which the sordid wretches engaged in carrying on the haphazard game of common life are so anxious and expert to cast upon them'.[108] As in his earlier article, whereas 'the majority of mankind are condemned to pass through life either as ciphers or in the sole pursuit of their own individual interests or amusements', men of genius 'can never be content with so narrow and selfish a sphere of action' (p. 681). One of Brydges's purposes in writing these articles is to prove to *Fraser's* readership that he is one of those who, as he puts it, 'are born for higher things'. Through describing the relationship between genius and society, Brydges is himself engaged in the sort of generalizing activity that is the province of genius and is making a claim about his own intellectual superiority:

> I am fully aware of the surprise with which many persons view these sort of discussions, which they call not merely idle but vexatious. It is not to be denied that many are not at leisure to pursue them, and many are not formed with a capacity to pursue them; but there are others, who have both the leisure and the capacity, and in whom it seems a desertion of duty not to pursue them. A part of mankind are as much destined for speculation as others are for mere action: to them, it is not sufficient to go round in the same mechanical steps, like a blind horse in a mill.
>
> (p. 675)

The claim that philosophical speculation is the duty of those who have both 'capacity' and 'leisure' clearly reveals the aristocratic origins of his theory of genius. However, as the essay continues, Brydges seems to become uncertain as to exactly where his duty lies, stating that he is 'puzzle[d]' and 'harrass[ed]' by the question of 'to what extent we may be allowed to drink oblivion to our own private concerns, by draughts of the seductive cup of literature' (p. 677).

Here, Brydges's valorization of the role of the genius or philosophical speculator is threatening to collapse. The issue is not simply the extent to which such a man should ignore his own 'concerns' (private interests, including the welfare of his family) by engaging in literary pursuits for the public good. For such pursuits are described as 'seductive' and intoxicating, an 'indulgence' for which Bridges says he has 'been unjustly and cruelly blamed' (p. 677). A few sentences on he asks, 'why am I not given the ordinary latitude for the defects of frail humanity?' and complains that 'to indulge in innocent and elevating amusements is a crime in ME' (p. 677). So Brydges has raised two linked obstacles to the argument he makes earlier in the article. The first is that literature may be pursued not as a public duty, but as a pleasurable diversion from one's private cares, and second is that as a result it may be more of a personal amusement than an activity for the benefit of mankind. These problems are enacted on the level of genre, as Brydges's supposedly disinterested discussion of genius in a public journal becomes increasingly undermined by his use of the autobiographical language of private sensibility.

Brydges goes on to suggest that society should be ignored when it blames individuals for neglecting their private concerns but clearly realizes that this could be read as a claim about, in Jeffrey's phrase, *'the dispensing power'* of genius. Thus he anxiously states that he does not 'mean to be the apologist of vice, or to argue that genius is above the rules of moral obligation. I think the reverse; I think that it is difficult, though not impossible, for true genius to exist without a high degree of virtue' (p. 678). This reassertion of the probable connection between genius and virtue is necessary because Brydges has effectively weakened his own argument about the transcendence of genius by suggesting that literary pursuits might be no more than self-indulgent pleasures, rather than disinterested contemplation for the public good. It also shows that he is aware of the need to defend himself from complaints that an emphasis on genius threatened stable domestic life. As the essay continues, he again seeks to recover his position by emphasizing the distinction between the literary and the 'common mind', which is 'exercised principally in plotting for its own interest or its own vanity, or in the contemplation of gross amusements or gross indulgences'. Literature, on the other hand, 'detaches, enlarges, raises, softens…It tends to expel personalities and localities, and to draw off the poison of evil passions, by letting in the air of heaven upon them' (p. 679).

Brydges's tendency to write about himself when discussing genius nicely dramatizes the difficulties he had in representing the literary man as a disinterested figure, and is also apparent in his 'An Essay on Originality of Mind' (1837). Here he suggests that 'in this iron age there is an attempt to decry and extinguish all real genius, and to substitute in its place a bastard kind of gaudy assumption' by those 'who lead the public mind'.[109] The perils of original thought are such that 'happiness consists in the absence of genius and talents', for men of genius are incapable of contending with the 'self-interest' and 'dissimulation' that prevail in society:

> I contend that this is the triumph of Satan, which Providence can permit only as a punishment. I take it, that hard-heartedness, false-hood, deceit, and cunning, will always triumph over delicate and sensitive virtue. Lord Byron was a great genius; but he had a good deal of the devil in him; and it must be admitted that it was *this* which carried him forward triumphant through the world.[110]

Byron's success, then, was due to the evil, selfish elements in his nature; his contemporary fame was based on his transgressive personality rather than his poetic abilities. This separation of the poet's genius from any criminal or radical aspects of his persona is, of course, exactly what happens in Lockhart's reviews of Shelley.[111]

There are three important aspects of Brydges's account of genius. First, his emphasis on the link between genius and morality; the man of genius has much greater sensibility than the mass of mankind and is disinterested and virtuous rather than cunning and selfish. *This* is why there is a tension between the genius and society and *not* because genius is in any way a pathological or transgressive principle. Second, all the articles are defensive in tone, because Brydges's assertions about the importance of genius exist alongside a profound uncertainty about the utility of literature and abstract speculation. And third, there is a strong autobiographical element in his discussions. Readers of *Fraser's* would have been well aware, particularly after his appearance in the magazine's 'Gallery of Illustrious Literary Characters' in February 1834, that when he complained about the dissonance between the genius and society, Brydges spoke from bitter experience.[112] His use of 'we' is not a journalistic convention, for his name is appended to all his articles, but is meant to place himself in a select band of neglected genius.[113] And at other times he uses the first person and complains explicitly about the remarks of his detractors.

Brydges's *Autobiography* (1834) refers at great length to the sufferings that he has endured at the hands of his malevolent fellow men, and reveals a persecution complex of almost Rousseauvian dimensions. The tone of the book is very similar to that of the *Fraser's* articles, for his continual assertions of his own merit are clearly prompted by the serious and only partially concealed doubts that he has as to whether he truly is a poetic genius. Bulwer, writing in the *ER*, was unconvinced by Brydges's claims, describing him as an example of a particular 'species of literary character... that has all the acute sensibilities of poetical genius, without its energy and power'.[114] Brydges's dislike of society and his complaints about various individuals in the book are, he argues, a result of a dangerous and selfish egotism, which can be distinguished from the more benevolent egotism of Rousseau, Byron or Milton. In such cases, periods of solitude can be healthy and restorative, 'but a solitude that is the aliment of misanthropy – the den of hatred – the mephitic and noisome cave from which evil oracles are emitted – is the retreat, not of genius, but of envy, which is at war with genius'.[115] This emphasis on sociality is interestingly similar to Jeffrey's criticisms of the Lake Poets, especially in the review of the *Excursion*, as well as his remarks on the 'Burnsian' account of genius. Like Jeffrey, Bulwer seeks to keep the creative artist operating well within the public sphere, although his idea of the scope of this sphere is quite different from Jeffrey's. Whereas the latter looked back to an eighteenth-century model of gentlemanly taste, Bulwer looks forward to an early Victorian ideal of the professional man of letters who is engaged in a wholesome, mutually improving relationship with a reformed society – both models are clearly opposed to an account of Romantic genius, which relies on an alienation, or at least a distance, between the writer and society.[116]

As editor of the *NMM* in the early 1830s, Bulwer played an important role in the development of a campaign for the 'Dignity of Literature', which sought to improve both the social and financial status of authors.[117] The campaign drew upon complaints about the neglect of men of genius: Bulwer stated in *England and the English* that 'the respect we pay to wealth absorbs the respect we should pay to genius' and he was inspired by D'Israeli's writings.[118] However, extreme complaints such as Brydges's were an embarrassment, because they seemed to suggest that literature was inevitably at odds with a commercial society, and had no way of understanding rapid popular success (such as Bulwer's) other than as a sign of artistic failure. Bulwer claimed that the new generation of writers had a 'more wholesome and masculine frame of mind' than that of many of their 'immediate predecessors'. Furthermore, 'as the political constitution becomes more popular, genius of every description is, perhaps, insensibly compelled to become more social'. Because many of his fellows will be involved in politics, the modern writer becomes familiar 'with the affairs of the actual world. The agitation, the stir, the ferment – the lively, the unceasing, the general interest in political concerns, which it is in the nature of popular governments to create – meet him in every circle'.[119]

So political reform, and the agitation surrounding it, is beneficial to genius by saving it from an 'effeminate' withdrawal into the private realm. Increased democracy forces 'masculine', modern literary characters to become more comfortable with contemporary society. This argument leads Bulwer to a Utopian representation of the relationship between the modern writer and more public figures, which perfectly encapsulates his reformist ideal of authorship:

> This it was which so singularly characterized the literature of Athens; bringing
> in close contact the statesman and the student – giving vitality to the dream of
> the poet, and philosophy to the harangues of the orator. And by a necessary

reaction, the same causes which render the man of letters more interested in the affairs of men of action, interest the men of action in the aims and character of men of letters. The connexion is as serviceable to the world as to the scholar; it corrects the dreaminess of the last – it refines the earthlier calculations of the first; and thus popular institutions insensibly become the medium of exchange, which barter and transfer from the most distinct quarters, the most various commodities in the intellectual commerce of mankind.[120]

This sympathetic, mutually improving exchange between the writer and the politician is provocatively couched in the language of trade, thus dismissing Brydges's construction of an antagonism between genius and economic society. Rather, Bulwer sees a coming together of men of letters and men of action, who, by following their individual interests, contribute to the public good. And the claim that this exchange will take place through 'popular institutions' – presumably the apparatus of a reformed government – undercuts Brydges's attacks on 'the mob'.[121]

Brydges responded in an article which, while manifestly prompted by his insecurity about his literary gifts, attempted to argue that he was a poetic genius. He also claimed that 'the irregularities and morbidnesses which commonly accompany genius' were an integral part of its essence, thus defending and valorizing his personal dislike of society.[122] The interesting issue here is not the quality of Brydges's poetry, but what the exchange between him and Bulwer tells us about the problem of genius in the 1820s and 1830s. The belief that suffering, neglect and alienation were often the concomitants of genius gave unsuccessful authors such as Keats, Brydges and Richard Henry Horne (see later) the mental strength to persist in their careers, but many others, like Bulwer, refused to accept this account of the relationship between the writer and society. Those who relied on deferring their rewards to posterity were thus not only faced with the obvious psychological and financial pressures that went along with this, but an ideological pressure that came from the contrast between two very different notions of the role of literature in modern Britain.

John Stuart Mill and the *Monthly Repository*

Brydges's view that literary genius was threatened by an unholy alliance of political economy and democratic politics was not unique. In the 1822 edition of *The Literary Character*, Isaac D'Israeli attacked 'a new race of jargonists, the barbarous metaphysicians of political economy, [who] have struck at the essential existence of the productions of genius in literature and art . . . rejecting whatever does not enter into their own restricted notions of "utility" '.[123] The increasing power of utilitarian discourse was conflated by Romantic conservatives with theories of political economy, the explosion of periodical writing for a 'mass' readership, and the diffusion of democratic ideas, into a vision of a debased culture in which genius could not flourish. Notable examples of this view are Thomas Carlyle's remarkable and influential *ER* essays 'Signs of the Times' (1828) and 'Characteristics' (1831). Literature, for Carlyle, had succumbed to the modern obsession with 'Mechanism': 'were Homer and Shakspeare [*sic*] members of any beneficed guild, or made Poets by means of it? ... No; Science and Art have, from first to last, been the free gift of Nature; an unsolicited, unexpected gift; often even a fatal one'.[124] And furthermore, the 'prevalence of Reviewing' revealed 'the diseased, self-conscious state of [modern] Literature', where there is no place for the spontaneous inspiration of true genius.[125]

But the sense that genius was under threat was not just felt by those who disliked the increasing democratization of society – in the early 1830s, John Stuart Mill wrote interestingly on the subject in the *Monthly Repository* (*MR*), a Unitarian miscellany founded in 1806.[126] In 1828, the Unitarian preacher W. J. Fox became editor and began turning it into a much more reformist, utilitarian-influenced journal, with more political and literary – and less theological – content. At the end of 1831, he became the journal's owner, and the *Repository* began expressing such liberal views that it was disowned by the Unitarian Association. As Isobel Armstrong has argued, Fox aimed 'to deepen and enrich the Benthamite tradition by correcting misapprehensions of it and associating it above all with literature. His reading of Benthamism meant in the first place, the dissemination of pleasure in its widest sense, the democratization of literature and the exploration of the links between literature and politics'.[127] Fox himself wrote in 1835 that 'the cultivation of a popular enjoyment and philosophy of Art, is amongst the primary objects of real Reformers'.[128] In order to fulfil his aims, the *Repository* had to show that an increasingly democratic society was not inevitably damaging to genius.

In August 1832, only a couple of months after the passing of the Reform Bill, the journal contained an anonymous article entitled 'Some Considerations Respecting the Comparative Influences of Ancient and Modern Times on the Development of Genius'. The writer, taking issue with the claim that 'the present age is singularly hostile to genius', gave a good account of the way in which such arguments were often formulated:

> that the mind cannot grow and thrive on the unnumbered medicaments which modern civilisation drugs it with; that with all our schools, and schoolmasters, and mechanics' institutes – with all our reviews, and magazines, and newspapers – with all our cyclopaedias, and digests, and abridgments ... we are on a wrong track; that the vaunted march of mind is but a 'rickety hobble;' that in losing the institutions and maxims of our gothic progenitors, we have lost all the higher and brighter manifestations of intellectual power.[129]

This passage brings out nicely the conservative nostalgia that was often implicit in attacks on modern civilization as damaging to the creative mind. But although the writer goes on to suggest that this is not the case, a continued emphasis on the threats facing genius in the present day – such as *'the intense and unintermitted rapidity with which outward forces and influences assail us'*[130] – rather weakens the power of his or her counter-arguments. The first of these is that there are new discoveries to be made in poetry and science. The second and concluding suggestion, elaborated on in an article the following month, is that Christianity will empower genius to resist those forces in the modern world that threaten it.[131]

John Stuart Mill, writing in the October 1832 number of the *Repository*, was signally unconvinced by these arguments, stating, first, that 'genius stands not in need of access to new truths', and, second, that Christian societies have not 'proportionally abounded in men of genius' compared to those of the ancients.[132] Mill, of course, had no desire to return to 'the institutions and maxims of... gothic progenitors', and yet he argued that the modern world *was* weak in genius compared to the Greeks and the Romans because modern education was obsessed with imparting knowledge ('cram') and did not teach people to think for themselves. Genius, for Mill, is no more than the capacity for independent thinking, and need not be 'a rare gift bestowed on few. By the aid of suitable culture all might possess it, although in unequal degrees'.[133] This is hardly a surprising statement for a utilitarian to make, but it is important to note that it is very different from the idea of genius often expressed in *Fraser's*. In order to try to reconcile a more democratic society with an emphasis on genius, Mill redefines the term so that it becomes, at least to some extent, available to all. Although Mill was strongly influenced by Carlyle at this time, his account of genius shows that their ideas about the relationship between the exceptional individual and society were always fundamentally different, and this would become more apparent over the next three decades. And by making modern education's obsession with 'facts' (which Mill, unlike Dickens, does not associate with utilitarianism) the sole scapegoat for the apparent decline in genius, Mill disassociates himself from the conservatism normally associated with such complaints.

However, some of the Mill's other writings at this time show that he was also aware of concerns about the pernicious effects of the periodical press and burgeoning 'mass' audience on original thought. In his 1833 article 'Writings of Junius Redivivus', a review of William Bridges Adams's *The Producing Man's Companion*, he argues (in an obviously Carlylean passage) that the main importance of books is that they allow us to know the souls of their authors. However,

> it is one of the evils of modern periodical writing, that we rarely learn from them to know their author. In those sibylline leaves wherein men scatter abroad their thoughts, or what seem their thoughts, we have little means of identifying the productions of the same sibyl; and no one particular oracle affords by itself sufficient materials for judging whether the prophet be a real *soothsayer*. It is so easy in a single article to pass off *adopted* ideas and feelings for the genuine produce of the modern mind; it is so difficult on one trial to detect him who, aiming only at the plausible, finds and converts to that meaner purpose the same arguments which occur to him who is earnestly seeking for the true.[134]

Anonymous periodical writing makes it hard to distinguish those writers who are truly inspired from those who take others' ideas in order to sound plausible to their readers. Thus the democratization of culture threatens to occlude, or perhaps even dissolve, the Romantic distinction between the genius author and the hack writer. The answer, Mill believes, is that journalists should follow Adams's example of a consistent *nom de plume*.[135] This consistency is to Adams's credit, yet he is '*not a great* writer'.

At this point, the argument becomes highly distinctive and sheds its Carlylean clothing. Because for Mill, Adams's lack of greatness is no bad thing – in the current state of social and political crisis, voluminous and able writers are needed who can 'popularize among the many, the more immediately practical results of the thought and experience of the few' through the medium of the periodical press. Any writer who seeks to do more than this will 'forgoe immediate usefulness' in the hope of reaching posterity and can have no role in 'the great intellectual business of our time'.[136] Literary greatness is superfluous in a culture dominated by ephemeral periodical writing, but Mill does not lament this because of his sense that he is writing at a moment of cultural crisis when rapid change is necessary. In his *Repository* articles, Mill articulated a widespread sense among reformers that the Romantic conception of genius as a quality belonging to a tiny elite who affected society in a 'subterraneous' (Brydges) or 'unacknowledged' (Shelley) fashion, or whose works could only be comprehended at some indefinite point in the future, was no longer useful in a modernizing culture.

Fraser's and the (in)dignity of literature

Writing in 1834, the poet Allan Cunningham concluded his *Biographical and Critical History of the British Literature of the Last Fifty Years* on a melancholy note:

> some one has desired me to describe the influence which men of genius have in this land: this can be done in a word – they have none. The editors of two or three leading newspapers have more to say with the country and the government, than all the bards which have breathed for these last fifty years. The influence of genius is recorded in its fortunes. Chatterton drank poison, because he could not find bread; Johnson was refused the means of improving his health abroad; Burns, at his death, had neither bread in his house, nor a penny in his pocket; Crabbe died a poor parson – preferment did not find him out; Scott crushed himself attempting independence, and his country refuses to save his books from the auctioneer; Byron was exiled and died all but cursing the land his genius adorns; Coleridge has been deprived of his small pension; Wordsworth lives by distributing stamps; Southey has a pint of thin wine a-day from the king; Moore has found verse, like virtue, it own reward; Hogg picks a mutton bone on Yarrow, and Wilson lives by moral philosophy. I bid the subject farewell.[137]

If Cunningham was just describing the sufferings of literary characters then this passage would be fairly unexceptional but his claim that they have no 'influence' with the country and the government is striking; here he is relying on both the archaic and modern uses of 'influence'. 'Men of genius' have no access to those in positions of power (the archaic usage) – this is reflected in their lack of adequate patronage and consequent poverty – and they also have little effect on public and governmental opinion (the modern usage), unlike the 'editors of two or three leading newspapers'. Reviewing Cunningham's book in *Fraser's*, Maginn wrote that he hoped to convince him that

> the number of those who have cause to quarrel with their genius is marvellously small. Genius is by no means such a slayer as people would sometimes make it appear, though certain causes must produce their natural effects in men of genius, as in men of meaner mould.[138]

In a similar way to Heraud, Maginn refuses to accept that the sufferings of authors are the result of their genius, although this is not exactly Cunningham's argument. It was important for *Fraser's* to keep genius 'pure' in this way in order to maintain its association with Christian virtue and Tory social ideology. However, the extended refutation of Cunningham that Maginn promised did not appear until 1838, in a leading article entitled 'Genius and the Public'.[139] This was also, in part, a very belated review of an anonymous book published in 1833, entitled *Exposition of the False Medium and Barriers Excluding Men of Genius from the Public*, written by the young poet, Richard Henry (later Hengist) Horne.[140] As Ann Blainey has shown, in the early 1820s, Horne had become an obsessive 'subscriber to Romantic poetic beliefs', and believed that his 'dissimilarity to other men' proved that he had a poetic vocation. He saw his heroes – Keats, Shelley and Hazlitt – as men of genius who had been victimized by a corrupt society.[141] His book is a rather histrionic depiction of the sufferings of writers, artists and scientists, which are, he argues, due in part to the ignorance and greed of the reading public and the government. In particular, he makes a scapegoat of publishers' readers, who make up the 'false medium' of his title. He is keen to emphasize that writers cannot generally be held personally responsible for their sufferings, stating that there is only 'a very limited degree of truth' in the idea that 'the personal misconduct or imprudence of men of genius, is the chief cause of their misfortunes'.[142] Instead, Horne argues that generally the transgressions of 'superior men' are due to 'strong passions that can find no proper vent [and which] must either destroy the individual with their smouldering and wasting fire, or else break forth in wrong directions'.[143]

Horne's claim that the crimes and sufferings of genius were caused by the conjunction of its powerful energies with the pressures of worldly want and neglect seemed to his reviewer to be a tendentious attempt to excuse the serious errors of immoral individuals, for not one of the 'eternally quoted list' of Chatterton, Otway, Savage, Burns and Sheridan:

> owed his misery to any thing more or less than to the very sufficient cause of an utter want of conduct. Talk of their genius ruining them, indeed! Had these men been *true to themselves*, their genius would have commanded the homage, as it did the admiration, of their contemporaries. Instead of this, by an entire disregard of all social restraints, they contrived to make the judicious grieve, and to bring the very name of poet into contempt among the sober-minded portion of the community.[144]

Here the alienation between the author and society is not inevitable, but the result of the misdemeanours of individuals who happen to be poets. And, although Horne's argument is much more about the neglect of genius by society than it is about the nature of genius, his reviewer uses this opportunity to attack the idea that genius was inherently eccentric:

> Can any effect be more pernicious than that produced, or likely to be produced, by such men, on those who come after them, and who, in the glory of their youth, and under the exaggerating influence of what is called the poetic temperament,

are but too ready to regard life under an illusive aspect, and to sneer at the suggestions of a sound judgement? Is not the plain English of all that is said on this subject by the sentimentalists, male and female, simply this, that the possession of genius is of itself a sufficient emancipation from ordinary moral and social restraints – that honesty, decorum, industry, and foresight, are for the humdrum drudges of everyday life; but that the ethereal essence of genius is far above all this, and that its extravagances, errors – nay, crimes – are to be palliated by the convenient creed, that 'the light which leads astray is the light from heaven?'[145]

Horne's reviewer, like Barbara Hofland and the writers of the *SMA*, identifies the claim that genius is an alibi for transgression as a threat to society. But this seems to me to be a deliberate misreading of Horne's argument, albeit one that is aided by the excesses of his rhetoric. I would suggest that what the reviewer really dislikes is the reformist agenda inherent in Horne's complaints about the neglect of genius. For the *Exposition* is not only dedicated to Bulwer, but also embraces the 'March of Intellect', panegyrizes Hazlitt (who had died in 1830), and argues that genius should be on the side of the many against the powerful few.[146]

Assuming that 'Genius and the Public' was written by Maginn, or one of his disciples, then it gives rise to an interesting irony, because during the early Victorian period his scandalously Bohemian lifestyle – exhibiting as it did a distinct lack of 'honesty, decorum, industry, and foresight' – was seen as a prime example of the eccentricities of the literary character. After his death from consumption in 1842, Maginn's family were forced to apply to the Royal Literary Fund for financial help. On the application form, Francis Mahony described the writer's wife and children 'as the casualties of a life wholly dependent on literature'.[147] This seems close to the argument that 'Genius and the Public' attacked, for here Maginn's profession is blamed for the sufferings of his family, rather than his own indigence and irresponsibility. It is probable that for much of the 1830s Maginn's income from journalism was about 1000 pounds a year, so he was hardly a neglected genius.[148] In 1850, Thackeray, once a writer for *Fraser's*, prompted a controversy surrounding the 'Dignity of Literature' with his representation of the literary life in *Pendennis*, in particular his portrayal of the periodical writer Captain Shandon, who was based on Maginn.[149] In one passage, the young Pendennis tries to defend Shandon's improvidence by stating that 'we must deal kindly with the eccentricities of genius, and remember that the very ardour and enthusiasm of temperament which makes the author delightful often leads the man astray'. This is too much for his sensible friend George Warrington, who denies

that there are so many geniuses as people who whimper about the fate of men of letters assert there are. There are thousands of clever fellows in the world who could, if they would, turn verses, write articles, read books, and deliver a judgement upon them … If a lawyer, or a soldier, or a parson, outruns his income, and does not pay his bills, he must go to jail; and an author must go, too.[150]

Warrington's complaint is that the term 'genius' is used as an alibi for the transgressions of authors because it represents writing as a special vocation with special privileges.

As far as he is concerned, it is a profession like any other, and thus authors must submit to the same rules as other members of society. Later in the novel, Thackeray (or the narrator) himself expresses his disagreement with the 'doctrine' 'that men of letters, and what is called genius, are to be exempt from the prose duties of this daily, bread-wanting, tax-paying life, are not to be made to work and pay like their neighbours'.[151] For Thackeray, such arguments were unnecessary because, as he made clear to his critics in 1850, he believed that 'literary men had earned for themselves a place in society quite as satisfactory as that enjoyed by other professional men'.[152] However, for writers like Dickens and Forster, who felt that 'literary men' were still socially and financially undervalued, Thackeray's portrayal of literary Bohemia seemed likely to damage their prospects of turning authorship into a respectable and well-rewarded profession that exhibited middle-class values such as 'self-discipline, hard work, methodical habits and temperate living'.[153] 'Genius' was at best an equivocal term for proponents of this model of authorship for three reasons. First, because it was associated with a model of literary production that valorized the products of 'inspiration' and denigrated those who practised literature as a 'trade'. Second, because, as we have seen, it was linked with eccentric and excessive forms of behaviour. And third, because it seemed to have become devalued through overuse and was associated with shallow celebrity and literary 'lionism'. Thus in the early Victorian period, the term 'genius' tends to be employed with more circumspection than was the case earlier in the century, and is more frequently used ironically. For example, in Dickens's early novels, malignant or insignificant characters such as Fagin in *Oliver Twist*, Simon Tappertit, Dennis the executioner, and Grip the raven in *Barnaby Rudge*, and Chevy Slyme in *Martin Chuzzlewit*, are all described as geniuses with conscious or unconscious irony depending on whether the describer is the narrator, or one of their sycophants.

This trend is also apparent in the anonymous two-part moral tale, 'A Most Talented Family', published in *Fraser's* in July and August 1836. This title may be a subtle hit at Bulwer, who, according to the *OED*, was the first writer to use 'talented' in its modern sense in his novel *Falkland* (1827). In 'Genius and the Public', it is described as an 'intolerable word', which the writer associates with the complaints of second-rate authors who do not deserve to rise above neglect. However, in 'A Most Talented Family', it is actually the word 'genius' that is represented as a sort of 'cant' term concealing moral transgression, self-interest and mediocrity. The story, therefore, has some similarities with Hofland's *The Son of a Genius*, but 'A Talented Family' is also clearly in the service of *FM*'s Tory politics.

The narrative is a simple one. Mr Foster, a country gentleman, is in despair at the lack of genius displayed by his otherwise worthy children, whom he compares unfavourably with his much-lauded niece and nephews, a fashionable belle with singing talents, a successful Radical politician, and a novelist whose fictional heroes include a body-snatcher and a savage otter hunter. However, when he visits the Seymour family in London, he discovers that the true situation is very different: Arthur, the politician, is an adventurer who has no loyalty to his party and seeks only his own preferment; his sister Julia is a dangerously irresponsible coquette; and Augustus, the novelist, writes meretricious, Bulwer-esque productions. The family life of the Seymours is desperately unhappy, for Foster's sister and her husband spend all their time worrying about the success of their offspring, who obviously have no respect for them. The young geniuses move in a society of 'brisk, shallow, second-rate' people, all 'Radicals', who are influenced solely by the pursuit of celebrity – the appearance of genius rather than its reality. This desire for present popularity, rather than true fame, is destructive not only to modern literature, but to family life:

> the love of notoriety... unknits the links of family tenderness, by rendering parents and children, brothers and sisters, even husbands and wives, careless and independent of the affections of each other, and only solicitous of the praise and admiration of a world of strangers.[154]

The story ends with a comeuppance for all three geniuses, and Foster is delighted to return to the bosom of his own 'dear, good, happy family'.

At the beginning of the story, Foster complains that his wife fails to value 'the gift of *genius*', and she replies that

> I am quite sensible that a certain something which is called *genius* is the idol set up by the good people of the nineteenth century, as the object of their preposterous adoration; but it's impossible for me to regret the absence of this quality in my family – for I am not quite certain that I comprehend what it is.[155]

Foster attempts to enlighten his wife through his nephew's discussion of the subject in his romance 'Scrapegrave, the Body-snatcher', a typical late Romantic account of genius as a sort of spiritual energy and sensibility to beauty which leads to strong passions and an aspiration for fame. Mrs Foster is signally unimpressed by her nephew's effusions, and states that she is delighted that her virtuous, healthy and handsome children do not possess 'this highly popular quality [which] may be regarded as the result of a strong tendency to madness, acted upon by an inordinate degree of selfishness and vanity'.[156] Although the course of the story shows Mrs Foster's preference for her own children to be correct, it does not *necessarily* support her definition of genius. 'A Most Talented Family' critiques the way in which the term is used in contemporary culture, and the way in which it is confused with transitory popularity. For it soon becomes clear to the reader – and Foster – that his relatives certainly lack genius in the spiritualized 'Heraudian' sense in which the term tended to be used in *Fraser's*. However, there is more going on here than the typical Romantic distinction between true genius and false celebrity. Foster is only able to discover that his relatives have been puffed up by newspaper panegyric by coming face-to-face with them – as these direct encounters are impossible for most of the public, the implication is that it is safer to avoid having anything to do with 'this highly popular quality'. The suggestion that the word 'genius' can conceal not only hollow pretensions, but a disdain for social morality which endangers the fabric of middle-class domestic life is entirely in keeping with the Evangelical arguments we examined earlier in the chapter. And 'A Talented Family' goes even further by linking this misuse of 'genius' with 'Radical' politics – thus the readers of *FM* are encouraged to treat the word with a great deal of suspicion.

Conclusion

The Romantic celebration of the creative artist is a truism of literary history, but accounts of genius in early nineteenth-century literary magazines were also highly contested. The figure of genius was frequently produced as a response to perceived cultural pressures, in particular the rise of the periodical press and the associated democratization of culture. Although writers like Coleridge saw critics and the reading public as enemies of genius, magazines like *Blackwood's* and *Fraser's* found the term highly useful. Genius was put forward as a redemptive, conservative force and great efforts were made to cleanse it of unfortunate associations. At the same time, there were frequent opposing claims that too much emphasis on genius could weaken respect for hard work, religion and possibly even damage the social fabric. In particular, two arguments associated with genius were identified as pernicious: first, that that it was often neglected by society, and second, that it was naturally prone to imprudence or even immorality. Although these claims often appeared in close proximity, they are distinct. But writers who opposed them tended, probably in order to have a bigger target at which to aim, to conflate them into the (imaginary) assertion that genius was an excuse for various forms of transgression, and that society was to blame for the sufferings of men of genius.

Two main factors associated with the increasing power of the middle classes lay behind this pressure on genius in the 1820s and 1830s: literary professionalization and a growing climate of moral earnestness. The massive expansion of the periodical press and the success of the serial novel led to the emergence of a large number of relatively well-paid writers who sought social respectability. For them, 'genius', with its possible associations with transgression, antisociality and disdain for the reading public, was not always a useful term. Evangelicals were also suspicious of a term that seemed to suggest that creative ability was a justification for the neglect of private duties. The result of this was that the discourse of genius was forced to adapt in order to survive, and did so principally through an association with Christian spirituality in its highest form. It also seems to have become increasingly confined to discussions of poetry and the poet's role, for many early Victorian critics had a grandiose conception of the poet as seer which they had largely inherited from Coleridge and Shelley. But, particularly in the 1830s, it often seemed that there was no active contemporary poet who could live up to this ideal, although the vogue for writing religious epics shows that many people were willing to try. Thus it was the Romantics, Wordsworth in particular, who were put forward, often nostalgically, as transcendent, redemptive figures whose works might aid spiritual–social rebirth. The problem for literary biographers was that this was often the principal justification for writing about the Romantic poets, but at the same time such figures could only be made interesting and sympathetic to readers by emphasizing their human qualities and failings. It is this tension between the 'ideal' and the 'real' that I examine in the following two chapters.

2 Literary biography and its discontents

Writing in 1809, Samuel Taylor Coleridge described the early nineteenth century as an 'Age of Personality' and suggested that contemporary literature was infected by an obsession with 'literary and political *Gossiping*'.[1] A few months later, he returned to the same theme, arguing the boundary between public and private was becoming dangerously blurred:

> In the present age (emphatically the age of personality!)...there are men, who trading in the silliest anecdotes, in unprovoked abuse and senseless eulogy, think themselves nevertheless employed both worthily and honourably, if only all this be done '*in good set terms*,' and from the Press, and of *public* Characters: a class which has encreased so rapidly of late, that it becomes difficult to consider what Characters are to be considered as private...A crime it is...thus to introduce the spirit of vulgar scandal, and personal inquietude into the Closet and the Library, environing with evil passions the very Sanctuaries, to which we should flee for refuge from them![2]

Coleridge was not alone in claiming that the 'sanctuary' of private life was threatened by press intrusion and, as was often the case, his views were, in part, a conservative reaction to the expansion of the reading public. However, he was correct that writers and readers during the Romantic period were generally more interested in the private lives of 'public characters' than their eighteenth-century forebears had been. This was especially true with regard to authors, who, perhaps for the first time in history, could become celebrities in the sense that their personalities and, in extreme cases, their private lives, could be an integral part of the marketing and consumption of their works. The development of the idea of original genius during the preceding decades meant that literary texts were seen increasingly as expressions of the inner selves of their creators. It was inevitable that there would be a strong upsurge in biographical writing on writers at the same time as their works began to be approached as self-revelation and, in some cases, to invite such an approach. Genius, it was widely believed, could be discovered and comprehended through examining the appearance, personal habits, and private manners of authors – and thus it was sometimes argued that 'reading' the life was a vital adjunct to reading the text.

This claim was challenged by a strong anti-biographical discourse that constructed an absolute boundary between a person's public life – their writings, speeches and so on – and private life – their personal character, appearance and relationships with family and friends. In the early nineteenth century, the home was being increasingly idealized as a refuge from the tensions and conflicts of the public sphere and therefore even the most hagiographic writer had to be wary of crossing the line between the two: at best, it might be seen as a breach of the rules of social propriety, and, at worst, it could be perceived as an act of terrible betrayal.[3] This chapter will examine Romantic-period debates about that validity of literary biography and, in particular, the central problem facing literary biographers: how to distinguish a legitimate interest in 'genius' from pernicious gossip.[4]

Biographical debates: William Wordsworth and Thomas Carlyle

The scope of the Romantic debate about the value and limitations of literary biography can be understood by looking at two accounts of the genre, both of which were prompted by biographies of Burns. Wordsworth's *A Letter to a Friend of Robert Burns* (1816) was written at the request of Gilbert Burns, who sought Wordsworth's advice as to the best way of restoring his elder brother's battered reputation through a defence of the poet to be attached to a new edition of his poetry that Gilbert was superintending. Carlyle's *Edinburgh Review* (*ER*) article on Burns was published twelve years later, ostensibly as a review of Lockhart's *Life of Burns* (1827). These two essays mark out the parameters of Romantic discourse on the biography of authors. By the end of the *Letter*, Wordsworth has utterly denigrated literary biography; by the end of his review, Carlyle has turned it into a vital act of spiritual interpretation.

Although they discuss different biographies, the particular criticisms made by the two men are interestingly similar. Both argue that past biographers of Burns have not shown true insight into his mind and motivation. Wordsworth argues that Currie has damaged Burns's reputation due to his 'superficial knowledge' of the poet, which has led him to concentrate on the external events of Burns's biography, rather than his inner life:

> here is a revolting account of a man of exquisite genius, and confessedly of many high moral qualities, sunk into the lowest depths of vice and misery! But the painful story, not withstanding its minuteness, is incomplete – in essentials it is deficient; so that the most attentive and sagacious reader cannot explain how a mind, so well established by knowledge, fell – and continued to fall, without power to prevent or retard its own ruin.[5]

Because Currie's biography does not aid the reader to understand what lay behind Burns's behaviour, it has harmed his reputation by giving a catalogue of debauchery. The dangers of biography that merely compiles facts are also identified by Carlyle in his review of Lockhart. He praises him for giving a better account of Burns's character than his predecessors, and makes a distinction between mere 'lives' and true biographies, stating that if an individual is deserving of biography, then 'we have always been of opinion that the public ought to be made acquainted with all the inward springs and relations of his character'.[6] Carlyle develops this view in his

1830 article on 'Jean Paul Friedrich Richter' where he argues that most biographies fail because they concentrate on the facts of the subject's life to the exclusion of his spiritual being; thus they are 'mere Indexes of a Biography'.[7]

Wordsworth and Carlyle agree that biography fails if it deals merely with the material and the external. Instead, the biographer must engage in a sympathetic way with his subject in order to reveal his (or, very occasionally, her) psychological complexities. However, Wordsworth goes on to argue that 'true' biography is impossible because (a) only a close friend of an author can know enough about his life and 'internal springs' so as to be a truthful biographer, but (b) such a friend would have too much sympathy to reveal the author's foibles to the world (p. 120). The impossibility of reconciling sympathy and knowledge also affects the publication of an author's correspondence. Most readers, lacking sympathy with the subject, will not know how to read his letters properly, to distinguish sentiments expressed 'to gratify the tastes of several correspondents', or 'for the momentary amusement of the writer's own fancy', from 'those which his judgement deliberately approves, and his heart faithfully cherishes' (pp. 120–1).

This argument is similar to the criticisms that were to be levelled at Thomas Medwin's and Leigh Hunt's biographies of Byron by reviewers such as Thomas Love Peacock and John Gibson Lockhart. It was claimed that both biographers often took Byron's conversation and letters too seriously and that he enjoyed saying outrageous things to them purely for effect. This may have been true, but the criticism was also a means for partisan reviewers to construct Byron according to their own ideological template; to dismiss as insincere any of his reported utterances – on religion, for example – that were inconsistent with the image of the poet that they were trying to create. Furthermore, this argument served to emphasize the distinction between the genius, his biographer and the reading public. Not only the majority of biographers, but also most readers were represented as incapable of properly interpreting the private conversations – or even the private lives – of geniuses, for (it was claimed) they could not read critically and took everything at face value. Wordsworth's aim in the *Letter* is to show that the private life of genius is not fit for public consumption because a mass readership cannot properly understand the eccentricities that men like Burns often exhibit: 'it is the privilege of poetic genius to catch, under certain restrictions of which perhaps at the time of its being exerted it is but dimly conscious, a spirit of pleasure wherever it can be found' (p. 124). But, conversely, in the hands of Carlyle, this argument about the ignorance of readers could also be used to elevate literary biography by valorizing the role of the biographer or critic as a crucial interpreter and mediator of the conversation, appearance and actions of exceptional individuals to the reading public.

Wordsworth's fear is that the ability to judge between the conflicting demands of the subject's right to privacy, and legitimate public interest in biography,

> runs a risk of becoming extinct upon us, if the coarse intrusions into the recesses, the gross breaches upon the sanctities, of domestic life, to which we have lately been more and more accustomed, are to be regarded as indications of a vigorous state of public feeling.
>
> (p. 122)

This passage strongly echoes Coleridge's lament on the 'age of personality'. Significantly, during the period in which Wordsworth composed the *Letter* (December 1815 to early February 1816), Byron's separation from his wife was prompting intense speculation and savage attacks in the press. It seems likely that the 'gross breaches upon the sanctities of domestic life' to which Wordsworth referred would have made contemporary readers immediately think of the controversy surrounding Byron's marriage, and this context, I think, partly explains the vehemence of Wordsworth's antipathy to biographical approaches to poets. Byron was an example and a warning to other literary figures of the strange, double-edged nature of celebrity, the way in which public adulation could quickly turn into public revulsion. He had encouraged and manipulated public interest in his private life, but was ultimately driven from England by the very culture of 'personality' which he had helped to foster.

The crux of Wordsworth's argument in the *Letter* is that there is an essential difference between the biographies of authors and those of men 'who have borne an active part in the world'. In the case of the latter, the knowledge of their character gained 'by the scrutiny of their private lives, conduces to explain not only their public conduct, but that of those with whom they have acted'. In the case of authors, however, he argues that 'our business is with their books – to understand and enjoy them. And, of poets more especially, it is true – that, if their works be good, they contain within themselves all that is necessary to their being comprehended and relished' (p. 122). Poets like Burns are particularly unsuitable subjects for biography, for 'the principal charm' of their writings 'depends upon the familiar knowledge which they convey of the personal feelings of their authors'. For Wordsworth, the danger here is that the discrepancy between the poet's character, as revealed in his (or possibly her) work, and the character represented in their biography, may diminish the enjoyment and instruction that the reader gains from their poetry. Burn's 'poetic' character, although based on his 'human' one, is 'airy and spiritual': 'plague, then, upon your remorseless hunters after matters of fact . . . when they would convince you that the foundations of this admirable edifice are hollow; and that its frame is unsound!' (p. 123).

By the mid-1810s Wordsworth was a well-known cultural figure and was aware at the time he wrote the *Letter* that he was a potential subject for biography. His affair with Annette Vallon in the early 1790s and the existence of his illegitimate daughter meant that he had much to hide from the inquisitive. It is also possible that he was aware of rumours about his relationship with Dorothy and feared that they might be made public after his death. Like Coleridge, Wordsworth used his attack on the contemporary popularity of biography as a way of justifying his own lack of readers, representing it as a sign of the debasement and ignorance of the reading public who cared more about gossip than art. So the *Letter* should be considered in tandem with the *Essay, Supplementary to the Preface* (1815) in that both texts represent genius as alienated from contemporary literary culture, which consists of reviewers and biographers who pander to readers hungry for literary controversy and tittle-tattle.

Whilst Wordsworth tries to show that the knowledge of the 'genius' of Burns that can be extrapolated from his works is all that the reader requires, Carlyle claims that the story of the poet's life is much more important and powerful than his poetry: 'True and genial as his poetry must appear, it is not chiefly as a poet, but as a man, that he interests and affects us'.[8] For Carlyle, Burns's poetry did not give true expression to his genius due to the peculiarly troubled circumstances of his life, and its brevity. Thus 'the Writings he has left', offer 'no more than a poor, mutilated fraction of what was in him; brief, broken glimpses of a genius that could never show itself complete'.[9] As Carlyle then embarks on a lengthy and panegyrical critique of Burns's poetry, he implicitly concedes that this account of it is an exaggeration. However, about halfway through the essay, he again emphasizes the greater importance of the poet's life history. 'Far more interesting than any of his written works', Carlyle claims,

> are his acted ones: the Life he willed and was fated to lead among his fellow-men. These Poems are but like little rhymed fragments scattered here and there in the grand unrhymed Romance of his earthly existence; and it is only when intercalated in this at their proper places, that they attain their full measure of significance.[10]

This extraordinary statement represents a new extreme in the Romantic interest in the creative artist as a private individual. It is not only that Burns's poems can be properly appreciated only within the context of his biography, but that his most important production was his life, his 'acted' works.[11] For Carlyle, the facts of this life are there to be sensitively and charitably interpreted; just like his poems, the narrative of Burns's existence is there to be *read*.

It is only towards the end of the article that Carlyle attempts to show why he believes literary biography to be so important. He invokes the example of Byron in order to argue that wealth or social status would not have made Burns happy, for suffering is the inevitable consequence of genius. As 'missionaries to their generation', both men existed 'in dim throes of pain, this divine behest lay smouldering within them; for they knew not what it meant, and felt it only in mysterious anticipation, and they had to die without articulately uttering it'.[12] This notion of the poet, or man of letters, as missionary, prophet and seer ('*vates*') is of course central to Carlyle's thought and is further developed in his other biographical essays, such as those on Richter, as well as *On Heroes and Hero-Worship* (1841). Men like Burns and Byron are important for Carlyle because they are messengers to mankind who reveal the essentially spiritual nature of reality, 'a perpetual Priesthood . . . teaching all men that a God is still present in their life; that all "Appearance," whatsoever we see in the world, is but as a vesture for the "Divine Idea of the World" ' (Carlyle's quotations are from Fichte).[13]

However, Carlyle argues in both 'Burns' and *On Heroes and Hero-Worship* that Burns is important not as a successful missionary, but as a failed one. Paradoxically, such failure may be more interesting and important than success, as Carlyle implicitly concedes by discussing 'failures' such as Rousseau, Johnson and Burns in 'The Hero as Man of Letters', rather than Goethe, who, he claims, was a successful prophet. In this lecture, suffering 'every species of worldly Distress and Degradation' is represented as an essential part of the life of a heroic author – yet, in the article on 'Burns', Carlyle asserts that worldly circumstances prevented the poet from carrying out his prophetic mission in his lifetime. This is the rich paradox at the heart of Carlyle's theory of heroic genius. The hero is a Christ-like figure whose suffering is his success and whose life story offers others the possibility of redemption. The biographer, by drawing attention to the failure of the author's life, can help to transcend this failure and allow the expression of the spiritual truth to take place. He does this partly by bringing out the true qualities of the author, which were misunderstood in his lifetime, but mainly by showing that the neglect of such a genius is an important sign of the failings of the society in which he lived. So Carlyle completes Burns's task through his narrative of the poet's life, and thus, by implication, is himself a heroic man of letters.

Carlyle and Wordsworth have related views with regard to the messianic status of the poet, yet they disagree strongly about the usefulness of literary biography. Whereas Wordsworth feared that he might become a victim of the culture of celebrity that he saw around him, Carlyle's championing of biography not only had much to do with his philosophical and political interest in 'Great Men' but also effectively validated his own role as an up-and-coming literary critic and biographer. In 1828, these genres were much powerful in comparison to poetry than had been the case in 1816. The publication of 'Burns' in the *ER* is also important, for as a potent symbol of Scottish culture and national identity, the poet was a locus of symbolic conflict between periodicals such as the *Edinburgh* and *Blackwood's*. Jeffrey's criticisms of the poet in his 1809 review allowed Tories like Wordsworth and Lockhart to represent him as an enemy of poetic genius, and to claim Burns for their own. Furthermore, as F. R. Hart has shown, in both *Peter's Letters to His Kinsfolk* and the *Life of Burns*, Lockhart used the treatment of the poet during his lifetime as a way of attacking the Scottish Enlightenment, which he associated with Whig dominance in Edinburgh, and the rise of the *ER*.[14] Thus the position of Carlyle's article within the *Edinburgh* can be seen as an attempt to present the periodical as supportive of Scottish literature in order to supersede Lockhart's championing of the poet in his recent biography, and to wrest Burns back from the Tories.

Biographical debates: William Hazlitt, Thomas De Quincey, Isaac D'Israeli

In an 1820 review of a new edition of Joseph Spence's *Anecdotes, Observations, and Characters of Books and Men*, William Hazlitt responded to Wordsworth's criticisms of literary biography: 'It has been made an objection to the biography of literary men, that the principle events of their lives are their works; and that there is little else to be known of them, either interesting to others, or perhaps creditable to themselves.'[15] There is something rather sly about the way in which Hazlitt describes the poet's argument, for the slightly ironic 'perhaps' serves to suggest that Wordsworth's position is fundamentally defensive and self-interested. In contrast, Hazlitt argues from the position of the curious reader, rather than the self-protective writer:

> It is the very absence of grave transactions or striking vicissitudes that turns our attentions more immediately upon themselves [literary men], and leaves us at leisure to explore their domestic habits, and descry their little

peculiarities of temper... We draw down genius from its air-built citadel in books and libraries; and make it our play-mate, and our companion. We see how poets and philosophers 'live, converse, and behave,' like other men. We reduce theory to practice; we translate words into things, and books into men. It is, in short, the *ideal* and abstracted existence of authors that renders their personal character and private history a subject of so much interest. The difficulty of forming almost any inference at all from what men *write* to what they *are*, constitutes the chief value of the problem which the literary biographer undertakes to solve.[16]

For Hazlitt, it is the fact that there is no *necessary* connection between the character of a writer and that of his works that makes literary biography so interesting. He goes on to give Johnson as an example of the difference between author and man; this reference is particularly apt, for Johnson had himself remarked on such a discrepancy, stating that 'there has often been observed a manifest and striking contrariety between the life of an author and his writings'.[17] This view was still fairly commonplace during the early nineteenth century; however, Hazlitt's argument is interestingly original in that he makes this 'contrariety' the sole justification for literary biography. Unlike Johnson he does not claim that the life narrative of a genius can offer moral teaching to the reader; neither does he, like De Quincey and others, claim that literary biography is useful or interesting in that it sheds light on the works of the author, or on his 'intellectual characteristics'.

Hazlitt is able to take up a position in which the aim of literary biography is principally the satisfaction of 'a curiosity... that has its origin in enthusiasm' because he is neither trying to defend himself from potential biographers, nor is he seeking to justify his own biographical practice.[18] However, Thomas De Quincey was in a very different position when he came to write his first article on William Wordsworth for *Tait's Edinburgh Magazine* (TEM) in January 1839. His *Tait's* articles on the recently deceased Coleridge in 1834–5 had prompted a hysterical response among the Grasmere circle, who had seen their publication as an appalling act of betrayal motivated by greed and envy. Carlyle recorded that Robert Southey, in particular, was apoplectic with rage and had told Coleridge's son, Hartley, that he ought to go to Edinburgh with 'a strong cudgel... and give De Quincey, publicly in the streets there, a sound beating – as a calumniator, cowardly spy, traitor, base betrayer of the hospitable social hearth, for one thing!'.[19]

This controversy seems to have informed De Quincey's careful attempt in the first of the Wordsworth articles to discriminate between his approach to his subject and mere literary gossip.[20] He begins by claiming that not only is Wordsworth 'destined to be had in the everlasting remembrance by every generation of men', but that as a great poet who has made himself 'necessary to the human heart', he will be remembered with an intensity of feeling, which is not accorded to the memories of great philosophers, reformers and so on. This leads on to a fantasy of cultural imperialism in which, due to the spread of English throughout the world, Wordsworth's poetry will be loved by those who 'have any depth of feeling... in every clime and every land'.[21] This global popularity, De Quincey argues, will inevitably lead to a desire for information about the poet himself.

> Commensurate with the interest in the poetry will be a secondary interest in the poet – in his personal appearance, and his habits of life, *so far as they can be supposed at all dependent on his intellectual characteristics*; for, with respect to differences that are purely casual, and which illustrate no principle of higher origin than accidents of education or chance position, it is a gossiping taste only that could seek for such information, and a gossiping taste that would choose to consult it.[22]

Legitimate interest, and the biography that serves it, will only seek information that is relevant to an understanding of the subject's 'intellectual characteristics', and thus, presumably, their works. On the other hand, gossip deals in the 'casual' or chance attributes of its subject, those which are purely the result of the happenstance of his past 'education' – which means more than simply 'schooling' – and present situation in life. Although the passage is a little unclear, I do not think that De Quincey is thus implying that such cultural factors have no *effect* on the subject's 'intellectual characteristics', but rather that they also produce other effects that are entirely unconnected with those characteristics, and which are not the legitimate province of biography.

In the second part of the justification, De Quincey attempts to defend himself further from potential accusations of gossip:

> Meantime, it is under no such gossiping taste that volumes have been written upon the mere portraits and upon the possible portraits of Shakspeare; and how invaluable should we all feel any record to be, which should raise the curtain upon Shakspeare's daily life – his habits, personal and social, his intellectual tastes, and his opinions on contemporary men, books, events, or national prospects! I cannot, therefore, think it necessary to apologize for the most circumstantial notices past or to come of Wordsworth's person and habits of life.[23]

At first, De Quincey seems to be on the verge of contradicting himself, for the desire for *any* record, that, as he puts it, 'should raise the curtain on Shakspeare's daily life', is surely dangerously close to revealing, in his own terms, a 'gossiping taste'. But his examples of what lies behind this curtain can clearly all be related to Shakespeare's 'intellectual characteristics' and thus the original distinction is maintained. In the final sentence, however, it is again threatened, for De Quincey's explicit refusal to apologize for the 'most circumstantial notices' only serves to make his discomfort with them all the more plain, as he clearly feels that his readers might be, perhaps even should be, expecting such an apology.

The passage that I have been discussing comes towards the end of the first instalment of the Wordsworth reminiscences, after De Quincey has spent some time describing the poet's personal appearance. Considering the prevalent physiognomical assumptions of the period, it is easy to see how the discussion of Wordsworth's face can be justified as legitimate, but it is much less clear that the account of the poet's bad legs, 'mean appearance', and the fact that he walks like an insect, is not, in De Quincey's own terms, pandering to a 'gossiping taste'. For he makes no attempt to connect these attributes to the poet's genius – of course, the purpose of the justification we have discussed is to convince the reader that everything that De Quincey relates, or has related, about Wordsworth is bound to shed light on his 'intellectual characteristics'. Thus this passage is, in part, a piece of sophistry, for De Quincey gives the reader no way of distinguishing between biography and gossip, except on the biographer's say-so.

Naturally, Wordsworth and his family were horrified by the articles, especially as De Quincey had gone further than most biographers in writing about the living. But it is the remarks above on 'the most circumstantial notices', rather than the relatively inoffensive content of the 'portraits', that can help us to understand why Wordsworth was so opposed to literary biography throughout his career. He clearly realized that if people believed that an author's genius was evident in his private life, then the biographical remit was potentially infinite. Many Romantic biographers presented the smallest details of their subject's appearance or manners as offering insights into their particular psychological makeup; for example, in the essay 'My First Acquaintance with Poets', Hazlitt makes Coleridge's walk a sign of his intellectual and political instability, and the size of his nose supposedly reveals his lack of willpower.[24] Biographical readings of the subject's physiognomy were commonplace, and the currency that phrenology gained in England during the 1810s shows a cultural obsession with reading the signs of character or genius in the most apparently insignificant details of personal appearance.

However, those who linked authorial and textual character were faced with a problem where there was a clear discrepancy between an individual's writings and his behaviour in private life. One contemporary response to this difficulty was by recourse, not always explicitly, to the concept of 'genius' as the author's 'best self'. This is similar to the classical/Renaissance model of the inspired artist; genius, in this view, is something that possesses the author for a short time as he writes, departing as he returns to his everyday affairs.[25] That there was an essential contradiction between this theory, and the biographical approach that constructed 'genius' as omnipresent in the quotidian, is evident in the work of Isaac D'Israeli. In the 1818 edition of *The Literary Character*, he suggests that 'an author and an artist may yield no certain indication of their personal character in their works',[26] but refuses to conclude that therefore writing is a mere exercise or performance: 'can he whose secret power raises so many emotions in our breasts, be without any of his own? . . . An alien to all the wisdom and virtue he inspires? No!'[27] His solution to this problem seeks to reconcile both anecdotal evidence and his belief in authorial sincerity:

> An author has, in truth, two distinct characters; the literary, formed by the habits of his study; the personal, by the habits of his situation. And, however the personal character may contrast with that of their genius, still are the works themselves genuine, and exist as realities for us – and were so doubtless to themselves, in the act of composition. In the calm of study, a beautiful imagination may convert him whose morals are corrupt, into an admirable moralist, awakening feelings, which yet may be cold in the business of life.[28]

D'Israeli's account goes further than Wordsworth's, for although the latter had represented Burns's 'poetic' character as a purified version of his human one, he also implied that the two were strongly linked. On the other hand, D'Israeli represents the author's imagination as allowing him to transcend the personal character produced by his circumstances and to put on, in seclusion, the mantle of genius.[29]

The difficulty with D'Israeli's argument is that while it offers a solution to the problem of the discrepancy between life and art, it undermines the project that it is meant to support. For if the literary work is produced in seclusion, 'under the influence' of genius, then the personal life and character of the writer should be of little relevance to understanding his work. Why then does D'Israeli spend a whole book attempting to describe, through biographical anecdotes, the 'literary character', which he claims consistently reveals the same personality traits and personal habits? Of course, like most of his contemporaries, D'Israeli ultimately assumes that there *is* a link between the private life and public utterances of an author, and his theory of genius as a form of temporary inspiration is simply trying to account for those writers who do not fit easily into this model. However, there is a tension between positing a potential *separation* between a writer's personality and his genius, at the same time as attempting to give an account of the peculiar personality traits *associated with* genius. This tension, which is also apparent in many biographical articles, results from the popularization of the Romantic model of genius during the early nineteenth century.

Genius is meant to be the possession of the gifted few. It cannot be explained by system, or reduced to rules. Its workings are ineffable, incomprehensible to ordinary mortals and perhaps even to men of genius themselves. In the 1820s and 1830s, periodical writers sought to emphasize the transcendent nature of genius whilst at the same time mediating it to their readers through biographical accounts of particular authors. They were thus faced with the task of revealing the spiritual through the quotidian, whilst at the same time showing the spiritual to be utterly separate from the quotidian. The only writer to deal effectively with this problem was Carlyle, who did so by breaking down the distinction between the spiritual world of art and the material world of biography: 'there is no heroic poem in the world,' he argued, 'but is at bottom a biography, the life of a man: also, it may be said, there is no life of a man, faithfully recorded, but is a heroic poem of its sort, rhymed or unrhymed'.[30] However, for Carlyle, it would require an exceptional individual to bring out the poetry of his subject's life: the criticisms that were made with regard to Hunt's inability to comprehend Byron could be applied to anyone, and the only way that biographers could circumvent this was to set themselves up, implicitly or explicitly, as the peers of their subjects. Ultimately, it would take a genius to interpret and mediate the life of another genius to the reading public.

The problem of 'personality'

In an essay published in the *London Magazine* (*LM*) in November 1820, its editor, John Scott, launched a powerful assault on *Blackwood's Edinburgh Magazine* (*BEM*), accusing its writers of fraud, misuse of anonymity and 'the most licentious personal abuse'. He took particular issue with the 'Cockney School' articles, claiming that they were *ad hominem* attacks which contained 'no genuine criticism', and repeated his accusations in the following two numbers.[31] These articles led to Scott's death following a grotesquely mismanaged duel with John Gibson Lockhart's friend, John Christie, at Chalk Farm in February 1821.[32] This event is still a well-known example of the excesses of literary warfare in the early nineteenth century, and at the time it seemed to confirm the idea that *Blackwood's* was infecting literary culture with 'personality'. But were things really that simple? In an important article, Peter Murphy has examined the magazine's 'obsessive interest in the interaction, attachment and slippage between authors (published names) and persons (bodies indicated by names)'.[33] He shows that *Blackwood's* writers constructed an abstract written world which effaced individual personality through the use of a variety of pseudonyms that could not easily be related to the real authors of the magazine. Paradoxically, this destabilization of public identity by sundering it from the private realm was accompanied by a controversial form of criticism that, as in the case of Hunt, sought 'to punish written egotism by a fierce obtrusion of the bodily into the written', that is, through references to the appearances and private lives of *Blackwood's* victims.[34]

In the 'Cockney School' articles, 'Z.' (Lockhart) constructs a highly detailed comic character who is ostensibly an extrapolation from Hunt's poetry, but who inevitably serves to represent Hunt as an actual individual. This strategy is most apparent in the following well-known passage:

> The poetry of Mr Hunt is such as might be expected from the personal character and habits of its author. As a vulgar man is perpetually labouring to be genteel – in like manner, the poetry of this man is always on the stretch to be grand. He has been allowed to look for a moment from the antichamber into the saloon, and mistaken the waving of feathers and the painted floor for the *sine qua non's* of elegant society. He would fain be always tripping and waltzing, and is sorry that he cannot be allowed to walk about in the morning with yellow breeches and flesh-coloured silk-stockings. He sticks an artificial rose-bud into his button hole in the midst of winter. He wears no neckcloth, and cuts his hair in imitation of the Prints of Petrarch.[35]

Is this detailed description of Hunt put forward purely as a metaphor for his poetical pretentiousness, or is Lockhart also describing Hunt's real physical appearance? The confusion is probably deliberate, but his comments on the morality of *The Story of Rimini* seem much more clearly to be a personal attack. Hunt's 'Muse' is described as a vulgar prostitute, and the reader is informed that 'his mind seems absolutely to gloat over all the details of adultery and incest'. The point is to insinuate that Hunt himself is as depraved as his poem, and Lockhart goes on to claim that

> the very Concubine of so impure a wretch as Leigh Hunt would be to be pitied, but alas! for the Wife of such a Husband! For him there is no charm in simple Seduction; and he gloats over it only when accompanied with Adultery and Incest.[36]

The 'immorality' of *The Story of Rimini* reveals Hunt to be a monster in private life, but Lockhart's reference to Hunt's wife was excessive even for *Blackwood's*, and William Blackwood cut this passage in later editions of the magazine.[37] Unsurprisingly, the removal of a couple of sentences from the first 'Cockney School' article did not mollify Hunt, who demanded that 'Z.' reveal his true identity, and threatened that, if it remained concealed, the publishers of the 'foul scandal' would have to face 'the consequences of their delinquency', that is, a libel action.[38] His attacker dismissed Hunt's complaints in *Blackwood's*, stating that 'when I charged you with depraved morality, obscenity, and indecency, I spoke not of Leigh Hunt the man...I have no reason to doubt that your private character is respectable'. This is disingenuous, and Lockhart goes on to imply that he has *every* reason to doubt Hunt's respectability: 'I judged of you from your works, and I maintain they are little calculated to support such a conclusion'.[39] Lockhart's claim that he had merely attacked Hunt as an author failed to convince his victim, who noted that 'Z.' had misrepresented 'my actions, my motives, my very reading, nay, my personal manners and very walk'.[40] Three months later, Lockhart, possibly emboldened by the lack of court proceedings, came up with a much stronger formulation of the relationship between author and text than previously:

> There can be no radical distinction between the private and public character of a poet. If a poet sympathizes with and justifies wickedness in his poetry, he is a wicked man. It matters not that his private life may be free from wicked actions. Corrupt his moral principles must be – and if his conduct has not been flagrantly immoral, the cause must be looked for in constitution, &c. but not in conscience. It is therefore of little or no importance, whether Leigh Hunt be or be not a bad private character. He maintains, that he is a most excellent private character, and that he would blush to tell the world how highly he is thought of by an host of respectable friends...In such a case, the world will never be brought to believe even the truth.[41]

Poetry, then, reveals the personal character of its author, and may actually give a more accurate impression of this than the author's private life, for, in the case of Hunt, it reveals the true perniciousness of his desires. Lockhart concedes that Hunt may be a respectable private man, but claims that this is simply because he is not strong enough for immoral conduct – perhaps a reference to Hunt's tendency to inform the readers of the *Examiner* about the state of his health.

It was not simply the need to avoid a libel action that initially made Lockhart slippery on the issue as to whether or not Hunt was immoral in private life, for, as Murphy has shown, the writers of *Blackwood's Magazine* continually played on contemporary confusion about the relationship between author and text. Taken as a whole, what is particularly intriguing about the 'Cockney School' articles is that they inhabit both sides of the *Blackwood's* paradox of authorship. On the one hand, they bring Hunt, Keats and Hazlitt into the world of semi-fictional characters that supposedly wrote the magazine, such as 'Christopher North', 'Morgan Odoherty' and 'Philip Kempferhausen', and although this is an act of coercion, it is also an elaborate joke that seemed to sunder *Blackwood's* victims from their real physical existence, and turn them into (sometimes affectionate) caricatures. Although the seriousness of the 'Cockney School' attacks should not be underestimated, by the early 1820s Hunt was treated with a familiar raillery which was similar to the way in which the magazine dealt with 'friends' such as Hogg and De Quincey in the *Noctes Ambrosianae*. On the other hand, the use of *ad hominem* references, such as to Keats's training as an apothecary, Hunt's family life, or Hazlitt's alleged sexual misdemeanours in the Lake District, clearly entailed an obtrusion of the material into this supposedly abstract world of authorship, and one which intended to damage the real prospects of the magazine's victims.

It is no wonder then that enemies of *Blackwood's* found themselves caught up in its paradoxes, for when they sought to attack its use of 'personality', they were confronted by a confusing world of fictitious and semi-fictitious characters which protected the identities of the magazine's real authors. Murphy notes that John Scott's recourse to 'the rhetoric of clarity and exposure' with regard to personal identity is weakened by the fact that he himself attempts to speak for others such as Coleridge, who, as it turned out, supported the magazine. I would add that this rhetoric also proved contradictory when Scott attacked Lockhart as the true editor of the periodical, for in fact the editorship was a combined effort between Wilson, Lockhart and Blackwood, with the last-named probably having the final editorial say-so.[42]

Difficulties similar to those of Scott were experienced by Macvey Napier, the probable author of the anonymous pamphlet *Hypocrisy Unveiled and Calumny Detected in a Review of Blackwood's Magazine* (1818).[43] Napier complains that *Blackwood's* exploits the worst proclivities of the reading public: 'All the privacies of life are ransacked – all the sanctuaries of our nature explored and violated, for the purposes of feeding an insatiate and depraved appetite for scandal and detraction.'[44] He goes on to accuse the magazine of 'exhibiting personal defects and innocent peculiarities to the broad gaze of the public', and then attacks John Wilson in very personal terms, partly through a brief parody of the infamous Chaldee Manuscript.[45] Napier fears that 'no man would be safe, nor could any one of us promise himself a moment's happiness, if all the errors of his life might be raked up at every moment, and thrown in his teeth at the discretion of a scoundrel',[46] but finishes by stating his familiarity with the 'names, characters and schemes' of the *Blackwood's* writers and threatens that if 'they shall persist in their work of calumny and defamation, we shall in no respect spare them' – clearly a case of 'an eye for an eye'.[47] The pamphlet is meant to be an attack on 'personality', but ends up simply repeating the exaggerated rhetoric of personal vilification to be found in *Blackwood's*.

Later in the nineteenth century, the high-spirited attacks of *Blackwood's* early years were often put forward as the *ne plus ultra* of 'personality'. As part of his campaign to reform literary culture in the early 1830s, Edward Lytton Bulwer argued strongly against anonymous criticism, claiming that it was frequently a cover for vicious personal remarks. *Blackwood's* was his favourite example of this tendency:

> in order to obtain a sale, those bad passions in human nature which adore malice and garbage on personalities, were to be addressed . . . It called names, blustered,

and blackguarded: when it talked of an author, it informed you that he was 'pimpled', and never ridiculed his writings without abusing his face.[48]

In the course of a similar discussion in *England and the English* (1833), he exclaimed, 'what purpose salutary to literature is served by hearing that Hazlitt had pimples on his face?'[49] However, Bulwer was clearly unaware that, as Hazlitt himself had pointed out during his lifetime, he did not have a 'pimpled' complexion. The adjective was first used entirely gratuitously by Lockhart in the rhymed 'Notices' to the March 1818 number of the magazine – 'pimpled Hazlitt's coxcomb lectures' – and then became a running joke, probably because the magazine's writers knew that the term really annoyed its victim. But in the early 1820s, it was claimed that the epithet referred to Hazlitt's *writings*: 'none of us knows anything of his personal appearance – how could we? – But what designation could be more apt to mark the scurvy, verrucose, uneven, foully-heated, disordered, and repulsive style of the man?'[50] Just as in the case of Hunt, what was apparently an *ad hominem* attack was later justified as being a metaphorical comment on the author's work, rather than his person. Bulwer, by reviving the myth of Hazlitt's pimples, not only ended up viewing one of his idols through a lens supplied by *Blackwood's*, but repeated the personal references that he was trying to attack.[51] The magazine's rhetoric was highly infectious, I would suggest, because its equivocations about the relationship between private man and public author exposed the contradictory way in which early nineteenth-century culture represented literary genius. Writers like Bulwer demanded criticism directed at works rather than individuals, but at the same time were happy to feed an increasing public demand for anecdotes and gossip about authors. In the same editorial in which he attacked anonymous criticism, he celebrated the suitability of the *New Monthly* for biographical articles.[52] But what *Blackwood's Magazine* had showed ten years earlier was that *ad hominem* criticism was an inevitable result of such an interest: the whole literary world was obsessed by 'personality'.

3 Magazine biography in the late Romantic period

By the 1820s, literary magazines were feeding the demand for information about the private lives of authors and other public figures with a variety of memoirs, literary portraits, *ad hominem* reviews, conversations, reminiscences and recollections. Scholars have generally regarded these articles merely as sources of biographical information and there have been very few attempts to assess their significance within the culture of the period. And yet they *were* significant, both for their impact on nineteenth-century authors and readers, and for their role in the construction of Romanticism and the Romantic canon. This chapter begins the task of rectifying this omission by considering some of the most notable examples of late Romantic magazine biography in the context of the journals in which they first appeared.

The only critical study of fragmentary or collective biography during the Romantic period – which of course was the type of biography that most suited the periodical press – is Annette Wheeler Cafarelli's acute and scholarly *Prose in the Age of Poets*.[1] However, her emphasis on the influence of Johnson's *Lives of the Poets* on Romantic biographers elides differences between Johnson's approach – which was generally to discuss writer and work as separate entities – and the more complex and troubled attempts of his early nineteenth-century descendants to describe the connections between author and text.[2] This shift in emphasis, which reaches its apogee in the writings of Carlyle, has been well described by M. H. Abrams. He argues that before the Romantic period,

> the writing of the lives of poets and artists was carried on as one branch of general biography, intended to memorialize men of note in all areas of endeavor. But once the theory emerged that poetry is primarily the expression of feeling and a state of mind – and even, in its extreme form, that poetry is the fictional gratification of desire – a natural corollary was to approach a poem as a revelation of what Carlyle called the 'individual specialties' of the author himself.[3]

The very different biographical writings of Carlyle, Hazlitt and De Quincey evince a much greater interest in the particular psychological characteristics of the authors they describe than do *The Lives of the Poets*, and they also reveal a stronger fascination with the *relationship* between the details of the author's appearance and habits of life, his genius and his works. The emergence within literary magazines of a new sub-genre that straddles the genres of biography and criticism – the literary portrait – is symptomatic of the shift that Abrams describes.

Cafarelli also pays insufficient attention to the role that biographical texts played within particular magazines. Sometimes this was very simple: publishers had an interest in increasing the public profile of particular authors in order to foster the sales of their writings, or biographies of them.[4] It was also the case that by supporting the claims to genius of particular authors, magazines could position themselves against other publications and writers who denied those claims, and, as it were, invest their own symbolic capital in these figures in the hope of being able to partake of some of the glory resulting from their past or future successes. On an ideological level, magazines could use accounts of particular writers with strong political or cultural identities in order to support their own views, either by association, or by contrast. So although genius was often put forward as a force that transcended a contested literary world, in fact biographical accounts of authors helped magazines and their readers to achieve self-definition. This was not, of course, a smooth or simple process, in particular because writing on individual genius could not always easily be subsumed into the 'transauthorial' attitudes and rhetorical patterns of the journals in which it appeared.

Literary portraits: William Hazlitt and William Maginn

Most of the literary magazines of the early nineteenth century contained series of portraits of authors. These articles tended to be general discussions of their subject's intellectual characteristics – they also sometimes provided information about his or her life history, personal character and appearance (some included actual portraits) but mostly sought to avoid, as John Scott put it in 1814, 'the contamination of individual slander'.[5] Modern critics have paid very little attention to these series, despite the fact that they played an important role in canon construction during the late Romantic period.[6] Although they often promised a synoptic overview of the contemporary literary world, their inclusions and omissions were always conditioned by the ideologies of their authors and of their host magazines. One reason why, until recently, female and working-class writers who were popular during the early nineteenth century had tended to slip through the cracks of literary history is that they rarely appeared in the literary galleries of the time.[7]

The best-known Romantic gallery is Hazlitt's *The Spirit of the Age* (1825), which began as a series of five 'Spirits of the Age' (Bentham, Irving, Horne Tooke, Scott and Eldon) published in the *New Monthly Magazine* (NMM) in 1824. Although there has been some fine criticism of Hazlitt's book, only Mark Parker has considered the relationship between those five essays and the *New Monthly*.[8] However, his analysis is inadequate: first, because he underestimates the journal's engagement with the politics of its day, and second, because he overlooks an article by Cyrus Redding, the *New Monthly's* subeditor, which was published shortly before Hazlitt's series began and which had a significant impact on it. In his account of the *New Monthly* in the 1820s, Parker emphasizes its tendency to aestheticize personal experience, while Marilyn

Butler has suggested that it was 'so preoccupied with the epiphenomena of urban social life and amusements that it seemed to live by and for them'.[9] In fact, the magazine was considerably more wide-ranging and serious than these assessments suggest. Edited by the Whig poet Thomas Campbell, it sought to avoid literary and political partisanship and, as Nanora Sweet has shown, was well adapted to the 'new liberalism' of its day, which cut across party lines in support of freer trade and constitutional reform.[10]

Redding was probably the journal's most 'liberal' voice and, in the issue for November 1823, he published an article entitled 'The Good Old Times', which attacked as irrational and pernicious the tendency to admire old customs and habits at the expense of modern ones, arguing that the view that 'every recent improvement is an unwarranted innovation upon the sacred system of the past...prevents legislation from keeping pace with the circumstances of the age'.[11] In the course of his defence of modernity, Redding brings in several different arguments but it is notable that he mentions only two contemporary figures by name: the preacher Edward Irving and Walter Scott. Towards the beginning of the article, he remarks that 'the moral depravity of the age is another theme of depressing comparison, echoed from the Rev. Mr Irving's chapel to the hall of Westminster, and back again'.[12] Irving appears again towards the end, after a passage in which Redding evokes the civil and religious conflicts of previous centuries:

> It may be very well for Mr. Irving and others to invoke the names of brave men who sealed the cause of liberty or religion with their blood...but while we admire these glorious instances...what more can they be to us than subjects of admiration? In these much-abused modern times we have no demand for similar *auto da fés*.

Although, Redding argues, there is still 'religious intolerance' in modern Britain (the *New Monthly* supported Catholic Emancipation), people no longer have to die for their beliefs and the implication is that there is no place in such a society for fire-and-brimstone fanatics like Irving.[13] Scott is similarly a retrogressive figure, and one who not only evokes a barbaric past, but who also glamorizes its inequalities:

> Let the feudal system and its barbarous customs be compared with the present horror of vassalage and the contempt for pretensions grounded on the tawdry emblazonments of the Heralds' College – with the manly spirit of freedom, which will brook no insult from fellow-man, let his rank be what it may, and which the superior in rank and fortune is, *owing to the better spirit of the age*, equally restrained from offering to an inferior. Let the Border-robbers be stripped of the gaudy colouring in which the deceptive charm of antiquity and the magic pencil of Scott have arrayed them, and what were they but lawless barbarians deeply dyed in blood, rioting in the plunder of the defenceless?[14] [my italics]

The reference to Scott's 'magic pencil' tellingly alludes to his critical sobriquet: 'The Great Magician'. The novelist's conjuring, Redding suggests, creates an illusion that blinds his readers to the violence and oppression of the feudal system.

Hazlitt was contributing to the *New Monthly* throughout 1823: he undoubtedly read Redding's article and sought to respond to its assumption that the 'spirit of the age' was entirely progressive. In his *Plain Speaker* essay 'On the Pleasure of Hating', composed during the last two months of 1823, he defines it as 'the progress of intellectual refinement, warring with our natural infirmities'.[15] As Patrick Story has pointed out, this definition makes explicit 'a fundamental contradiction between his political commitment in support of the progressive, historical change he witnessed during his lifetime, and his traditional, unhistorical moral concept of "human nature" as fixed, even tainted'.[16] The influence of Redding's article is apparent in a passage in 'On the Pleasure of Hating' that implicitly takes issue with his claim that there is no modern demand for *'auto da fés'*. Although the refining tendency of the spirit of the age, Hazlitt argues,

> no longer allows us to carry our vindictive and headstrong humours into effect, we try to revive them in descriptions, and keep up the old bugbears, the phantoms of our terror and our hate, in imagination. We burn Guy Faux in effigy, and the hooting and buffeting and maltreating that poor tattered figure of rags and straw makes a festival in every village in England once a year. Protestants and Papists do not now burn one another at the stake: but we subscribe to new editions of *Fox's Book of Martyrs*.
>
> (XII, p. 129)

'Progress' will always be patchy and problematic, because human beings are drawn atavistically back to more barbaric times when their 'infirmities' were given freer reign. This serves to explain the popularity of the Scotch novels (something that Redding cannot do convincingly):

> they carry us back to the feuds, the heart-burnings, the havoc, the dismay, the wrongs and the revenge of a barbarous age and people – to the rooted prejudices and deadly animosities of sects and parties in politics and religion, and of contending chiefs and clans in war and intrigue. We feel the full force of the spirit of hatred with all of them in turn. As we read, we throw aside the trammels of civilisation, the flimsy veil of humanity.
>
> (XII, p. 129)

Readers can only be bamboozled by Scott's 'magic pencil' because they want to be – they enjoy the opportunity to escape from the repression of civilization and revel in hatred and bloodshed. And this also explains the popularity of Irving, who has 'rekindled the old, original, almost exploded hell-fire in the aisles of the Caledonian Chapel ... to the delight and astonishment of his fair audience' (XII, p. 129).

'The Spirits of the Age', and the subsequent book, continue this critique of Redding's optimistic liberalism despite Hazlitt's sympathy for the political position from which Redding writes. This is most strongly apparent in the articles on Irving and Scott. The February 1824 account of Irving depicts him as an intellectual prize-fighter, who fascinates the public with the violence and sweep of his battle with modernity: 'he has revived exploded prejudices, he has scouted prevailing fashions. He has opposed the spirit of the age, and not consulted the *esprit de corps*' (XI, p. 44). This attack on Irving as a reactionary fits in well with the *New Monthly's* liberalism.

But the article as a whole is a characteristically complex piece of writing: for Hazlitt, Redding's simple opposition between those who support progress and those bigots who laud the 'good old times' is inadequate. Irving's fashionability reveals the extent to which the modern consciousness is fascinated with the idea of a return to 'barbarism' and delights to dwell on the possibility of its own destruction. The preacher 'makes war' upon the modern world 'and leaves nothing standing but himself, a mighty land-mark in a degenerate age, over-looking the wide havoc he has made':

> It is not very surprising that when the whole mass and texture of civil society is indicted as a nuisance, and threatened to be pulled down as a rotten building ready to fall on the heads of the inhabitants, that all classes of people run to hear the crash, and to see the engines and levers at work which are to effect this laudable purpose.
>
> (XI, p. 42)

The pleasure that people take in such a spectacle – reminiscent of the vogue in the 1820s for the apocalyptic paintings of John Martin – signifies for Hazlitt the extent to which civilized 'improvement' is challenged by the self-destructive, retrogressive tendencies of humankind.

Redding's article also clearly influenced Hazlitt's April 1824 essay on Scott. This article did not contain the long final paragraph that appears in *The Spirit of the Age*, which strongly attacks the novelist for having degraded his genius through his political partisanship and association with *Blackwood's Magazine* (XI, pp. 67–8). However, I cannot entirely agree with Mark Parker that 'the version that appears in the *New Monthly* provides a curiously unpolitical reading of the Scotch novels...and takes pains to show Scott as a reconciler of extremes and a clarifier of prejudices'.[17] It is certainly true that Hazlitt argues that the Scotch novels are not partisan and give the lie to their author's politics:

> Does he really think of making us enamoured of the 'good old times' by the faithful and harrowing portraits he has drawn of them? Is he infatuated enough, or does he so doat and drivel over his slothful and self-willed prejudices as to believe that he will make a single convert to the beauty of Legitimacy, that is, of lawless power and savage bigotry, when he himself is obliged to apologise for the horrors he describes.
>
> (XI, p. 65)

But a passage like this is hardly 'unpolitical': it is, in fact, a direct attack on Scott's Toryism, which, for the sake of argument, uses his own writing against him. Hazlitt takes particular issue with a passage in volume three of *Ivanhoe*, where Scott suggests that the crowd that had gathered to see the execution of Rebecca has its modern analogues:

> Even in our own days, when morals are better understood, an execution, a bruising match between two professors, or a meeting of radical reformers, collects at considerable hazard to themselves immense crowds of spectators, otherwise little interested, excepting to see how matters are to be conducted, and whether the heroes of the day are, in the heroic language of insurgent tailors, *flints* or *dunghills*.[18]

Writing shortly after Peterloo, Scott is trying to downplay the importance of such meetings by suggesting that the vast majority of those present are merely interested in viewing an exciting spectacle and have no investment in radical politics. Hazlitt characterizes the passage slightly unfairly, arguing that Scott is having 'a sneer at the people' as '*flints* and *dungs*': this is quixotic, he claims, at a moment in the narrative when the reader's anger will be directed at 'the revolting abuses of self-contained power'. 'It is thus', Hazlitt writes with heavy irony, that Scott 'administers charms and philtres to our love of Legitimacy, makes us conceive a horror of all reform, civil, political, or religious, and would fain put down the *Spirit of the Age*' (XI, p. 66). Here 'the spirit of the age' is used in exactly the same way as in Redding's article – to refer to a modern interest in reform and progress. But whereas Redding believes that Scott's writing tends to glamorize the past, Hazlitt suggests that actually it reveals the 'barbarity' of the 'good old times'.

Hazlitt's other three 'Spirits of the Age' can also be related to the *New Monthly's* liberal emphasis on 'progress', although moderated somewhat by his views about humanity's bad tendencies. The account of Bentham in January 1824 is notably sympathetic, emphasizing his worldwide influence and his stature as a disinterested philosopher rather than a 'Legitimate' ruler: 'he is a beneficent spirit, prying into the universe, not lording over it; a thoughtful spectator of the scenes of life . . . not a painted pageant, [or] a stupid idol' (XI, p. 7). But Hazlitt also takes him to task for failing to allow for 'the caprices and irregularities of human nature' (XI, p. 8). Horne Tooke, in March 1824, is treated less sympathetically than Bentham: despite his apparent radicalism, Hazlitt claims, Tooke's political opinions were 'of the last age' (XI, p. 47) and he was a political '*trimmer*' rather than a disinterested patriot (XI, p. 52). The essay ends on a dark note as Hazlitt claims that the greater popularity of Lindley Murray's *Grammar* over Tooke's great work *The Diversions of Purley* is 'a curious example of the *Spirit of the Age*' (XI, p. 56). He suggests that this is because politicians and the clergy dislike Tooke's politics: 'is there nothing above the reach of prejudice and party-spirit? It seems in this, as in so many other instances, as if there was a patent for absurdity in the natural bias of the human mind' (XI, p. 57). So what starts as a critique of Tooke as a representative of the selfishness and cynicism of a vanished age ends with the apparent suggestion that political partisanship is inevitable. Hazlitt's sustained attack on Lord Eldon's opposition to reform and support for the abuses of power (XI, pp. 145–6) in the last of 'The Spirits of the Age' (July 1824) is entirely consonant with the *New Monthly's* liberalism, but his suggestion that Eldon's fixed views are due to his 'good-natured' character rather than mere ignorance also suggests the cynicism about human nature that pervades *The Spirit of the Age* volume.

Aside from the felicities of Hazlitt's style and his stature as a thinker, the reason that *The Spirit of the Age* is so much better than other literary galleries of the time is that the adversarial attitude the essayist takes towards many of his subjects creates a fascinating sense of intellectual tension and conflict. As John Kinnaird has pointed out, Hazlitt's approach influenced the efforts of later series to achieve 'thematic continuity', but they signally failed to match his 'critical relationship to his time'.[19] The literary galleries of the late Romantic and early Victorian period – although they are important in terms of the reception history of particular authors and contain some excellent writing – generally stayed within the familiar generic conventions of careful, balanced criticism and biography that studiously avoided 'personality'. The (in)glorious exception that broke these rules was William Maginn's 'Gallery of Illustrious Literary Characters' (*FM*, 1830–6), which, as well as manifesting the Irishman's satirical flair, also played an important role within its host magazine.[20]

Maginn had already subverted literary portraiture in his short series of 'Humbugs of the Age' (1824), which began in the scurrilous *John Bull Magazine* just as Hazlitt's series ended in the *New Monthly*.[21] These articles were direct and unabashed personal attacks: for example, in the first, he viciously mocked De Quincey's appearance, and hinted that his first child had been conceived before his marriage. The seventy-nine literary portraits in *Fraser's* were less ferocious, relying for their effect on giving the reader a sense of personal familiarity with the authors described, but, as they were in a fairly prestigious magazine, mostly (although not always) avoiding gossip and scandal. The articles, always a page in length, were based on Daniel Maclise's accompanying drawings, which often depicted the subject in a state of private, domestic relaxation. Maginn's tone was generally irreverent, even when praising writers of whom *Fraser's* approved, and enemies of the magazine (Whigs and Radicals) got a rough ride. Thus most of the article on Samuel Rogers consists of jokes about the fact that he resembles a corpse, and Thomas Moore is described (with some accuracy) as looking like 'something between a toad and a cupid'.[22]

The main point of the series was to place the recently launched *Fraser's* securely in the literary firmament by positioning it in relation to a number of friends and enemies. The sheer number of portraits, and their incisiveness, meant that this was achieved with greater success than in any other magazine.[23] The January 1835 issue was particularly important as it contained Maclise's sketch of 'The Fraserians' (Plate 1), which depicted twenty-six of the gallery's subjects seated at a convivial dinner over which Maginn presided, and which was described in his accompanying article. Patrick Leary has pointed out that 'from the first issue, *Fraser's* self-consciously projected itself as the product of a distinct literary coterie', and that this projection was partly mythical, for some of the figures in 'The Fraserians' had published very little in the magazine, and six of them – Southey, Murphy, D'Orsay, Hook, Jerdan and Coleridge (who had died three months earlier) – had contributed nothing at all.[24] Particularly in the case of Coleridge, Maginn was representing himself and *Fraser's* as being on familiar terms with literary genius in order to increase the journal's prestige. Thus in his early three-part article 'The Election of Editor for *Fraser's Magazine*', in which Maginn ventriloquises through a host of contemporary literary characters, Coleridge, 'the first genius of the age', is elected editor.[25]

Part of *Fraser's* success, as Leary argues, 'lay in breaking through the traditional anonymity of the periodical press by ushering the reader into vicarious informal fellowship with some of the leading writers of the day', and this task was mainly carried out by Maginn's literary gallery.[26] Much more than was the case with other such series, its subjects were interwoven into the fabric of the magazine's identity, and this gave *Fraser's* the aura of being closer to the pulse of genius than its competitors. But as we saw in Chapter 1, *Fraser's* also tended to produce an elevated conception of

THE FRASERIANS.

Plate 1 Daniel Maclise, 'The Fraserians', *Fraser's Magazine*, January 1835. Reproduced by permission of the Syndics of Cambridge University Library.

genius which removed it from the failings and limitations of mankind. Generally speaking, its readers are 'invited to imagine a subjectivity [which is] fundamentally *different* and inaccessible from their own'.[27] Thus the 'informal fellowship' that they were offered with men like Coleridge, Carlyle and Goethe could only go so far. Maginn's impudent literary portraits – which brought genius down to earth – were balanced with its mystification in other parts of the magazine.

Unlike most similar series, the 'Gallery of Illustrious Literary Characters' included women: this may simply have been a result of its large number of portraits. That there are no women in *The Spirit of the Age* should remind us that the individuals who are included constitute just one possible view of the cultural firmament in the mid-1820s. Hazlitt ignores all the successful female authors of his day, several of whom were considerably better-known than some of the male authors whom he includes (Felicia Hemans, Joanna Baillie and Maria Edgeworth spring to mind).[28] Hemans was enormously popular in the late Romantic period, and yet she is absent from its literary galleries: she does not even appear in *Fraser's*, which is astounding when one considers some of the obscure male authors who do get in. The highest proportion of women in all the galleries that I have looked at is to be found in Richard Henry Horne's *New Spirit of the Age* (1844). Here, eight out of thirty-nine portraits are of women – this may have had something to do with the fact that Elizabeth Barrett contributed to the book.

Writing in *Blackwood's* in 1824 as 'Ensign Morgan Odoherty', Maginn and Lockhart put forward a deliberately provocative view of women's writing:

> What stuff in Mrs Hemans, Miss Porden, &c. &c. to be writing plays and epics! There is no such thing as female genius. The only good things that women have written, are Sappho's Ode upon Phaon, and Madame de Stael's Corinne; and of these two good things the inspiration is simply and entirely that one glorious feeling, in which, and in which alone, woman is the equal of man. They are undoubtedly mistress-pieces.[29]

Although most critics of the period would not have denied the existence of 'female genius' quite so strongly, it was often argued or assumed that whatever genius women had was limited to sentimental works about love: 'mistress-pieces' (also a pun on 'masterpiece', of course). More 'liberal' voices tended to allow female genius a greater range and women in general a greater capacity for education without, of course, necessarily suggesting that women could be active citizens in the same way as men. For example, writing in the reformist *NMM* in 1832, Edward Lytton Bulwer argued that female intellectual cultivation should be encouraged, not so that women would be enabled to act in the public sphere, but so that they would better influence their husbands and sons, especially through an appreciation of 'Public Virtue'.[30] In a review of his friend Letitia Landon's novel *Romance and Reality* in 1831, he described her as 'a lady of remarkable genius',[31] and criticized those who argued against female education: 'does knowledge make men bad husbands? Why should it make women bad wives? . . . The soul of a woman is as fine an emanation from the Great Fountain of Spirit as that of a man'.[32]

Despite his Romantic rhetoric, Bulwer's position on female genius and education had some similarities with that articulated a generation earlier by the influential Evangelical writer Hannah More in her *Strictures on the Modern System of Female Education* (1799). More had argued that well-educated women could help to prevent a revolution by influencing men to reform society and claimed that 'women of real genius and extensive knowledge... have been, in general, eminent for economy and the practice of domestic virtues'.[33] She was considerably more suspicious of 'sensibility' and women writers than Bulwer, but their overall emphasis on the congruity of genius and domesticity is similar: despite their differences, both authors are at heart conservative reformers. It is interesting that a more radical view can be found in an anonymous *Fraser's* article on 'The Female Character', which argued strongly 'that in the arts and sciences, in the noblest efforts of mortal genius, and in the highest aspirings of human intellect, the female mind has and can rival that of the other sex'.[34] Furthermore, the writer claimed,

> no age has been so fruitful in female genius as the present. From all ranks of society women have come forth, and have distinguished themselves in almost every department of literature. Even politics, so long monopolised by mankind, finds partisans in the other sex; and Harriet Martineau is considered by her party their oracle on political economy. What females of any age possessed genius of a higher order than Joanna Baillie and Felicia Hemans? Who have given us moral sentiments more exalted than Hannah More and Caroline Bowles?[35]

'Female genius', then, indubitably exists – although whether it is quite as powerful and extensive as male genius is perhaps still unclear – and women are capable of distinction in a variety of forms of writing. This article reveals *Fraser's* capacity to contain views which conflicted with its general ideological stance, for the writer even goes on to suggest that the fitness of women for political offices should be tested and praises Mary Wollstonecraft.[36]

In contrast, the 'Gallery of Illustrious Literary Characters' generally carefully confined women's writing within the domestic sphere, and did not support anything other than the production of 'mistress-pieces'. For example, in the portrait of Letitia Landon, Francis Mahony 'defended' the writer from her critics:

> There is too much about love in them, some cross-grained critic will say. How, Squaretoes, can there be too much of love in a young lady's writings? we reply in a question. Is she to write of politics, or political economy, or pugilism, or punch? Certainly not. We feel a determined dislike of women who wander into these unfeminine paths; they should immediately hoist a mustache – and, to do them justice, they in general do exhibit no inconsiderable specimen of the hair-lip. We think Miss L. E. L. has chosen much the better part. She shews every now and then that she is possessed of information, feeling, and genius, to enable her to shine in other departments of poetry; but she does right in thinking that Sappho knew what she was about when she chose the tender passion as the theme for women.[37]

Emphasizing the limitations of female genius may have been particularly important for *Fraser's* because its writers (with some exceptions) tended not to take the line that genius was intrinsically anti-domestic, and this at least opened up the worrying possibility that women, even if primarily domestic beings, could be geniuses in the same way as men. Neither Bulwer, nor the *Fraser's* writer of 'The Female Character' would have had a problem with women writing about 'politics' or 'political economy', but Mahony relies on the traditional argument that such pursuits were alien and damaging to femininity. It is not even that Landon lacks genius, or is ignorant about things other than love, but that she rightly chooses to limit her writing to that one subject – she knows her place and does not challenge masculine ideas of the 'poetess'.[38] To a modern critic like Anne K. Mellor, Landon's acceptance of 'her culture's hegemonic definition of the female' led her into an artistic dead end, but for Mahony, it is to be celebrated.[39]

A year after the publication of 'The Fraserians' there appeared its female counterpart – 'Regina's Maids of Honour' (Plate 2) – comprising all the women writers who had appeared in Maginn's 'Gallery', as well as Anna Maria Hall, who was included a few months later. The participants, from left to right, are Hall, Landon, Mary Russell Mitford, Lady Morgan, Harriet Martineau, Jane Porter, Caroline Norton and Countess Marguerite Blessington. Whereas *Fraser's* male contributors enjoy a raucous, alcohol-soaked dinner, the 'Maids of Honour' take part in a genteel drawing-room tea party. In contrast to the openness of the picture of 'The Fraserians', 'Regina's Maids of Honour' is given a frame and a relatively detailed backdrop, which serves to emphasize that it depicts the enclosed private space of the home.

The accompanying article, written in rhyming prose, is Maginn at his ingenious worst. For example:

> What are they doing? what they should; with volant tongue and chatty cheer, welcoming in, by prattle good, or witty phrase, or comment shrewd, the opening of the gay new year. Mrs. Hall, so far and fine, bids her brilliant eyes to glow – eyes the brightest of the nine would be but too proud to shew. Outlaw he, and Buccaneer, who'd refuse to worship here. And next, the mistress of the shell (not the lobster, but the lyre), see the lovely L. E. L. talks with tongue that will not tire. True, she turns away her face, out of pity to us men; but the swan-like neck we trace, and the figure full of grace, and the mignon hand whose pen wrote the *Golden Violet*, and the *Lit'rary Gazette*, and *Francesca's* mournful story. (Isn't she painted *con amore*?)[40]

Maginn's description of 'L. E. L.' bears out Mellor's observation that Landon was often represented in the period, and indeed 'constructed herself and her poetry', as 'the icon of female beauty'.[41] But the ostensibly innocent final sentence of the passage has a dark subtext. Landon had first emerged as a writer in 1820, at the age of eighteen, when her poem 'Rome' appeared in the powerful *Literary Gazette*. Its editor, William Jerdan, became a strong supporter and during the 1820s she was employed as the periodical's chief reviewer, a remarkable position for a young woman. Landon remained unmarried and by 1826 rumours were circulating about her relationship

REGINA'S MAIDS OF HONOUR.

Plate 2 Daniel Maclise, 'Regina's Maids of Honour', *Fraser's Magazine*, January 1836. Reproduced by permission of the Syndics of Cambridge University Library.

with her mentor. As she became increasingly well-known as a poet, scandal continued to dog her and in 1830 her friends apparently received anonymous letters accusing her of being the mistress of a married man. One possible candidate was Maginn, a close friend who had worked with her on the *Literary Gazette*; another was Bulwer, with whom she seems to have had a mildly flirtatious friendship. In the 1830s, Landon's unconventional friendships with men continued to give rise to scandal, and in 1835, further rumours about her relationships with Bulwer, Maginn and Daniel Maclise, the illustrator of the 'Gallery of Illustrious Literary Characters', forced her to break off her engagement with the editor of the *Examiner*, John Forster.[42] So the question 'Isn't she painted *con amore?*' is at best insensitive, and at worst seems meant to suggest that the rumours surrounding Landon and Maclise were based on fact. Furthermore, Maginn had made a similar insinuation three years earlier in his literary portrait of Bulwer, where he mentions that Landon had described the author in *Romance and Reality*: 'we shall not say *con amore*, lest that purely technical phrase should be construed literally'.[43]

Maginn was a notorious scandalmonger and Michael Sadleir has argued that he probably wrote (or instructed his associate Charles Westmacott to write) the letters that so damaged Landon's reputation in order to revenge himself on her for having rejected his advances.[44] He also argues that Bulwer may have been involved in thwarting these advances and that this helps to explain the *Fraser's* policy of targeting of the novelist. This theory does seem to be supported by the first '*con amore*' remark, and, in that case, 'Regina's Maids of Honour' would be the final twist of the knife after the collapse of Landon's engagement. However, Sadleir's claims are highly speculative and are unlikely for several reasons.[45] It seems unnecessary to posit a private animus behind the attacks on Bulwer when his personality and politics made him a natural *Fraser's* target. Furthermore, there is no evidence of a breach between Maginn and Landon at any time – *Fraser's* generally treats her very positively. The only evidence that Maginn did make offensive advances to Landon is the utterly unreliable testimony of Grantley Berkeley. There is also no evidence that any of Landon's friends thought that the letters were by Maginn and, as Malcolm Elwin has suggested, it is even possible that the letters themselves never existed (although the existence of scurrilous rumours surrounding Landon is not in doubt).[46] Putting the issue of the letters to one side, it is possible that Maginn and Landon had some sort of intimate relationship: Landon's literary executor, Laman Blanchard, wrote to E. V. Kenealy with regard to his own biography, that he avoided mentioning Maginn when discussing Landon, 'from the knowledge I have of everything relating to him and to her on several grave points of their experience', although he also emphasized Maginn's 'devotion to her welfare'.[47] But I am not aware of any stronger evidence for this, and Elwin states that 'all Maginn's acquaintances, though commenting on his irresponsibility and fatal failing for the bottle, unanimously testify to his devotion to his wife and children'.[48] I think, therefore, that we have to read the '*con amore*' references as sly, perhaps even cruel, insinuations about Landon's relationships with Bulwer, Maclise and Maginn himself, but not as evidence of anything more sinister. In that sense, and despite the article's emphasis on Landon's femininity, Maginn is treating her in the same boisterous bantering fashion with which he deals with many of the male authors in the 'Gallery of Illustrious Literary Characters'.

In 1836, Landon met George Maclean, Governor of Cape Coast Castle in West Africa, and despite some confusion about whether or not they became officially engaged, and Maclean's second thoughts regarding the match, they eventually married in June 1838 and travelled to Africa. A few months later, Landon died of an overdose of prussic acid, which may or may not have been accidental. Mellor argues that

> by writing her self as female beauty, Landon effectively wrote herself out of existence: she became a fluid sign in the discourse that constructed her, a discourse that denied her authenticity and overwrote whatever individual voice she might have possessed. For a modern reader, both her life and her poetry finally demonstrate the literally fatal consequences for a woman in the Romantic period who wholly inscribed herself within Burke's aesthetic category of the beautiful.[49]

This seems a little too glib in its conflation of life and literature. The scandal greatly damaged Landon's reputation and literary *cachet*, but there is no way of showing that the contrast between her public and private persona had 'literally fatal consequences'. However, Mellor is right to draw attention to this contrast. Landon was simply unable to conform to the stereotype of female authorship put forward in the 'Gallery of Illustrious Literary Characters' and, to a certain extent, also in her poetry. Her association with scandalous aristocrats like Lady Caroline Lamb and Countess Blessington; her social spontaneity; and her close friendships with men like Jerdan, Maginn and Bulwer would have made her more suitable for the boozy dinner depicted in 'The Fraserians', rather than the genteel tea party of 'Regina's Maids of Honour'. But it was very difficult for women to play the role of the eccentric Bohemian writer during the Romantic period. Even though Landon was generally represented as a female genius – and although a number of male writers may have treated her as an equal – ultimately she lacked the social privileges that were often allowed to similarly gifted men.

Maginn's emphasis on Landon's desirability is also strongly apparent in his descriptions of Caroline Norton and Marguerite Blessington. And like Landon, these women were also unconventional figures. Norton had been separated from her abusive husband for several years and in June 1836 was to be tried on the charge of 'criminal conversation' with Lord Melbourne, then Prime Minister (she was acquitted). Blessington's husband had died in 1829, but long before then she had formed a scandalous relationship with the Comte D'Orsay. So although 'Regina's Maids of Honour' rather mockingly places women writers in a genteel domestic setting, Maginn also offers his readers a frisson of scandalous excitement with sexualized portrayals of those – Norton, Landon and Blessington – whose lifestyles challenged the strict boundaries of domestic propriety. His self-consciousness about the way in which this article 'peeps' into the private realm and seeks to titillate is apparent in the account of Blessington:

> O, gorgeous Countess! gayer notes for all that's charming, sweet, and smiling, for her whose pleasant tales our throats are ever of fresh laughs beguiling. Say, shall we call thee bright and fair, enchanting, winning...Go, try to read,

although his quill is too mean and dull what she inspired even in so great a
sumph as Willis; and if that Yankee boy admired, who can a Christian person
blame, if he, all Countess-smit, pretends that, if she lets him near the flame of
her warm glance he'd think it shame that, like her book, she and he should look
as nothing nearer than Two friends.[50]

This passage refers to, and to some extent parodies, the effusive account of
Blessington given by the American journalist Nathaniel Willis in a newspaper article
written in 1834, which was incorporated in his book *Pencillings By the Way* (1835).[51]
Willis was a controversial figure because he had breached the bounds of hospitality
by publishing details of his encounters as a guest in private houses such as
Blessington's (although her salon might be construed as 'semi-private'), especially as
he was not always diplomatic in his remarks.[52] It is not just that Maginn is suggesting that there is a degree of lust evident in Willis's description of the Countess –
which does indeed dwell on her charms – but that he is trying to distinguish between
Willis's weak and foolish lust ('Countess-smit') and the more controlled and ironic
desire present in 'Regina's Maids of Honour'. Whereas Willis is foolish enough to fall
for the real Blessington and then to publicize his folly, Maginn and his readers find
the allure in the authorial persona depicted, a figure that lies somewhere between the
'real' and the textual. This is not just the case with Blessington: throughout the
article, there is a deliberate conflation of writers and works; for example, when
the character of the Wandering Jew from Norton's poem *The Undying One* is imagined viewing her 'sunny eyes, her locks of jet'.[53] If women writers, supposedly, were
sentimental creatures capable only of expressing themselves in a direct and unso-
phisticated manner, 'Regina's Maids of Honour' consciously drew attention to the
way in which their authorial identities were constructed and limited by the masculinist
preconceptions of critics and readers, while doing exactly that.[54]

Literary reminiscences: Leigh Hunt and
Thomas Jefferson Hogg

The dubious status of the literary reminiscence in the early nineteenth century is
shown by the fact that it was often the last resort of periodical writers in desperate
financial straits: when Hazlitt wrote 'My First Acquaintance with Poets', he was
under house arrest for debt; Hunt claimed in his preface to the first edition of *Lord
Byron and Some of his Contemporaries* that if he had not owed money to Henry Colburn,
he would rather have consigned the book to the flames than have it published; and
De Quincey composed most of his articles on the Lake Poets whilst on the run from
his creditors. Authors knew that by making public the personal lives of their friends
and acquaintances they were open to accusations of betrayal, but they were also aware
that their recollections would be eagerly snapped up by publishers who were happy
to feed the public demand for such information. Apart from what they tell us about
the cultural climate of the early nineteenth century, contemporary literary reminiscences are important because they have played a significant role in mediating the
Romantic poets to later audiences.[55] The rest of this chapter considers the relationship

between genius and politics in the Romantic period by focusing on reminiscences in the *NMM*, *Fraser's Magazine* (*FM*) and *Tait's Edinburgh Magazine* (*TEM*).

Lord Byron and Some of his Contemporaries (1828) prompted a great deal of adverse press coverage and did some harm to Leigh Hunt's reputation. Although it was published in book form, so much of it was quoted and discussed in advertisements, puffs (in Colburn's periodicals) and reviews that it is useful to examine it in the context of magazine biography. In his preface to the first edition, Hunt admitted that in writing the book, he 'had involuntarily felt a re-access of the spleen and indignation which I experienced, as a man who thought himself ill-treated'; however, he also emphasized that he had written nothing about Byron that he did not believe to be true.[56] Hunt's bitterness is apparent throughout his account of the poet, for he gives Byron's every action and comment the worst possible construction, representing him as selfish, avaricious, incapable of love, absurdly proud, cowardly, capricious, jealous, superstitious, effeminate and ignorant. At the end of this piece of literary iconoclasm, Hunt takes the moral high ground, claiming that he has written it in order to counteract the misconceptions about the poet that have been caused by earlier memoirs and attacks 'the pensive public' for its sensationalism.[57] However, Hunt's justification for *Lord Byron and Some of his Contemporaries* – that it is a disinterested attempt to set the record straight on Byron for the public good – is weakened by his admission that his financial circumstances have forced him into publishing his recollections of the poet. And Hunt's explanations and equivocations in the prefaces to both the first and second editions, as well as in letters to the *Morning Chronicle*, show that he was deeply troubled by the impropriety of his conduct and anxious that he was merely pandering to the public's appetite for 'sensation'. This, of course, was one of the main criticisms aimed at him: for instance, Lockhart stated that the book contained 'the meanest details of private gossip – dirty gabble about men's wives and men's mistresses – and men's lackeys, and even the mistresses of lackeys'.[58]

Cafarelli has described the relationship of *Lord Byron and Some of his Contemporaries* to the development of the idea of 'the pathology of genius' during the Romantic period. She argues that

> there is a critical dissonance between the poets' idealization of the poetic calling and what was increasingly becoming evident in Romantic biography and criticism, the dark side of the alienage and marginality of the artistic community, which poets were reluctant to see explored . . . The archetype of the sick artist that emerged in the critical dialogue of Hazlitt and Leigh Hunt illuminated the poet as a cultural outsider.[59]

Her suggestion that Hazlitt's argument in his *Round Table* essay 'On the Causes of Methodism' that poetry is a symptom of the physical and mental sickness of its creators (IV, p. 58) greatly influenced Hunt's book, is an intriguing one. However, it does not stand up to close scrutiny. There were, of course, accounts of genius in the Romantic period that emphasized its transgressive, deviant nature, but Hunt has little recourse to these in *Lord Byron and Some of his Contemporaries*. Although it is written against the public's tendency to idealize genius, Hunt does not link Byron's infirmities to his poetical abilities, even though his *fame* has not done his character any good: 'Perverse from his birth, educated under personal disadvantages, debauched by ill companions, and perplexed between real and false pretensions, the injuries done to his nature were completed by a success, too great even for the genius he possessed.'[60]

Byron's many flaws, for Hunt, are the result of an innate ill temper, bad parenting, bad company and the pressures of celebrity. Hunt's attack is aimed at Byron as a man, not as an author, and the possibility that the light of Byron's poetry might be dimmed by our knowledge of his personal flaws becomes a source of regret for his biographer:

> I subscribe so heartily to a doctrine eloquently set forth by Mr Hazlitt – that whatever is good and true in works of a man of genius, eminently belongs to and is a part of him, let him partake as he will of common infirmity – that I cannot without regret think of the picture I have drawn of the infirmities of Lord Byron, common or uncommon, nor omit to set down this confession [i.e. the preface] of an unwilling hand.[61]

Cafarelli is certainly right that Hunt's depiction of Byron is a long way from Shelley's or Coleridge's claims that genius is necessarily virtuous, but it is also a long way from an account of genius that sees it as inevitably debauched, dangerous, mad or sick. Hunt's book is, in part, a study of Byron's pathology but it is certainly not a pathology of genius. For if Hunt had used such an argument, this would have been to try to excuse Byron's behaviour – and Hunt wanted to attack the poet, not to defend him.

If *Lord Byron and Some of his Contemporaries* is biography as revenge, then Thomas Jefferson Hogg's 'Percy Bysshe Shelley at Oxford' (*NMM*, 1832) is biography as vindication.[62] We saw in Chapter 1 that the *Blackwood's* reviews of Shelley in 1819 and 1820 attempted to separate his 'pernicious' opinions from his poetic genius. In an excellent article, Neil Fraistat has shown how Mary Shelley's edition of Shelley's *Posthumous Poems* in 1824 produced an 'etherealized, disembodied, and virtually depoliticized poet', but that this account was contested by piracies of his work by 'radical pressmen', in particular William Benbow's *Miscellaneous and Posthumous Poems of Percy Bysshe Shelley* of 1826.[63] The attempt to 'purify' the poet and his writings was continued in 1828 by a panegyrical article in the *Athenaeum's* series of 'Sketches of Contemporary Authors'. Its author, Frederick Denison Maurice, strongly denied that Shelley was really an atheist, and represented him as a true poet whose great achievement was to show that real improvement and reform must take place within the self, rather than in 'outward circumstances'.[64] Maurice was the inspiration for the group of Cambridge Apostles – Thomas Sunderland, Arthur Hallam and Richard Monckton Milnes – who argued in favour of Shelley at an Oxford Union debate in November 1829 on whether he or Byron was the greater poet (some of their opponents claimed not to know who Shelley was). As Richard Cronin has argued, the Apostles' version of Shelley was usually 'safely enclosed within a Wordsworthian wise passiveness', and their opposition to the Reform Bill entailed some tempering of their enthusiasm for him.[65] But their championing of the poet – which included the first

English publication of *Adonais* in 1829 – contributed to the rise in Shelley's reputation among middle-class readers.

Hogg's articles consummated this first phase in the poet's afterlife and sought to contradict the view that was sometimes propagated by the Tory press in the 1820s, which was that he was an immoral and deranged writer of infidel poetry.[66] So much criticism of Shelley was *ad hominem*, that Hogg's account of him as a young man was as much a defence of his work as of his personal character. 'Percy Bysshe Shelley at Oxford' concentrates on his many eccentricities: his untidy appearance; his enthusiasm for chemical experimentation; his awful voice; his strange sleeping habits and his childish delight in making paper boats. However, Hogg also continually emphasizes that he was eminently sane, virtuous and brilliant, and claims that on their first meeting these qualities were apparent in his facial features, which

> breathed an animation, a fire, an enthusiasm, a vivid and preternatural intelligence, that I never met with in any other countenance. Nor was the moral expression less beautiful than the intellectual; for there was a softness, a delicacy, a gentleness, and especially (though this will surprise many) that air of profound religious veneration, that characterizes the best works, and chiefly the frescoes...of the great masters of Florence and of Rome.[67]

Despite his religious scepticism, which Hogg tries to downplay as a sin of youth, Shelley, as in Maurice's account, is represented as a highly spiritual being who is superior to ordinary people.

One gets a sense of the careful way in which Hogg deals with Shelley's enthusiasms if his representation of the poet is compared with Hazlitt's pen-portrait in the *Table-Talk* essay 'On Paradox and Common-Place' (1821):

> The author of the Prometheus Unbound...has a fire in his eye, a fever in his blood, a maggot in his brain, a hectic flutter in his speech, which mark out the philosophic fanatic. He is sanguine-complexioned, and shrill-voiced. As is often observable in the case of religious enthusiasts, there is a slenderness of constitutional *stamina*, which renders the flesh no match for the spirit. His bending, flexible form appears to take no strong hold of things, does not grapple with the world about him, but slides from it like a river...He is clogged by no dull system of realities, no earth-bound feelings, no rooted prejudices, by nothing that belongs to the mighty trunk and hard husk of nature and habit, but is drawn up by irresistible levity to the regions of mere speculation and fancy, to the sphere of air and fire, where his delighted spirit floats in 'seas of pearl and clouds of amber'.

> (VIII, pp. 148–9)

Hazlitt's Shelley is a deranged monomaniac whose restless desire for revolution is the product of a weak constitution. The comparison with 'a religious enthusiast' continues the argument about the pathology of genius to be found in 'On the Causes of Methodism'; because of his physical infirmities, Shelley is drawn into a dream world which bears little resemblance to the realities of 'nature and habit'. Hazlitt elaborates on this view of the poet through the use of a series of metaphors taken from the natural sciences, and, considering Shelley's enthusiasm for chemistry whilst at Oxford, these are clearly, in part, an *ad hominem* reference.

> There is no *caput mortuum* of worn-out, thread-bare experience to serve as ballast to his mind; it is all volatile intellectual salt of tartar, that refuses to combine its evanescent, inflammable essence with any thing solid or any thing lasting. ... He puts every thing into a metaphysical crucible to judge of it himself and exhibit it to others as a subject of interesting experiment, without first making it over to the ordeal of his common sense or trying it on his heart.
>
> (VIII, p. 149)

Caput mortuum is a chemical term meaning the residue remaining after the distillation or sublimation of a substance, though it was also used figuratively in the eighteenth and nineteenth centuries to refer simply to a worthless residue. Of course here it is meant ironically, for Hazlitt does not believe experience to be 'worn-out' or 'thread-bare'. 'Salt of tartar' is now know as potassium carbonate; Hazlitt's knowledge of chemistry seems to be at fault here because it is neither volatile nor inflammable. However, if one recalls the action of potassium when put in water – an experiment which some readers may recall from school chemistry lessons – then one gets a sense of the image of Shelley that is being constructed. His ideas appear at first to be bright, fiery and exciting, but prove to be highly unstable and quickly dissolve away.

Regardless of their scientific inaccuracies, these metaphors have a powerful rhetorical effect, emphasizing that Shelley's mania for experimentation leaves him insensible to the demands of 'common sense', or human sympathy ('his heart'). Thus Hazlitt gives a Burkean defence of custom and prejudice – 'the hard husk of nature and habit' – against Shelley's 'speculation and fancy'. The poet is shown as a scientific mountebank conducting 'electrical experiments in morals and philosophy', which 'though they may scorch other people . . . are to him harmless amusements, the coruscations of an Aurora Borealis, that "play round the head, but do not reach the heart"' (VIII, p. 149). Like later writers on the poet, Hazlitt emphasizes his unearthliness: but this does not (as it does for Maurice) suggest the healthy spirituality of a poetic genius, but rather the dangerous enthusiasm of a fanatic.

Hogg's account of the poet's relationship with chemistry makes very different claims. When they first meet, Shelley is obsessed by the science, and discourses to Hogg with wild-eyed excitement about future discoveries. But Hogg is careful to emphasize that despite Shelley's joy in seemingly pointless and potentially hazardous experiments, the poet firmly believes that scientific progress will end poverty and hunger and that this is the reason for his obsession with the subject.[68] His 'electrical experiments' are meant to help mankind, not shock them; his schemes and fantasies are always, for Hogg, benevolent ones, because Shelley's virtuous nature commands his enthusiasm. This is made very clear by an anecdote in the final part of 'Percy Bysshe Shelley at Oxford'. On a visit to London, Shelley drags his friend to a pawnbroker's shop and explains that on a previous visit, 'some old man had related to him a tale of distress' and asked for ten pounds: 'five of them he drew at once from his pocket, and to raise the other five he had pawned his beautiful solar microscope!'[69] We are told that this was 'a favourite plaything' of Shelley, and he had kept it long after 'he had parted with all the rest of his philosophical apparatus'. But in Hogg's story, the poet's desire to aid the unfortunate is shown to outweigh all other consid-erations, even his personal hobby-horses – thus Hogg attempts to give the reader an 'impression of the pure and genial beauty of Shelley's nature'.[70] Whereas Hazlitt uses science, in the form of a semi-personal, metaphorical critique, to argue that Shelley lives in a fantasy world of wildly speculative radicalism, Hogg uses it, in the form of biographical anecdote, to represent the poet as a man deeply concerned with *practical*, paternalistic benevolence.

The publication of the Shelley articles occurred during a time of intense political agitation surrounding the Reform Bill. Late in 1831, Edward Lytton Bulwer took over the editorship of the *New Monthly* from Samuel Carter Hall (who was demoted to sub-editor), and transformed it from a quietly liberal miscellany into a campaign-ing, reformist journal.[71] It might be thought that this would have made it a good vehicle for Hogg's articles, but there was a tension between their account of an eccen-tric genius like Shelley and the ideal of the new man of letters that Bulwer was prop-agating at this time. As I argued in Chapter 1, in the early nineteenth century many professional authors became increasingly dubious about the notion of the literary genius as an isolated or transgressive figure. Bulwer, in particular, demanded a new breed of post-Reform writers who could aid social progress by communicating with ordinary people. He was opposed to the artistic elitism represented by, for example, Maurice in the *Athenaeum*, a periodical which Bulwer attacked in *Paul Clifford* (1830) as ' "The Asinaeum," which was written to prove, that whatever is popular is neces-sarily bad'.[72] Although Hogg worked very hard to downplay the transgressiveness of Shelley's life and opinions, his account of the poet's otherworldliness jarred with Bulwer's notions of the type of author suitable for a newly reformed society.

In his *Life of Percy Bysshe Shelley* (1858), Hogg states that, due to Bulwer's interfer-ence with his reminiscences, he had to speak of Shelley 'not exactly as I would, but as I might'.[73] He prints a letter from his editor, dated 12 January 1832, responding to Hogg's complaints about omissions from the first article. Bulwer tells him, that 'if an editor lays before him one great – paramount – consistent object in a periodical', that is, Reform, then 'alteration and omission become of frequent necessity...an oneness of opinion in all the papers is then requisite'.[74] Hogg is warned that the articles will not be published if changes cannot be made to them, and that this will probably be neces-sary in the future, for 'your natural affection for Shelley carries you a little beyond that estimate of what he has left to the world, which as yet we are authorised to express'.[75] Furthermore, Bulwer rejects Hogg's proposal of an article on Shelley's poetry.[76]

It is interesting that the High Tory *Fraser's* published a very positive account of Shelley's poetry in 1831 and yet there is no place in the reformist *New Monthly* for a similar article.[77] Despite his opposition to 'personality', Bulwer was only interested in biographical anecdotes of Shelley because, although he believed him to be an important figure in understanding the intellectual spirit of the time, he was suspicious about the merits and influence of his poetry. In December 1831, he wrote that Walter Scott 'in his wildest flights, never loses sight of common sense – there is an affinity between him and his humblest reader; nay, the more discursive the flight, the closer that affinity becomes'. Shelley, however,

> disdains common sense. Of his 'Prince Athanase', we have no earthly comprehension – with his 'Prometheus' we have no human sympathies; and the grander he becomes, the less popular we find him. Writers who do not in theory know their kind, may be admired, but they can never be popular. And when we hear men of unquestionable genius complain of not being appreciated by the herd, it is because they are not themselves skilled in the feelings of the herd.[78]

Echoing Hazlitt's earlier criticisms of the poet (and we should recall that Hazlitt was one of Bulwer's heroes), Bulwer finds Shelley to be too unworldly to be an effective communicator; for both writers, his lack of 'common sense' alienates him from normal people.

Bulwer's suspicions seemed to be borne out by Hogg's account of Shelley's politics. Although the poet is described as having been 'entirely devoted to the lovely theory of freedom' – by which Hogg means classical republicanism – he is represented as a fundamentally speculative politician, 'eminently averse at that time from engaging in the far less beautiful practices wherein are found the actual and operative energies of liberty'.[79] Hogg reports a conversation with Shelley when the poet spoke of his 'aversion' to political articles in the press, and his disdain for the men he had seen at the House of Commons. However, according to Richard Holmes, Shelley became increasingly politically committed at Oxford, *largely due to Hogg's influence*, and was a keen reader of Hunt's *Examiner* and Cobbett's *Political Register*.[80] In a move that would be repeated in the *Life of Percy Bysshe Shelley*, Hogg greatly understates his friend's youthful radicalism and totally conceals his own:

> Ordinary rules may guide ordinary men, but the orbit of the child of genius is essentially eccentric. Although the mind of Shelley had certainly a strong bias towards democracy, and he embraced with an ardent and youthful fondness the theory of political equality, his feelings and behaviour were in many respects highly aristocratical . . . The unbleached web of transatlantic freedom, and the inconsiderate vehemence of such of our domestic patriots as would demonstrate their devotion to the good cause, by treating with irreverence whatever is most venerable, were equally repugnant to his sensitive and reverential spirit. As a politician, Shelley was in theory wholly a republican, but in practice, so far only as it is possible to be one with due regard for the sacred rights of a scholar and a gentleman; and these being in his eyes always more inviolable than any scheme of polity, or civil institution*, although he was upon paper and in discourse a sturdy commonwealth-man, the living, moving, acting individual, had much of the senatorial and conservative, and was, in the main, eminently patrician.[81]

In reality, Shelley was deeply involved in practical politics as a young man – for example, he travelled to Ireland in 1812 and 1813 to support local demands for Catholic emancipation and repeal of the Act of Union of 1800. But in Hogg's article, the poet appears as a sort of aristocratic dilettante, whose republicanism is purely the result of a classical education and who is, in practice, a conservative. Thus Hogg continues and strengthens the 'deradicalising' of Shelley begun by *Blackwood's Magazine* and continued by the *Posthumous Poems* and the Apostles. It is perhaps not surprising that Hogg would knowingly propagate such a false view of Shelley – he had his own position to consider as a successful Tory barrister and he also may have felt that he was serving the poet's memory by disassociating him from popular radicalism at a time when its effects were widely feared among the middle and upper classes. It is interesting, however, that Bulwer was willing to take Hogg's account as fact. His waspish footnote to 'civil institution' in the above quotation is 'after all, we fear, from this passage, that our poet must have had very confused notions of the true scope and end of "Schemes of Polity" and "Civil Institutions" '.[82] The irony is that although Bulwer was fiercely reformist in the early 1830s, his views were nothing like as radical as those of the young Shelley or Hogg.

Hogg's account of Shelley's politics was not left uncontested. Late in 1832, Leigh Hunt's edition of *The Masque of Anarchy* was published by Moxon. Shelley had originally sent the manuscript of the poem to Hunt in September 1819, but Hunt did not publish it in the *Examiner*, presumably due to fear of prosecution. Thirteen years later, with the increased public interest in Shelley, and the passing of the Reform Bill in June, it must have seemed like the right moment to publish the poem. Hunt seems to have come across Hogg's account of Shelley's politics around the time that he was correcting the proofs of the edition and he added a long passage to the preface in which he took issue with Shelley's biographer.[83] He is particularly keen to counteract the notion that Shelley was an abstract theorist of liberty: 'Mr. Shelley's countrymen know how anxious he was for the advancement of the common good, but they have yet to become acquainted with his anxiety in behalf of this particular means of it – Reform.'[84] And he also disagrees strongly with Hogg's suggestion 'that he was an aristocrat by disposition as well as birth', arguing instead that Shelley had no interest in 'high-bred manners' and cared only for the intrinsic worth of people:[85] 'if an aristocracy of intellect and morals were required', Hunt suggests, 'he was the man for one of their leaders'.[86] The clincher, as Hunt sees it, is a pamphlet Shelley wrote in 1817 entitled 'A Proposal for Putting Reform to the Vote through the Country' and he quotes a passage in which Shelley promises £100 a year (a tenth of his income at the time) to support plans for Reform: clearly a very different type of benevolence from that practised by the poet in Hogg's anecdote about the solar microscope. In another passage, Shelley proposes the introduction of 'Annual Parliaments' and seemingly anticipates the Reform Bill as part of a process that will eventually lead, when the 'public mind' is sufficiently 'improved', to universal suffrage.[87]

Bulwer, however, does not seem to have read *The Masque of Anarchy* volume. In an article on Tennyson, published the month after the final instalment of 'Percy Bysshe Shelley at Oxford', he developed his charge that Shelley's poetry was elitist:

> When poetry cannot touch the common springs of emotion – cannot strike upon the Universal Heart – there is a fault somewhere. Shelley would have been not a less, but a greater poet, if he had studied simplicity more...It is not philosophy to utter in grand words the rhapsodies of insanity.[88]

It is clear, I hope, that this critique is political as well as literary. We saw in Chapter 1 that, when criticizing Brydges in 1834, Bulwer argued that genius needed to become 'more social' and that modern men of letters exhibited 'a more wholesome and masculine frame of mind' than their predecessors.[89] He was willing to believe in Hogg's 'aristocratical' Shelley because he was already professionally and politically suspicious of the idea of eccentric genius that the poet seemed to represent. Although Shelley's work had been of interest to radicals during the 1820s, and was to become popular among the Chartists in the 1840s,[90] Bulwer learnt to associate him with an artistic and political elitism that was fundamentally undemocratic.

Literary reminiscences: Richard Pearse Gillies on Scott

Despite his political views, it was in the recently deceased Sir Walter Scott that Bulwer found the link between genius and the masses that he sought:

> There was in him a large and Catholic sympathy with all classes, all tempers, all conditions of men; and this it was that redeemed his noble works from all the taint of party, and all the leaven of sectarianism; this it was that made him, if the Tory in principle, the all-embracing leader in practice. Compare with what *he* has done for the people – in painting the people – the works of poets called Liberal by the *doctrinaires*...Out of print, Scott might belong to a party – in print, mankind belonged to him. Toryism, which is another name for the spirit of monopoly, forsook him at that point where his inquiries into human nature began.[91]

Bulwer was not the only reformer to panegyrize Scott after his death – for example, he was represented as a great moral teacher by Harriet Martineau in the January 1833 number of *Tait's*. Unlike Bulwer, Martineau believed that Scott did not understand the lower orders, but for both authors he seemed to offer a much more suitable version of genius for the modern world than the pathological, elitist principle that was often associated with Byron and Shelley.[92] Thus Bulwer wrote in his obituary that Scott's 'career was one splendid refutation of the popular fallacy, that genius has of necessity vices – that its light must be meteoric – and its courses wayward and uncontrolled'.[93] And Martineau stated that he had 'vindicated the character of genius by the healthiness of his own'.[94] As a popular but critically acclaimed writer who was widely considered to have led a notably virtuous life, Scott seemed like a suitable model for the modern literary character in a post-Reform Britain, regardless of his political principles.

Thomas Carlyle, as one might expect, was to take a different view, arguing in his review of Lockhart's *Life of Sir Walter Scott* (1837–8) that the novelist was too ordinary to be described as a great man and that he lacked the passionate, divine inspiration that was characteristic of genius: 'his life was worldly; his ambitions were worldly. There was nothing spiritual in him; all is economical, material, of the earth earthy'.[95] But despite, or perhaps because of, this lack of spiritual fire, he was 'an eminently well-conditioned man, healthy in body, healthy in soul; we will call him one of the *healthiest* of men'.[96] Lockhart's was the official biography, but an interesting account of Scott was published in book form by Richard Pearse Gillies in 1837, first appearing in *Fraser's* in four parts from October 1835 to January 1836.[97] We saw in Chapter 1 that, generally speaking, *Fraser's* strongly propagated a view of genius as a form of divine inspiration and tried to disassociate it from any transgressive qualities, and I want briefly to consider how Gillies's articles related to this project.

About a year before the articles began, *Fraser's* published a slashing review, probably written by Maginn, of James Hogg's book *The Domestic Manners and Private Life of Sir Walter Scott* (1834). Maginn complains, with breathtaking hypocrisy, that the account is typical of Hogg in that it shows him 'ready to take advantage of any opportunities injudiciously afforded him to break through the decencies and privacies of life, if by doing so he could furbish up materials for an article'.[98] This does not, however, stop *Fraser's* from reprinting the *whole* of Hogg's piece in the course of the review. But Maginn's complaint is not simply that that the article is improper, or that it is full of inaccuracies. The main problem is that someone of Hogg's rank cannot be expected to have understood Scott:

> If by domestic manners he had intended the manners of Sir Walter's domestics, there is no doubt that he is fully qualified, from taste, relationship, congeniality of sentiment, and considerable social intercourse with them; but as to the manners of Sir Walter himself, as well might we expect from a costermonger an adequate sketch of the manners of the clubs in St. James's Street.[99]

This inequality between biographer and subject is not just a matter of social background but one of genius and this, Maginn implies, should not surprise us, for 'the first rank in literature in our times has been attained by men of birth and family, or, at all events, of careful, learned, and expensive education'.[100] Geniuses, then, are always gentlemen, and therefore Scott's 'proper reverence for the established orders of the land' sits naturally alongside his 'true antiquarian and poetical feeling in favour of proud and long-descended names'.[101]

Although in the 1830s Gillies was an impecunious man of letters, he was also a gentleman who had inherited his father's landed estate in 1808. This meant that, unlike Hogg, he met the *Fraser's* requirements for the depiction of Scott. For Gillies, the novelist was exceptional in that he combined a powerful imagination with iron self-control and thus avoided the errors so often associated with genius: 'in his mind poetic sensibility and imagination, which have too often degenerated into irritability and caprice, were never allowed to assume any undue preponderance'.[102] Although Gillies argues that genius is innate and cannot be learnt, he also places great emphasis on the importance of Scott's rural upbringing in the development of his gifts. For 'in the crowded walks of social life, and amid the affairs of the working world, whether in high ranks or low, imagination is chilled and invention fettered'.[103] Anticipating Brydges's claim in *Fraser's* the following year that for the leisured man of genius, unlike other people, 'it is not sufficient to go round in the same mechanical steps, like a blind horse in a mill',[104] Gillies remarks that 'it is only by getting out of the mill-horse track IN THOUGHT, if not in reality, that such powers can have free scope . . . for the most part [society's] pleasures and duties are circumscribed and conventional'.[105] Great and lasting poetry is based on the *'lasting and universal'* imagery of nature, rather than a description of a particular society. Thus the poet whose work is:

> composed while wandering amid the mountain-solitudes and listening to the eloquence of Nature in her cataracts, winds, and waving forests, will have a far more powerful voice than the gentleman who wrote elegant, trim, and precise verses, at Eton or Harrow, proved acute in geometry at Cambridge, and who finally settles into his library in Grosvenor Street.[106]

This might be seen simply as the 'Romantic' account of artistic creation in its basic form, opposing as it does inspiration, natural sublimity and solitude, to poetic rules, town life and conventional society. But, bearing in mind the *Fraser's* emphasis on the gentlemanliness of genius, it is worth considering what sort of rural experience Gillies is describing. It is, of course, that of a leisured elite. Due to his bad health as a child, Scott is brought up in the country, away from public school, but he is just as gentlemanly as those who might have attended Eton or Harrow and gone on to Cambridge. (And Scott, of course, did attend Edinburgh High School and Edinburgh University.) Genius may be innate, but the development of the ability to escape from 'the mill-horse track' depends on a youthful freedom which is only available to a privileged few. This emphasis on the connection between Scott's social status and his art is continued in the fourth and last part of the essay, which describes his role as a land-owning gentleman, a 'member of an old Border family of the highest rank'.[107] Gillies argues against those, like Fox, who criticized him for being more interested in his social status than authorship – 'the laird destroyed the novelist'[108] – by emphasizing that Scott had 'no love of aristocratic display' and that his purchase and improving of Abbotsford was a rational endeavour that gave him pleasure through the exercise of good taste, and greatly benefited his tenants and neighbours.[109] Furthermore, Abbotsford is much more than an elegant estate – it is permeated by Scott's presence, and its grounds and apartments, like the Scotch novels, are 'imperishable monuments of his genius'.[110] This emphasis on the similarity between Scott's actual property and his literary property seeks to resolve any tension between his gentlemanliness and his role as a professional author.

Scott, as portrayed by Gillies, may seem like a perfect paradigm of genius for a Tory journal with a strong interest in the aesthetic. He is a landowning gentleman; his politics are strictly 'Church and King' but his novels appear strongly sympathetic to the lower orders; he is far enough from urban society not to be corrupted, but not so far as to be alienated; his final years are represented as a sort of martyrdom as he struggles to pay off his creditors even though he is not to blame for his business debts; his moral character is unimpeachable; and no genius has ever 'left behind him a reputation so completely without blot'.[111] Gillies was canny enough not to mention Scott's part in *Blackwood's Magazine's* rumbustious early years and the death of John Scott, for by this time it was a widely held view that the 'Cockney School' attacks had been excessive. Despite Scott's apparent perfection, however, it is noteworthy that he was not consistently fêted by *Fraser's* in the same way as Coleridge, for example. This may be partly to do with genre: critics in the 1830s were likely to consider poetry to be intrinsically more important than prose, even the Scotch novels. But it also has to do with biographical constructions of character: ultimately, there was something a little too 'earthy' about Scott for a journal that tended to propagate a highly spiritualized and elitist account of genius.

Thomas De Quincey's 'Lake Reminiscences' and *Tait's Edinburgh Magazine*

During the period from 1833 to 1841, De Quincey published over thirty personal reminiscences in *TEM*. The most well known of these are his four-part essay 'Samuel Taylor Coleridge', which began in September 1834, shortly after the poet's death, and his articles on Wordsworth, which appeared in 1839.[112] Although there have been some good accounts of the 'Lake Reminiscences', they have tended to focus on De Quincey's psychological need to assert himself against Coleridge and Wordsworth, and there has been no consideration of how their position within *TEM* should affect our reading of them. The journal, founded by William Tait early in 1832, was at first mainly a political organ, which sought to advance the Radical cause, and its early contributors included Utilitarians like John Stuart Mill and Richard Cobden. It also contained literary articles and reviews, but, because *Tait's* was inspired by utilitarianism rather than transcendentalism, genius was a far less important term for the journal than it was for *FM*. However, in an article published in May 1833, Leigh Hunt showed how the word could be attached to a reformist agenda, suggesting that the 'privilege' of 'the aristocratical and educated classes' had nothing to do with 'intellectual superiority':

> Genius has not made them lords and squires. It raises a man here and there; and in the first foundations of the present system of society, it may have laid a few of the stones; but accident, and subserviency, and brute force, laid by far the greater number. What may have been got by genius in the first instance, has certainly not been kept by it. Acquiescence and lying have been the great selfish conservatives.[113]

Hunt's target is the sort of writing on genius that linked it with the maintenance of the social hierarchy – this went back as far as Duff and Gerard, but, as we have seen, was also given powerful expression in *Blackwood's* and *Fraser's*. His account suggests that there is nothing inevitably reactionary about the concept of genius, even when genius is constructed as a form of subjectivity that transcends material considerations. To state explicitly that genius has little to do with politics or economics may weaken the power of the idea as a force for social change, but it can also weaken its power as a support for inequality:

> Genius, considered merely in itself, and as a thing full of resources, wants nothing but itself for its honour and dignity . . . . To common wants it is superior. Do we think that Sophocles, or Virgil, or Newton, or Locke, or Raphael, cared for any

thing in the world, provided they could indulge their intellectual impulses, and obtain admiration? Did Schiller or Wieland care? Does Mr. Wordsworth? ... We mean that, as a body, and as far as regards their salaries, they [men of genius] are indifferent to every other superiority over their fellow-men, than such as the consciousness of genius can supply. If all the world had been in a condition of rational equality, *they* would not have been the men to want ten-thousand beef-steaks a day, or parks ten miles round in the neighbourhood of starving weavers.[114]

Hunt's argument fitted in precisely with *Tait's* politics. De Quincey's instincts would probably have been to steer clear of such a Radical journal, but in the early 1830s he was in terrible financial difficulties and could not survive purely by writing for *Blackwood's*.[115] In 1834, he began a series of 'Sketches of Life and Manners; from the Autobiography of an English Opium Eater', which continued intermittently until 1841. As the majority of other articles in *Tait's* were anonymous, the 'Opium Eater' (who was widely known to be De Quincey) quickly became the most prominent character in the magazine, and the constant stream of autobiography must have given its readers a strong sense of personal acquaintance, perhaps even sympathy, with him. At the beginning of 1834, *Tait's* began a new series and the price was reduced from half a crown to one shilling. This made it more affordable for the lower middle-class and working-class readers who were its intended audience, and as a result, 'it became the largest selling magazine in Scotland and a surprisingly popular magazine in England'.[116] Another important change occurred in June of that year, when *Johnstone's Edinburgh Magazine* was incorporated into *Tait's*, and Christian Isobel Johnstone became the new 'hands-on' editor, although Tait maintained a strong role in the functioning of the magazine. Under Johnstone, the journal became much more of a literary magazine, but retained its reformist stance. The Opium Eater's contributions were an integral part of the new-look *Tait's* and must have aided its success. Robert Morrison has argued convincingly that the magazine offered a vehicle for the more 'liberal' side of De Quincey's character, and that he often expressed opinions in it which ran counter to the rabid Toryism of his contributions to *Blackwood's*.[117] Having said that, De Quincey was not a natural *Tait's* writer, and there was sometimes a certain *frisson* between some of the opinions expressed in his articles and the content of the rest of the magazine.

So when De Quincey began the essay on Coleridge in September 1834, the readers of *Tait's* were already familiar with the persona of the 'Opium Eater', and may have trusted his honesty even if they distrusted his politics. He started by emphasizing Coleridge's great genius, but quickly moved on to describe his plagiarisms, his procrastination, his unhappy marriage, his wife's jealousy of Dorothy Wordsworth and the personal misery caused by his opium addiction. These revelations were mixed up with erudite disquisitions on Kant and Schelling, the purpose of which may have been to make De Quincey and his readers more comfortable with the gossipy nature of the essay. In the next two parts, De Quincey continued to emphasize his subject's 'majestic intellect', but risked further annoying the poet's friends and relatives by arguing that he had first had recourse to opium due to his desire for 'luxurious sensations',[118] and by discussing his falling out with Basil Montagu.[119] In the final part of 'Samuel Taylor Coleridge', he completed his biography of the poet and moved on to try to justify the essay. He emphasized that it had been composed *'almost extempore* and under circumstances of...extreme haste', and half-apologized for its impressionistic style.[120] This sort of special pleading was also used after the Wordsworth articles, and we should note that William Tait wrote to Christian Johnstone in 1840 that 'every piece of MS...which he put into my hands bore many, very many proofs of having been read over and corrected...he has always told me that he composes very slowly'.[121]

De Quincey also stated that he intended to give 'a general glance...over the intellectual claims of Mr Coleridge', for 'those very claims constitute the entire and sole justification for the proceeding personal memoir.[122] As we saw in the case of his justification of the Wordsworth articles, he felt that he had to tread very carefully as a biographer by emphasizing that although he was fulfilling an understandable public interest in men of genius, this interest had to be related to the genius itself, rather just being irrelevant tittle-tattle. Thus he sought to justify his discussion of Coleridge's 'character' and 'manners':

> If Mr Coleridge had been merely a scholar – merely a philologist – or merely a man of science – there would be no reason apparent for travelling in our survey beyond the field of his intellect, rigorously and narrowly so called. But because he was a poet, and because he was a philosopher, in a comprehensive and most *human* sense, with whose functions the moral nature is so largely inter- woven, I shall feel myself entitled to notice the most striking aspects of his *character*,...of his disposition, and his manners, as so many indications of his intellectual constitution.[123]

This is all very well, but De Quincey did not perform the survey that he promised. Over the next few pages, he discusses Coleridge's politics and that is where the essay ends. It is a remarkable spectacle to see De Quincey, normally described as an ultra- Tory, trying to make Coleridge's views palatable to the reformist readers of *TEM*. He begins by arguing that the designations 'Whig', 'Tory' and 'Radical' do not apply to the 'vast majority of good citizens'. Most people, including Coleridge, are *'Reformers'*, with no party allegiance, who are 'favourably disposed to a spirit of ventilation and reform carried through all departments of public business'. Coleridge, we are told, was 'a friend to all enlightened reforms', including 'Reform in Parliament'.[124] The poet's association with the Tory party is described as simply a result of his opposition to Bonaparte. Whatever the complexities of Coleridge's conservatism, De Quincey's account is clearly tendentious, but the important point is that because he is writing in *Tait's*, he feels impelled to put forward an argument which goes against the grain of many of his other political utterances. Such a passage could never have appeared in *Blackwood's Magazine*.

Although the fourth part of 'Samuel Taylor Coleridge' ends with the editorial promise 'To be concluded in our next',[125] this promise was not kept. I do not know for certain why De Quincey never completed his account of the poet, but one reason might be that he realized that *Tait's* readers did not particularly care about judging Coleridge's 'intellectual claims'. They simply did not have any investment or interest in the conservative, transcendental philosophy which Coleridge represented in the 1830s, and which made him such an important figure for *Fraser's* audience of 'the metropolitan fashionable and educated elite'.[126] What De Quincey could never admit publicly was that the whole point of the Coleridge articles (and those on Wordsworth) was that they were *gossip* – they do not tell us much about either of the poet's works, but they do give a vibrant picture of the personal lives of two remarkable individuals. Despite De Quincey's obvious bitterness, the reader is mostly invited to sympathize with Coleridge's sufferings and failings, which are actually quite ordinary. It is fitting that the articles appeared in *Tait's*, because they deprived genius of the mystique with which it was associated by *Fraser's* and which so often had conservative ends.

As we saw in Chapter 2, De Quincey's explicit justification for the Wordsworth notices is similar to that of the essay on Coleridge: they are valuable because they shed light on the genius of an author whose work will transcend time and place. But at the same time, he clearly seeks to counteract contemporary representations of Wordsworth as a paragon of wisdom and virtue by including details of him which are meant to show that in some ways he is not a particularly impressive man – this is, of course, part of the attraction of the articles. De Quincey also takes great pains to show that genius is not self-sufficient: Wordsworth is only able to devote his life to his art due to the sacrifices of his friends and family, and his enormous good fortune.[127] Similarly, Coleridge is supported by a succession of friends and benefactors.[128] The problem is that De Quincey is so good at making his subjects seem human, so good at *embodying* genius, that it becomes hard for the reader to connect the felicities of Coleridge's or Wordsworth's poetry – which he also emphasizes – with the account of their appearance, habits and flaws. This has the effect of sundering man and work, and perhaps attacks implicitly the idea of the genius – which we find in Hogg's articles on Shelley, for example – as a person whose exceptional nature is revealed in all aspects of his life. However, this was probably not a conscious strategy on De Quincey's part, but rather the inevitable result of the personal bitterness behind these ad hoc productions, particularly with regard to Wordsworth. For when writing about genius in more abstract terms in the April 1846 number of *Tait's*, he distinguishes it from talent in a way in which the Lake Poets would have approved:

> Genius is that mode of intellectual power which moves in alliance with the *genial* nature, i.e. with the capacities of pleasure and pain; whereas talent has no vestige of such an alliance, and is perfectly independent of all human sensibilities...Besides its relation to suffering and enjoyment, genius always implies a deeper relation to virtue and vice: whereas talent has no shadow of a relation to *moral* qualities, any more than it has to vital sensibilities. A man of the highest talent is often obtuse and below the ordinary standard of men in his feelings; but no man of genius can unyoke himself from the society of moral perceptions that are brighter, and sensibilities that are more tremulous, than those of men in general.[129]

Here De Quincey is discussing George Gilfillan's claims, in his literary portrait of Keats, that 'men of genius' are *not* particularly prone to irritability or poverty. He argues that this is difficult to prove or disprove: but what can be shown is that they are not only intellectual superior to normal people, but also spiritually superior. This does not necessarily contradict the account of genius in the 'Lake Reminiscences', but is clearly different in emphasis. In his articles on the Lake Poets, De Quincey shows them as living, breathing, *flawed* individuals who cannot succeed without financial and social support, thus undercutting the extreme representation of the creative artist as a transcendent, Godlike figure that we find in different forms in the writings of authors like Heraud and Carlyle. Thus, whatever De Quincey's political views, the articles on Coleridge and Wordsworth had an egalitarian edge and fitted in well with the radicalism of *Tait's*. In Chapter 4, I will show how a personal account of Wordsworth as a private man in *Blackwood's Magazine* could have very different implications.

4 *Blackwood's Edinburgh Magazine* and the construction of Wordsworth's genius

In an essay published in *Tait's Edinburgh Magazine* (*TEM*) in August 1835, Thomas De Quincey argued that his 'appreciation of Wordsworth' as a young man had put him thirty years in advance of his contemporaries. Although now, he claimed, magazines 'habitually speak of Mr Wordsworth as *a* great if not *the* great poet of the age', during the first quarter of the nineteenth century, 'language was exhausted, ingenuity was put on the rack, in the search after images and expressions vile enough – insolent enough – to convey the unutterable contempt avowed for all that he had written by the fashionable critics'. According to De Quincey, for many years only one periodical supported the poet:

> *Blackwood's Magazine* (1817) first accustomed the public ear to the language of admiration coupled with the name of Wordsworth. This began with Professor Wilson; and well I remember – nay, the proofs are still easy to hunt up – that, for eight or ten years, this singularity of opinion, having no countenance from other journals, was treated as a whim, a paradox, a bold extravagance of the *Blackwood* critics . . . In short, up to 1820, the name of Wordsworth was trampled under foot; from 1820 to 1830 it was militant; from 1830 to 1835 it has been triumphant.[1]

De Quincey's account of *Blackwood's* as a lone voice crying in the critical wilderness is inaccurate, but the magazine was notable for its campaign to improve Wordsworth's reputation in the period from 1818 to 1822. This campaign contributed much to the later success of the poet, as well as to the construction of the 'Victorian' Wordsworth – 'a noble, morally pure priest of natural religion'[2] – whose person was as much an object of veneration as his poetry. The aim of this chapter is to examine how and why *Blackwood's* represented him as a great genius at a time when his position in literary culture was uncertain.

There have been a number of valuable recent accounts of Wordsworth's complex and troubled engagement with the literary marketplace, examining subjects such as his views on posterity and the reading public, his dealings with publishers and his campaign for copyright reform in the 1830s.[3] There are also some useful studies of the reception of his poetry during his lifetime.[4] But surprisingly little has been written on the construction of Wordsworth by his contemporaries – how they represented him as a writer, as a thinker and as a man.[5] 'Constructed', of course, can mean both 'made' and 'interpreted'. The making of Wordsworth as a successful poet was based, in part, on interpretations of his writings and character. Furthermore, the existence of journalistic narratives describing this success was an important precondition for more tangible forms of reputation such as public honours or sales. To understand the process by which Wordsworth came to be widely viewed as a sanctified poetic genius who produced works of great value requires that we imagine a time when a now – canonical writer was still in competition with his peers, a time when his reputation still had to be made. Wordsworth's fame is a result of the way in which he was marketed and mediated both during his lifetime and since; his reputation *could* have been constructed differently.

Blackwood's succeeded in convincingly interpreting aspects of Wordsworth's life and work that had previously been put forward as reasons for his artistic 'failure' – for example, his isolated existence in the Lake District – as evidence of his greatness. In doing so, it helped to popularize what we would now identify as a typically Romantic ideal of cultural production: a model that emphasizes the importance of originality, individuality and the transcendence of worldly concerns. But the magazine's notorious interest in 'personality' both underpinned and ironized its account of Wordsworth as a transcendent genius. For although this account was based, in part, on representations of him as a private man – most notably in John Wilson's 'Letters from the Lakes' (1819) – we shall see that the very existence of those representations in the pages of the magazine problematized its claim that he stood above the literary marketplace.

Wordsworth's reception

Despite De Quincey's remarks, Wordsworth's name was certainly not 'trampled under foot' until 1820; the story is much more complicated than that. The reviews of *Lyrical Ballads* were mostly positive, and each volume sold about 2000 copies over a seven-year period.[6] Wordsworth was not to achieve such commercial success again until the 1830s. In 1802, Jeffrey began his attacks on the 'Lake Poets' and other critics quickly followed suit.[7] The *Edinburgh's* influence was apparent in the critical and commercial response to Wordsworth's *Poems* of 1807, which represented the nadir of the poet's reputation and sales, and in the following few years, the critics tended to denigrate the Lake Poets, and Wordsworth in particular.[8] However, reviews of *The Excursion* (1814), and the *White Doe of Rhylstone* (1815) were generally positive, although Jeffrey's attacks continued unabated. Wordsworth's two publications of 1819, *Peter Bell* and *The Waggoner*, were badly received by most critics, but this is hardly surprising considering their subject matter: it is almost as if the poet was being deliberately provocative. These negative reviews had relatively little influence on his overall reputation, for by 1819 he had already published a considerable amount of poetry. The reviews of the *River Duddon* volume (1820) were mostly positive.

The good reviews enjoyed by Wordsworth in the 1810s did not have a strong effect on his sales, and one reason for this must have been because Jeffrey's attacks in the *Edinburgh*, which generally sold well over 10,000 copies (and was read by many more), had a far greater effect on contemporary readers than any number of appreciative articles in minor periodicals like the *Philanthropist* or the *British Critic*.[9] Writing in 1819, John Gibson Lockhart (in the guise of 'Peter Morris') lamented the influence of Jeffrey's version of Wordsworth on Scottish readers:

> The reading public of Edinburgh do not criticise Mr Wordsworth; they think him below their criticism; they know nothing about what he has done, or what he is likely to do. They think him a mere old sequestered hermit, eaten up with vanity and affectation, who publishes every now and then some absurd poem about a Washing-Tub, or a Leech-Gatherer, or a Little Grey Cloak. They do not know even the names of some of the finest poems our age has produced.[10]

Blackwood's writers tended to exaggerate the influence of *Edinburgh Review* (ER) in order to emphasize the 'heroism' of their battle with it, but the journal was certainly a powerful force during the 1810s, and the fact that Wordsworth, despite his professed aloofness from periodical criticism, was willing to invite ridicule by railing bitterly at Jeffrey in 1815 and 1816 shows his awareness of the damage that the critic had done to his reputation and sales.[11]

De Quincey's narrative of Wordsworth's reputation *is* suggestive in so far as 1820 can be seen as a turning point in his career. *Blackwood's* and, to a lesser extent, other new periodicals like the *London Magazine* (LM) and the *New Monthly Magazine* (NMM) played an important role in the steady rise of the poet's cultural status during the 1820s and 1830s. In the latter period of his life, as well as being treated with much more deference by the critics, he attracted numerous visitors to Rydal Mount, his sales gradually increased and he received a number of public honours culminating in the Laureateship in 1843.[12] The growing interest in Wordsworth around 1820 is apparent not only in reviews of his new volumes, but also in the appearance of a number of articles that offered general assessments of his work and 'genius'.[13] Although, as one might expect, these sometimes crossed the thin line between discussing his poetic abilities and describing his personality and private life, at that time it was only *Blackwood's* that published a directly personal, anecdotal account of the poet, in the form of the 'Letters from the Lakes'.

Blackwood's and Wordsworth

The *Blackwood's* approach to Wordsworth was initially rather inconsistent. In 1934, Alan Lang Strout showed that three anonymous letters on the poet's *Letter to a Friend of Robert Burns* (1816), which appeared in the magazine in June, October and November 1817, were all written by Wordsworth's friend John Wilson, who was himself seen as a member of the 'Lake School'.[14] The first attacked Wordsworth and defended Jeffrey from the poet's criticisms. The second was a vindication of the poet, and the third was another attack. Strout argues that these articles were as much a reflection of Wilson's 'extraordinary volatility' as a publicity stunt on behalf of a fledgling publication.[15] However, they must also be read in the context of the magazine's explicit disdain for 'unity of mind' and its capacity to contain conflicting arguments and opinions, a discursive heterogeneity apparent most strongly in the *Noctes Ambrosianae*.[16] As we shall see, Wilson certainly did have mixed feelings about his friend, but in the 1817 articles he was also, in a crude way, exploring different perspectives on Wordsworth and acting out the ongoing controversy surrounding the poet's merits. This combination of personal and structural ambivalence also led, I think, to the *Noctes Ambrosianae* of September 1825, in which Christopher North, the fictional editor of the magazine and Wilson's principal *Blackwood's* persona, stated that Wordsworth was 'a good man, and a bad poet' and that *The Excursion* was 'the worst poem, of any character, in the English language'.[17] When another victim of the same article threatened legal action, Wilson hid in the Lake District and sent letters to William Blackwood begging him not to reveal his name for fear that he would be exposed as Wordsworth's calumniator.[18]

The attacks of 1817 and 1825 bookend a period in which the *Blackwood's* attitude to Wordsworth was nearly always one of unqualified adulation. Wilson wrote the vast majority of articles praising him, though others such as Lockhart, Patmore and Moir also joined the chorus of approbation.[19] His genius was constantly celebrated and he was treated as a profound thinker, worthy of veneration. The following passage from 1818, with its religious overtones, is typical:

> With all the great and essential faculties of the Poet, he possesses the calm and self-commanding powers of the Philosopher . . . Hence he looks over the world of life, and man, with a sublime benignity . . . The pathos and the truth of his most felicitous Poetry are more profound than of any other, not unlike the most touching and beautiful passages in the Sacred Page.[20]

Blackwood's, of course, praised other contemporary poets at this time, but this sort of language was reserved for Wordsworth. He was marked out from 'all the other first-rate writers of the age', who, Wilson argued in 1822, 'have varied their moods and measures according to the fluctuations of popular feeling, sentiment, and opinion'. In contrast,

> Wordsworth buries his spirit in the solitary haunts and recesses of nature, and suffers no living thing to intrude there, to disturb the dreams of his own imagination. He is to himself all in all. He holds communings with the great spirit of human life, and feels a sanctity in all the revelations that are made to him in his solitude . . . His poetry is to him religion; and we venture to say, that it has been felt to be so by thousands. It would be absolute profanation to speak one word against many of his finest breathings; and as the author and promulgator of such divine thoughts, Wordsworth, beyond all poets, living or dead, is felt to be the object of the soul's purest reverence, gratitude, and love.[21]

For Wilson, Wordsworth's solitary and contemplative life gives him access to 'revelations' that are denied to his more worldly minded peers. But in the final sentence of the passage, he seems less like a holy hermit and more like a living God, the 'author' of 'divine thoughts' who should be revered above all other poets (including, presumably, Shakespeare and Milton).

What lay behind such high praise? The answer that Wilson and other *Blackwood's* writers were simply responding to Wordsworth's poetic gifts is inadequate, for there were also strong commercial and ideological factors behind their positive representations of the poet. Jeffrey N. Cox argues that the impetus behind the magazine's praise of Wordsworth was its enmity towards the 'Cockney School': '*Blackwood's* editors seem to decide that if the gathering of liberal and radical intellectuals around Hunt criticized Wordsworth and the Lakers, then *Blackwood's* would defend them: if you are my enemy's enemy, then you must be my friend'.[22] But Cox, I think, accepts at face value an opposition between the two 'Schools' that *Blackwood's* had actually very much exaggerated so as to pretend that it was the sole critical voice that was capable of recognizing the Lakers' genius. In fact, Hunt and Keats had also written favourably about Wordsworth in the previous year, and thus in order to protect the apparent exclusivity of *Blackwood's'* cultural investment in him, Lockhart took great pains in two of the 'Cockney School' articles to deny that the 'Cockneys' could truly have the taste to appreciate such a genius.[23]

Blackwood's used Wordsworth to help create a position for itself within the increasingly competitive marketplace for periodical literature. By this I do not mean that its support of him had a direct or immediate effect on its popularity, but rather that this support was a central part of the journal's identity – and ultimately the distinctiveness of this identity helped the journal to sustain its early success and compete with other journals, most notably the *Scots Magazine* and the mighty *ER*. In the magazine's early years, Wilson and Lockhart frequently attacked Francis Jeffrey, using his 'failure' to appreciate Wordsworth's genius as a prime example of his own weakness as a critic, the inadequacies of the *ER* and the lamentable ignorance and partisanship of the Edinburgh Whigs.[24] During the 1820s, it was customary for *Blackwood's* to claim that it had single-handedly rescued the poet from public obscurity and critical vituperation. For example, in 1826, Wilson and Maginn argued that the magazine's inception had quickly led to 'a revolution' in reviewing: 'no Zany-Zoilus in the Blue and Yellow [the cover of the *ER*] could any longer outcrow the reading Public. A long, prosing leading article in the Edinburgh, abusing Wordsworth, looked ineffably silly beside one splendid panegyrical paragraph in Maga on the Great Laker'.[25] It matters little whether or not this claim was accurate; the point is that *Blackwood's'* self-promotion was partly based on its professed opposition to the *ER*, and its support of Wordsworth was a powerful way of articulating this opposition.[26]

What other factors led *Blackwood's* to construct Wordsworth as a genius? The panegyric on him and Coleridge in the third of the 'Letters from the Lakes' (March 1819) may well have been partly designed to secure the latter's approbation. An article in the infamous October 1817 issue of the magazine had savagely attacked his *Biographia Literaria*.[27] But by 1819, William Blackwood was attempting to solicit him as a contributor and sent him the March 1819 issue.[28] In June of that year, William Davis (of Cadell and Davis, Blackwood's London agents) wrote to the publisher, stating that '[Coleridge] *must* be much influenced, I think, by what he has discovered of the altered manner in which both he himself and his friend Wordsworth have lately been mentioned in your Magazine'.[29] Another reason for the journal's support of Wordsworth is simply that his Toryism, which was becoming increasingly apparent (especially after his support for Lowther in the Westmoreland election of 1818), chimed in with *Blackwood's* own ideological stance. Finally, he was also valuable to the magazine because he could be used to strengthen its account of poetic genius as, ideally, an emanation of national culture that had to be restrained by custom and tradition – 'guarded alike by wisdom and reverence from all transgression' – as opposed to a dangerous force, which threatened social and political stability.[30]

The 'Letters from the Lakes'

John Wilson's 'Letters from the Lakes' are the most significant and interesting of the *Blackwood's* accounts of Wordsworth because their adulation takes the form of biography rather than criticism. They cannot be properly analysed without a brief account of the relationship between the two men. Following a brilliant career at Oxford, Wilson had settled at the Elleray estate near Windermere in 1808. He had already written Wordsworth a fan letter in 1802, and quickly became a close friend of the poet and his family.[31] Writing in August 1808, Dorothy Wordsworth told her friend Catherine Clarkson about Wilson's reverence for her brother, and the increasing intimacy between the two households.[32] In 1810, Wilson became godfather to Wordsworth's son William, and was also, he later claimed, allowed to read the manuscript of the *Prelude*.[33] *The Isle of Palms* (1812), Wilson's first volume of poetry, bears obvious marks of Wordsworth's influence: in one poem, 'The Angler's Tent', Wilson even self-deprecatingly compares his mentor's 'inspired song' with his own 'lowlier simple strain'.[34] Shortly after its publication, however, the friendship seems to have become strained, and by 1815 a breach between the two poets had developed. In February of that year, Henry Crabb Robinson reports the following piece of gossip by De Quincey:

> Wilson, the minor poet of the Lakes, is estranged from Wordsworth. Vanity among such men produces sad effects. Wordsworth was offended that Wilson should borrow so much without acknowledgment from him and his works, and has therefore given no praise to Wilson. This pains Wilson, who has, besides, peculiarities in his manners, etc., which Wordsworth does not spare.[35]

It seems that Wilson's hero-worship of the older man became tinged with the resentment of a friend who found his merits were not acknowledged, and perhaps also with the anxiety of a poet trying to emancipate himself from the influence of a literary forebear. Thus it is hardly surprising that, when Wilson began to write for *Blackwood's* after being forced to give up his life of gentlemanly leisure due to a heavy financial loss, he was capable of attacking as well as praising Wordsworth.

The 'Letters from the Lakes' purported to be translations of letters written by a young German, Philip Kempferhausen, while holidaying in the Lake District in the summer of 1818. The first letter describes his wanderings among the Lakes, the second concentrates on a trip to Ambleside and a meeting with Robert Southey and the third recounts a visit to Wordsworth at Rydal Mount. This letter treats the poet as a celebrity, and interestingly anticipates his status as a Lakeland oracle in the latter period of his life. Like most of Wilson's other articles on the poet, it seeks to defend Wordsworth's work from his critics, but in this case through a representation of his personal character and private life. He appears, in part, as a country gentleman immersed in a network of healthy, paternalistic social relations – this links him with *Blackwood's* Tory ideology, which emphasized rural virtue, the maintenance of social distinctions and religious orthodoxy. At the same time, despite its panegyrical tone, by breaching the boundaries between public and private in such a way the article represents a deliberate insult to Wordsworth, and reveals Wilson's ambivalent feelings about his former friend.

In the first letter, Kempferhausen writes of the beauties of the Lake District with great enthusiasm; he describes his time there as 'a month in Paradise' and recounts the uplifting effect this environment has had on his 'soul'.[36] It soon becomes apparent, to the initiated *Blackwood's* reader, that the German is also an enthusiast for Wordsworth. He quotes the first two lines of 'My heart leaps up' and his prose echoes 'Tintern Abbey': 'the spirit of human life breathed a peculiar music'.[37] His account of the people of the Lake District, emphasizing their beauty and primitive virtue, clearly has Wordsworthian resonances, and is meant to contradict those critics, like Hazlitt and Jeffrey, who had attacked the poet for writing about uncivilized peasants.

The second letter describes a visit to the house of Robert Southey at Keswick. Kempferhausen's unnamed correspondent, it transpires, is also a fan of the Lake Poets, and thus the young German feels enabled to reveal information about their private lives:

> I hope that I know too well what is due to the sanctity of the domestic life of men of genius and virtue, to utter one idle word about that bright scene of happiness which I was permitted, though a stranger and unknown, to behold and to enjoy – but to you who, like myself, regard these men at once as the most original of poets, and the most patriotic of citizens, I may be allowed to communicate something of what I felt in their presence.[38]

Here Wilson is playing with notions of public and private. Kempferhausen justifies his forthcoming account of the private lives of Wordsworth and Southey on the grounds of the respect that he and his friend have for them, and the private nature of their correspondence. As a document in a public journal, the article may of course be read by individuals who have no respect for the Lake Poets, so in its own terms, it seems to transgress the 'sanctity of the domestic life of men of genius and virtue', which Kempferhausen claims to value so highly. However, during 1818 *Blackwood's* had cajoled, instructed and *constructed* its readers as individuals who were capable of appreciating the Lake Poets and simply needed to be introduced to their merits. Through Kempferhausen, Wilson is addressing the entire readership of the journal and telling them that now they have been educated in Wordsworth's genius and virtue, they have earned the right to consume images of his private life – an assertion with which Wordsworth himself would certainly not have concurred.

Southey gives Kempferhausen an introductory note to Wordsworth, and the reader
is promised that 'of that extraordinary person – certainly the most original genius of
his day, at least of his country (for we must not yield our Goethe) – I shall endeavour
to speak in my next Letter'. On his walk back to Ambleside, Kempferhausen muses
on Southey's intellect, achievements and self-discipline, and, defending him from
the charge of apostasy, calls him 'a devout lover of his country'. For despite 'all the
prejudices of sectarian spleen – all the levity and indifference, real or affected, of mere
worldly men to the character and pursuits of a recluse poet and philosopher', Southey
has a 'splendid and noble' reputation among 'enlightened and good men, citizens,
and Christians'.[39] The claim that 'mere worldly men' have failed to appreciate
virtuous genius is repeated in the later description of Wordsworth.

In the third of the 'Letters from the Lakes', as Peter Swaab has argued, Wilson
situates Wordsworth in a pastoral context like that of *The Excursion*.[40] This is significant, for in part, the article attempts to mediate the persona that Wordsworth
adopted in that poem – the Miltonic philosopher-poet – to the readers of *Blackwood's*.
It also seeks to defend this version of genius from the criticisms of Hazlitt and Jeffrey,
who had represented Wordsworth as an alienated, antisocial figure in their reviews of
his epic.[41] Jeffrey in particular had argued that the faults of *The Excursion* stemmed
from the poet's isolated existence; that Wordsworth lacked 'taste' because of his desire
to distance himself from his contemporaries both geographically and artistically.[42]
Although he accepted that 'solitary musings' in the Lake District 'might no doubt
be expected to nurse up the mind to the majesty of poetical conception',

> the collision of equal minds – the admonition of prevailing impressions – seems
> necessary to reduce its redundancies, and repress that tendency to extravagance
> or puerility, into which the self-indulgence and self-admiration of genius is so
> apt to be betrayed, when it is allowed to wanton, without awe or restraint, in the
> triumph and delight of its own intoxication. That its flights should be graceful
> and glorious in the eyes of men, it seems almost to be necessary that they should
> be made in the consciousness that mens' eyes are to behold them – and that the
> inward transport and vigour by which they are inspired, should be tempered by
> an occasional reference to what will be thought of them by those ultimate
> dispensers of glory.[43]

In contrast to the Wordsworthian 'egotistical sublime', Jeffrey propounds
a Whiggish, dialogic account of artistic creation; the tendencies of imaginative
genius towards 'extravagance', 'self-indulgence' and 'intoxication' need to be curbed
by social interaction with 'equal minds'. Genius, he goes on to argue, can only succeed through 'an habitual and general knowledge of the few and settled permanent
maxims, which form the canon of general taste in all large and polished societies'.
Wordsworth's errors could have been avoided if 'instead of confining himself almost
entirely to the society of dalesmen and cottagers, and little children', the poet 'had
lived or mixed familiarly with men of literature and ordinary judgment in poetry'.[44]

If, as Raymond Williams claimed, the Romantic poets' emphasis on genius was
partly as a response to the alienation of the poet from his audience in an increasingly

commercialized literary world, then Jeffrey's critique of genius was based on a refusal to accept that this was a real problem.[45] As far as he was concerned, Wordsworth's failure was due to his self-induced separation from the reading public, and his disdain for its feelings. Conversely, *Blackwood's* attempted to show that the poet's position actually resulted from the inability of this public – misled by foolish critics like Jeffrey – to appreciate Wordsworth profound philosophical poetry, and at the same time insisted that *their* readers could be taught to admire him. In sharp contrast to Jeffrey's review, the third of the 'Letters from the Lakes' celebrates Wordsworth's sequestration in the Lake District and presents it as a guarantee of his poetry's merits.

Kempferhausen's description of his first meeting with Wordsworth is an important moment in the cultural fashioning of the poet:

> There seemed to me, in his first appearance, something grave almost to austerity, and the deep tones of his voice added strength to that impression of him . . . His mind seemed to require an effort to awaken itself thoroughly from some brooding train of thought, and his manner, as I felt at least, at first reluctantly relaxed into blandness and urbanity. There was, however, nothing of vulgar pride in all this, although perhaps it might have seemed so, in an ordinary person. It was the dignity of a mind habitually conversant with high and abstracted thoughts – and unable to divest itself wholly, even in common hours, of the stateliness inspired by the loftiest studies of humanity . . . Never saw I a countenance in which CONTEMPLATION so reigns. His brow is very lofty – and his dark brown hair seems worn away, as it were, by thought, so thinly is it spread over his temples.[46]

This early account of Wordsworth as a deep thinker is echoed in later nineteenth-century representations of him as a poet–philosopher–priest. The passage works against contemporary representations of Wordsworth and his work as puerile and childish: *this* man is not the writer of the widely mocked *Poems* of 1807, but the great genius who created *The Excursion*. Wilson is also careful to emphasize that Wordsworth's abstracted manner is not due to pride or egotism – epithets that were frequently hurled at the poet in the 1810s – but a sign of the 'dignity' and 'stateliness' of his extraordinary mind.

After describing the poet's idyllic home life and emphasizing his familial affections, Kempferhausen gives an account of a walk to Grasmere church with Wordsworth and his family. At this point in the article the poet appears as a philanthropic country gentleman who is venerated by the local peasantry: 'the old men, as they passed by, addressed him with an air of reverence, inspired no doubt by the power and wisdom of his conversation, and also by the benevolence and charities of his life' (p. 740). And Wordsworth's virtue outshines even his poetic genius: 'I less envied William Wordsworth his glory as a prevailing poet, than his happiness as a philanthropist and a Christian' (pp. 740–1). Whereas Hazlitt and Jeffrey had disparaged rural society, implying that it was bound to degrade a man like Wordsworth by removing him from intercourse with his equals, Wilson shows the poet as protected from the corruptions of city life, and fully embedded in a network of healthy, hierarchical social relations in a devout rural community. His poetry may be revolutionary, but his politics and private life are entirely sedate. The *Blackwood's* Wordsworth is an image of literary greatness which suggests that genius – far from being a dangerous, transgressive force *à la* Byron and Shelley – can be fully reconciled with Church and State.

Wilson balances the representation of Wordsworth as a sociable, family-loving gentleman with a portrayal of him as a reclusive genius. After the visit to Grasmere Church, the poet takes Kempferhausen to a 'tarn of deepest solitude' in Easedale, where, the young German states,

> Wordsworth informed me, that he had meditated, and even composed, much of his poetry; and certainly there could not be a fitter study for a spirit like his, that loves to brood, with an intensity of passion, on those images of nature which his imagination brings from afar and moulds into the forms of life. It was in this naked solitude that many of the richest and loftiest passages of the 'Excursion' were composed.
>
> (p. 741)

This account of Wordsworth creating his masterpiece in sublime isolation is intended utterly to contradict Jeffrey's argument that the poet should restrain his imagination through a dialogic relationship with his urban readership. Wordsworth has an exemplary private life, marked by both domestic affections and social duty, but here Kempferhausen emphasizes that his poetry comes from solitude. This is a typically Romantic, individualistic view of composition. The explicit mention of Wordsworth's epic poem serves to emphasize the extent to which the third letter works as an advertisement for *The Excursion*. Throughout, Wilson represents Wordsworth's impressive appearance, personal happiness, sagacity and virtue as guarantees for the merit of his philosophical poem.

A vital aspect of the Romantic account of literary production is that for the true genius, writing is not an occasional hobby or a mere trade, but a way of life. Wordsworth speaks of poetry 'like an inspired man', and his auditor declares that

> it was evident, that poetry was the element in which he lived, and breathed, and had his being. Other poets, at least all I have ever known, are poets but on occasions – Wordsworth's profession is that of a poet; and therefore when he speaks of poetry, he speaks of the things most familiar, and, at the same time, most holy to his heart. For twenty years has he lived in this grand country, and there devoted his whole soul to his divine art.
>
> (p. 741)

Poetry is not just something that Wordsworth produces when he feels like it; it is his *essence*. In reality, of course, literature was certainly not Wordsworth's main source of income; unable to make enough money from his publications to support his family, he had taken on the post of Distributor of Stamps for Westmoreland and Penrith in 1813. Wilson is using 'profession' mainly in its theological sense, meaning, in general, a declaration of faith and, more specifically, the vow made on entering a religious order. Poetry, for Wordsworth, is like the daily work undertaken by a monk or nun: 'most familiar' and 'most holy'. Thus although Kempferhausen emphasizes that he is generous in his praise for his contemporaries, he is marked out from them: 'it was clear that his soul was with them of elder times; and who shall say, but in this he obeyed the voice of truth – the only voice to which in his solitude Wordsworth cares to listen' (p. 742).

This account of Wordsworth's separation from the literary marketplace is emphasized further by his 'unqualified contempt' for 'the periodical criticism of Britain'. He states that

> the office of a periodical critic was one beneath the dignity of a great mind – that such a critic, in order to please, to startle, or astonish – without doing which he could acquire no character at all – must often sacrifice what he knew to be truth – that he must mingle truth with falsehood, or, at least, with error; and that he who wrote avowedly and professionally to the public, must respect, nay, take advantage, of its prejudices or its ignorance; and if so, surely, whatever might be the advantages or disadvantages of such writings to the public, they were not worthy [of] much notice from a poet who devoted his whole life to the study of his art, – who in his solitude sought truth, and truth alone; and who, unless he knew that it was amply deserved, and wisely bestowed, would be miserable under the world's applause.
>
> (p. 742)

Again, this is a typically Romantic account of authorship. Periodical writers, unlike poets, write 'avowedly and professionally for the public'; they pander to their readers and thus sacrifice truth to sales. They cannot be men of 'high intellect'. On the other hand, the poetic genius finds truth in solitude, caring nothing for the 'world's applause', and, by implication, the concomitant financial rewards. It may seem odd that Wilson would include an attack on periodical literature in the 'Letters from the Lakes'. However, as we saw in Chapter 1, disquiet about the influence of the press on authors and the reading public was a fairly common theme among magazine writers of the period, and in 1818 both Wilson and Lockhart had published articles which attacked the way in which literary critics sought to position themselves and their readers as judges of men of genius.[47] *Blackwood's* was often represented by its writers very differently: as a supporter of genius and as a journal, which sought to educate and improve its audience, rather than pander to its prejudices. Its readers were encouraged to believe that it should not be included as part of a pernicious magazine culture that could be so harmful to creativity. By reporting Wordsworth's comments on the press in his account of the poet, Wilson affirms the model of cultural production that pitches the disinterested genius against the debased critic, while suggesting at the same time that *Blackwood's* is the exception that proves this rule. In reality, Wordsworth would certainly not have exempted it from his remarks, and so Wilson is also having a joke at the poet's expense.

For the 'Letters from the Lakes' were seen as a breach of social decorum by Wordsworth and his family. The poet had disliked *Blackwood's* from its inception, having taken umbrage at Wilson's attacks on *A Letter to a Friend of Robert Burns*, and the magazine was banned from his household.[48] Around the time of the publication of the third of the letters, he wrote to Francis Wrangham expressing his disgust at the 'personal' nature of *Blackwood's* articles on him and his friends.[49] When the 'Letters from the Lakes' were reprinted in the *Westmoreland Gazette*, probably with De Quincey's connivance, he was angered and tried to prevent the publication.[50] Wilson must have known that Wordsworth would be offended by *Blackwood's* account of his private life; as I showed in Chapter 2, in *A Letter to a Friend of Robert Burns*, the poet had attacked the contemporary culture of 'personality', lamenting 'the coarse intrusions into the recesses, the gross breaches upon the sanctities, of domestic life, to which we have lately been more and more accustomed'.[51] Having written three articles on this text, Wilson can hardly have been unaware of Wordsworth's assertion that biography was unnecessary in the case of authors, whom he did not consider to be public figures.[52]

Despite their eulogistic content, 'The Letters from the Lakes' were criticized by an anonymous writer in the *NMM*, who complained of the *Blackwood's* practice

> of dragging the peculiarities, the conversation, and domestic habits of distin-
> guished individuals into public view, to gratify a diseased curiosity at the
> expense of men by whom its authors have been trusted. Such a course, if largely
> fulfilled, would destroy all that is private and social in life, and leave us nothing
> but our public existence. How must the joyous intercourses of society be chilled,
> and the free unbosoming of the soul be checked, by the feeling that some one is
> present who will put down every look and word and tone in a note-book, and
> exhibit them to the common gaze! If the enshading sanctities of life are to be cut
> away – as in Peter's Letters, or in the Letters from the Lakes – its joys will speedily
> perish. When they can no longer nestle in privacy, they will wither.[53]

Wilson's effusive praise of Wordsworth in the 'Letters from the Lakes' is, paradoxically, a sort of revenge for Wordsworth's refusal to praise Wilson's poetry. The article
is calculated both to improve Wordsworth's cultural status and to offend the poet by
revealing details of his private life to the readers of *Blackwood's*. Wordsworth's dislike
of 'personality' was due not simply to his sense of personal dignity, but to a desire to
control the ways in which he, or different versions of him, were mediated and consumed. Throughout his career, the poet wanted public success, but was horrified by
the possible development of the culture of celebrity, which is a hallmark of modern
capitalist society: the uncontrolled, commercialized proliferation of representations
of individuals in the public eye. By publicizing the poet's private life, Wilson usurps
Wordsworth's power to control representations of himself. He asserts the increasing
dominance of the periodical press in the literary marketplace and also, covertly, his
own power over the poet as a writer for a powerful journal. And by including
Wordsworth's disparaging remarks on the press in a journal that is conducting a public campaign in support of the poet, he draws attention to the symbiotic relationship
that commodity culture creates between the artist and the critic. For although he
clearly does not agree with Jeffrey that the poetic genius should accommodate his
work to the taste of the reading public, he implies that the task of the 'original'
poet – as Wordsworth famously put it, of '*creating* the taste by which he is to be
enjoyed'[54] – can be achieved only through the aid of sympathetic criticism and
biography. Wordsworth needs *Blackwood's Magazine* to mediate his work to early
nineteenth-century readers, whether he likes it or not.

5   William Hazlitt and the degradation of genius

Writing in *The Spirit of the Age* (1825) of Walter Scott's ability to create lifelike characters, Hazlitt exclaims 'what a power is that of genius!'.[1] But his delight in the Scotch novels was matched by his hatred of their author's politics, particularly Scott's association with *Blackwood's Magazine* and the *Quarterly Review* (*QR*), and he goes on to state that 'there is no other age or country of the world (but ours), in which such genius could have been so degraded!' (XI, p. 68). Throughout his journalistic career, Hazlitt was obsessed by what he saw as the corruption of literary culture by government influence and class prejudice. During the 1810s, his main concern was the 'apostasy' of the 'Lake Poets', all of whom had held strongly Jacobinical views in the 1790s but had gone on to become supporters of the Tory government and beneficiaries of its patronage. In later years, as an increasingly successful essayist and critic, Hazlitt suffered a number of attacks from Tory journalists, and this led him frequently to complain that literary reviewing was being used as a means of damaging the reputations and prospects of writers with oppositional opinions. The tragedy of his time, he claimed, was that the great mechanism that should have emancipated writers and readers from the power of the State and the aristocracy – the periodical press – had become the most effective means for power to perpetuate itself: authors struggled to maintain the principles when faced with a 'nefarious and organised system of party-proscription, carried on under the mask of literary criticism and fair discussion' (XI, p. 68). Hazlitt believed that through journals that the government either directly sponsored or indirectly influenced, the values associated with 'Legitimacy' – respect for rank, wealth, tradition – were imposed on literary culture and propagated to the burgeoning reading public.

This chapter will explore Hazlitt's writings on the relationship between literary genius and political power, focusing on two periods of his career: the winter of 1816–17, when he wrote for the *Examiner*, and 1823, when he was a contributor to the *Liberal* and the *Edinburgh Review* (*ER*). In the first period, Hazlitt published a series of damning articles on 'modern apostates', and even went so far as to argue that 'poetry is right royal' and inevitably opposed to democracy (V, p. 347). One of these attacks – a letter to the *Examiner* contrasting Coleridge's eloquence as a radical preacher in 1798 with the reactionary gibberish (as Hazlitt saw of it) of the *Statesman's Manual* – became the germ of the famous essay 'My First Acquaintance with Poets', which appeared in the third number of the *Liberal*. It is my contention that Hazlitt's association with this magazine served, for a short time, to modify his jaundiced view of literary culture, and that it is only by repositioning 'My First Acquaintance with Poets' within the context of its original publication that we can understand the peculiarly ambivalent nature of this influential literary reminiscence.

Genius and power

Hazlitt's first publication, *An Essay on the Principles of Human Action* (1805), has been identified by modern critics as containing a theory of the 'sympathetic imagination', which informs his later writings on aesthetics and the fine arts, and which influenced Keats's ideas about poetic creation.[2] The *Essay* argues against philosophers like Hobbes and Mandeville who had claimed that people were naturally selfish. Hazlitt claims that in fact that the human mind is naturally *disinterested*, and that both altruism and self-love result from the operation of the sympathetic imagination. A number of critics have argued that sympathy is one of Hazlitt's 'principle criteria for poetic excellence',[3] and there has been a tendency to confuse his theory of poetic genius with Keats's. As Uttara Natarajan has shown, the latter's ideal of the 'camelion Poet' who 'has no self' is based on Hazlitt's account of Shakespeare in the essay 'On Posthumous Fame' from the *Round Table* (1817)[4]: 'He seemed scarcely to have an individual existence of his own, but to borrow that of others at will, and to pass successively through "every variety of untried being" ' (IV, p. 23). She goes on to argue that in general Hazlitt tended to represent genius as characterized by intellectual 'bias' and self-assertion, and that the ultra-sympathetic Shakespeare is an exception to this rule.[5] This certainly seems to be borne out by a number of passages from Hazlitt's writings and Natarajan gives particular weight to the essay 'On Genius and Common Sense', published in the first volume of *Table-Talk* (1821), where Hazlitt states that 'Shakespeare (almost alone) seems to have been a man of genius, raised above the definition of genius... He was the Proteus of human intellect. Genius in ordinary is a more obstinate and less versatile thing' (VIII, p. 42).

It is clear from Natarajan's account that the distinction between these two types of genius is not analogous with the distinction between egotism and sympathy. As she remarks, the self-assertion of the biased genius exhibits 'Hazlitt's peculiar associative version of "sympathy" or "relation"... a manifestation of the "power" of the inspired self'.[6] She does not refer to the following passage on Rousseau, from the *Conversations of Northcote* (1830), but it supports her point:

> he stamped his own character and the image of his self-love on the public mind... Had he possessed more comprehension of thought or feeling, it would only have diverted him from his object. But it was the excess of his egotism and his utter blindness to every thing else, that found a corresponding sympathy in the conscious feelings of every human breast, and shattered to pieces the pride of rank and circumstance by the pride of internal worth or upstart pretension.
>
> (XI, p. 278)

As Gregory Dart has argued, here Rousseau is represented as having been able to secure the sympathy of his readers through the excessive egotism of his writings – they represent 'a democratic universalisation of the self'.[7] His single-mindedness, the 'bias' of his genius, allows him to resist power and support freedom. In this passage, genius is a radical principle which, by asserting the power of 'internal worth', shatters the ideology of the *ancien regime*.

Natarajan, however, tends to elide the contradictions in Hazlitt's approach to genius, particularly poetic genius, which are due to the significant tension in his writings between a celebration of the creative imagination as a progressive force, and an anti-Romantic argument that links it with the support of pernicious forms of political power. In the optimistic mode, the 'bias' of genius is a strength that enables it to resist power, and 'universal', or Shakespearean, genius is figured as a form of disinterested subjectivity that sympathizes with all human existence. However, in texts such as the *Examiner* attacks on the apostates, Wordsworth's 'bias' is represented as a dangerous arrogance that makes him hate the world around him, and Coleridge's 'universality' results in mental paralysis and an inability to hold on to important moral principles. Hazlitt's ambivalence about genius also affects 'My First Acquaintance with Poets', where he celebrates the youthful promise of Wordsworth and Coleridge whilst implicitly lamenting the degradation of their gifts, which he believes have been offered up to the idol of 'Legitimacy'.

So while Natarajan notes in passing that, for Hazlitt, Coleridge lacked the single-mindedness that he saw 'as a general rule of human achievement,'[8] she does not mention that, even while he lamented Coleridge's weakness, Hazlitt continually emphasized his genius. And her acute argument about Hazlitt's celebration of the 'power of the inspired self' downplays considerably his distrust of poetic egotism, as exhibited by, for example, Wordsworth and Byron. She states that 'the strong manifestation of a particular poetic self may excite Hazlitt's antipathy', but claims that 'nonetheless, such self-centredness is also always regarded by him as a strength'.[9] This seems to me to be too strong a claim: for instance, in the 'Reply to Z.', Hazlitt remarks that 'I have spoken of [Wordsworth's] intellectual egotism (and truly and warrantably) as the bane of his talents and of his public principles' (IX, p. 5). Hazlitt's account of Wordsworth's 'intellectual egotism' is certainly more complex that he makes it out to be here, but this particular statement is unequivocal.

Of all Hazlitt critics, John Kinnaird has given the most emphasis to his distrust of the poetic imagination.[10] He argues that, after 1805, Hazlitt moved from a benevolist psychological theory to one based on the innate propensity of human beings to sympathize with 'power', a term not limited to, but certainly including, political power.[11] Kinnaird rightly emphasizes that Hazlitt's late-Regency tirades against the imagination as a supporter of social inequality are not rhetorical divergences from his 'true' theory of the disinterested imagination, but result from his ideas about the psychology of power, combined with his concern about the state of literary culture and his desire to assert 'the independence of genius from all power but that of its own conscience'.[12] However, this does not fully register the extent of Hazlitt's ambivalence about the relationship between literature and political progress; in the 1810s, he cannot seem to decide whether or not poetry is favourable to liberty. And in the early 1820s, as single-volume poetry becomes unfashionable and magazine writing becomes the most powerful genre in the literary marketplace, he is equally unsure about the political effects of the diffusion of periodical literature. Hazlitt never rescinded his argument about the natural disinterestedness of the human mind and referred to the *Essay on the Principles of Human Action* with great pride throughout his life.[13] But later experiences, particularly of the political apostasy of Wordsworth and Coleridge, led him to develop a darker view of the imagination which certainly complicated his earlier metaphysics. In the mid-1810s, his attempt to understand how literary culture had been corrupted resulted in some remarkable newspaper articles in which he not only attacked his former friends, but even the idea of the sympathetic imagination itself.

Understanding apostasy

During 1816, England was in a state of acute crisis. High taxation (a legacy of the war), the collapse of manufacturing industries, agricultural foreclosures and a poor harvest left many of the lower classes without work and starving, prompting widespread debate about the 'Distresses of the Country'.[14] Popular unrest culminated in the Spa Fields riot on 2 December, which in turn led to the suspension of *Habeas Corpus* in March 1817. Hazlitt's increasingly savage writings during 1816 clearly evince this heightened political temperature, but were also informed by more personal provocations. Still reeling from the defeat of Napoleon at Waterloo, he had been dogged by ill health throughout the year and his youngest son had died in June.[15] It is also likely that he knew that Coleridge and Wordsworth had been spreading rumours about the 'Keswick incident' of 1803 when they helped him escape from a mob of angry villagers after he was accused of assaulting a local woman.[16]

The feud between Hazlitt and the Lake Poets had been gathering momentum since 1813. It is possible that he wrote an anonymous squib attacking Wordsworth for surrendering his independence by accepting the post of Distributor of Stamps for Westmoreland, which was published initially in the *Morning Chronicle* in April of that year (it later appeared in the *Examiner* and the *Champion*).[17] He was certainly irritated by Wordsworth's *Poems* of 1815, which were dedicated to Sir George Beaumont, and contained a sonnet celebrating the triumph of George III over Napoleon at Leipzig. And in April 1816, Wordsworth published the *Thanksgiving Ode* – the climax of his 'coming out' as a Tory.[18] Hazlitt had also criticized Southey in 1813 for accepting the post of Poet Laureate, and had mocked his *New Year Ode* of 1814.[19] Meanwhile, Coleridge was writing for the *Courier*, a government newspaper. It was only a matter of time before Hazlitt lashed out.[20]

The *Examiner*, the reformist Sunday newspaper conducted by the Hunt brothers, was the perfect vehicle for Hazlitt's attacks on the apostates, for it was committed to independence from party ties, and Leigh Hunt had himself attacked Wordsworth and Southey for not being true to their early political convictions.[21] Having written for the *Morning Chronicle* and the *Champion* at the start of his career, from early 1815, Hazlitt contributed solely to the Hunts' newspaper and worked in close collaboration with them. His 1816 campaign began with an article on Coleridge's *Christabel* volume on 2 June, in which he criticized the poet's lack of achievement, and, as Robert Lapp has shown, gave 'a politically inflected reading of the title poem'.[22] He followed this with a review of Southey's *Lay of the Laureate* on 7 and 14 July, which taunted the poet for his Jacobin past, accused him of intolerance and 'overweening self-opinion', and described the poetry of the *Lay* as 'beneath criticism' (VII, pp. 85–96). Two months later, Hazlitt returned to Coleridge with a proleptic review of the *Statesman's Manual*, before it had been published, or even written (VII, pp. 114–18).[23] At the end of the year, just as the political crisis was at its height, he expressed his anger against the apostates in a series of articles: 'The Times Newspaper' (1 December); a letter, signed 'Scrutator', entitled 'The Editor of the Times' (8 December); 'Illustrations of the Times Newspaper' (15 and 22 December); a sardonic review of the *Statesman's Manual* (29 December); 'The Times Newspaper' (12 January 1817), and a letter on 'Mr Coleridge's Lay Sermon' (12 January 1817), which was another attack on Coleridge in the guise of a reader's response to Hazlitt's review.[24]

Although it contained no personal remarks, the Lakers' apostasy clearly also influenced Hazlitt's well-known review of a Kemble production of *Coriolanus* at Covent Garden (15 December 1816), in which the poetic imagination is damned as an inevitable supporter of 'power'.[25] Hazlitt begins by arguing that although the play handles different political debates 'very ably', 'Shakespeare himself seems to have had a leaning to the arbitrary side of the question, perhaps from some feeling of contempt for his own origin'. At this time, Hazlitt is so politically sensitive that even the 'protean' Shakespeare is represented as a sort of apostate who dislikes those of his own social background. He goes on to argue that the play's apparent sympathy with the aristocracy also says much about the relationship between poetry and power:

> The cause of the people is indeed but ill calculated as a subject for poetry: it admits of rhetoric, which goes into argument and explanation, but it presents no immediate or distinct images to the mind, 'no jutting frieze, buttress, or coigne of vantage' for poetry 'to make its pendant bed and procreant cradle in.' The language of poetry naturally falls in with the language of power.

The quotations in this passage are from *Macbeth* (I.vi.6–8).[26] Banquo tells King Duncan that all the projections and corners of Macbeth's castle are used by nesting martins, which are attracted by the sweetness of the air. Thus poetry builds itself on the impressive symbols and images that power projects, perhaps without realizing that power itself is also a source of blood and terror.

This, one might think, is a strong enough claim, but as Hazlitt continues he shifts from a discussion of poetic language to a politicized account of the associative imagination, which differs markedly from that of contemporary aestheticians:

> The imagination is an exaggerating and exclusive faculty: it takes from one thing to add to another: it accumulates circumstances together to give the greatest possible effect to a favourite object. The understanding is a dividing and measuring faculty: it judges of things, not according to their immediate impression on the mind, but according to their relations to one another. The one is a monopolizing faculty, which seeks the greatest quantity of present excitement by inequality and disproportion; the other is a distributive faculty, which seeks

the greatest quantity of ultimate good, by justice and proportion. The one is an aristocratical, the other a republican faculty. The principle of poetry is a very anti-levelling principle. It aims at effect, it exists by contrast. It admits of no medium. It is every thing by excess. It rises above the ordinary standard of sufferings and crimes. It presents an imposing appearance. It shews its head turretted, crowned and crested. Its front is gilt and blood-stained. Before it, 'it carries noise, and behind it, it leaves tears.' It has its altars and its victims, sacrifices, human sacrifices. Kings, priests, nobles, are its train-bearers; tyrants and slaves its executioners – 'Carnage is its daughter!' Poetry is right royal. It puts the individual for the species, the one above the infinite many, might before right.

(V, pp. 347–8)

This extraordinary passage is difficult to analyse because, as is often the case with Hazlitt, he makes his point through a series of appositional statements, rather than through a logical, sequential argument. The most important thing to bear in mind is that he is not simply giving us a theory of the associative imagination, which is meant to contrast with his earlier view of the sympathetic imagination, for, as Natarajan has argued, Hazlitt does not generally separate these functions of the imagination: 'the associative chain may be recognized as authentic only when it realizes a sympathy between the inspired object and the objective material reality'.[27] In fact, this passage represents his 'dark' version of both functions: the associative process is here the mechanism for the expression of the imagination's innate sympathy with power. The association of ideas is a form of theft; the imagination seeks to aggrandize a 'favourite object' by loading it with a disproportionate number of associations which are, in effect, taken from other objects. Whereas the *understanding* is disinterested, for it seeks to comprehend the relations between things – the world as it is – the *imagination* takes a selfish pleasure in fetishising its favourites. This is the foundation of poetry, and thus it is bound to celebrate individuals at the expense of the multitude. The phrase 'Carnage is its daughter' ironically incorporates Wordsworth's infamous lines on God from the 'Thanksgiving Ode' into an argument about how those lines came to be written, and their likely effect.[28] Hazlitt claims that by bolstering 'Legitimacy' through its love of glory and distinction, poetry becomes responsible for the 'human sacrifices' that power demands.

There are some similarities here with Thomas Love Peacock's argument in the *Four Ages of Poetry* (1820), although the *Coriolanus* review is angrier and less ironic. Both authors represent poetry as essentially a reactionary force which is inevitably implicated in the celebration of oppressive power.[29] But the extent of Hazlitt's ambivalence on this issue becomes clear when we realize that at other times he was capable of occupying the position taken up by Shelley in his reply to Peacock, *A Defence of Poetry* (written in 1821, published in 1840). In the lecture 'On Poetry in General', delivered just over a year after the publication of the *Coriolanus* review, Hazlitt denies that poetry is merely 'a branch of authorship' and redefines it as any sort of emotional response to the world, 'the stuff of which our life is made'. The poetic imagination is what makes us human – 'man is a poetical animal' – and it is vital for our moral well-being: 'He who has a contempt for poetry cannot have much respect for himself, or for anyone else' (V, p. 2). This lecture may well have influenced Shelley, who was to make very similar claims two years later.[30]

The *Coriolanus* review, then, makes a transhistorical generalization about the faculty of the imagination; Hazlitt transforms the relationship between literary culture and political power at a given moment into a *fait accompli*. And yet in other *Examiner* writings of the same period, he suggests that corrupt literary culture that he sees around him is a result of the particular political situation in Regency England. Hazlitt's fire was initially directed mainly at the editor of the *Times*, John Stoddart, an ultra-royalist who had once been an equally extreme Jacobin, and who also happened to be Hazlitt's brother-in-law. The articles on the *Times* are savage, often excessive, accounts of Stoddart and the Lake Poets as examples of 'literary prostitution', and of the corrupting influence of political power. The very position of the essays in the *Examiner* served to emphasize the way in which political and literary concerns were intertwined. The newspaper usually began with a section entitled 'The Political Examiner', invariably containing an attack on the government and/or the Tory press. This would be followed by 'Foreign Intelligence', 'Provincial Intelligence', 'The Examiner' – normally comment on political events in France – and finally miscellaneous items such as poems, letters, 'Literary Notices' and so on. This schema held for almost all of 1816; but issue for December the 15th began with the first of the 'Illustrations of the Times Newspaper', under the rubric of 'Literary Notices'. The 'Political Examiner' was nowhere to be seen. Hazlitt's articles on apostasy showed that the usual distinction that the layout of the *Examiner* made between politics and literature had become untenable.

Hazlitt's most detailed account of poetic apostasy is in the second of the 'Illustrations', published on 22 December. Here he states, in direct contradiction of the *Coriolanus* review, that 'the spirit of poetry is in itself favourable to humanity and liberty; but, we suspect, not in times like these – not in the present reign' (VII, p. 142). This is because 'the spirit of poetry is not the spirit of mortification or of martyrdom' – it does not have the strength to stand up against the *status quo*. He goes on to argue that, in fact, poetry and reality are entirely incompatible, for

> poetry dwells in a perpetual Utopia of its own, and is, for that reason, very ill calculated to make a Paradise upon earth, by encountering the shocks and disappointments of the world . . . It has the range of the universe; it traverses the empyreum, and looks down on nature from a higher sphere. When it lights upon the earth, it loses some of its dignity and its use. Its strength is in its wings; its element the air. Standing on its feet, jostling with the crowd, it is liable to be overthrown, trampled on, and defaced.

(VII, p. 142)

Poetry may be favourable to 'liberty', but only in its transcendental, rather than political, form. If it tries to engage with the grubby realities of the material world, it loses its freedom and its power. This stark separation of art from life also applies to poets, who, Hazlitt claims,

> live in an ideal world, where they make every thing out according to their wishes and fancies . . . They are naturally inventors, *creators not of truth but beauty*: and

while they speak to us from the sacred shrine of their own hearts, while they pour out the pure treasures of thought to the world, they cannot be too much admired or applauded: but when, forgetting their high calling, and becoming tools and puppets in the hands of others, they would pass off the gewgaws of corruption and love-tokens of self-interest, as the gifts of the Muse, they cannot be too much despised and shunned.

(VII, pp. 142–3; my italics)

The distinction that Hazlitt makes between 'truth' and 'beauty' here reveals the extent of his distrust of the Romantic imagination at this time. He did not always hold this opinion, and he revised this passage when it was reprinted in the essay 'On Poetical Versatility' in the *Round Table* (1817); poets are here described as '*creators of truth, of love, and beauty*' (IV, p. 152; my italics). In 1816, however, they are represented as fantasists whose ability to 'feign the beautiful' makes them dangerous and useful tools for those in positions of power. This is not the same as the *Coriolanus* argument; there is a similar emphasis on the ability of the poetic imagination to support power, but here it does not appear to be an inevitable process, occurring only when poets forget their 'high calling'.

Although Hazlitt claims that the apostates are to be 'despised and shunned' for bringing poetry into disrepute, he also offers explanations for their behaviour, which make their political shifts seem almost inevitable. If the *Coriolanus* review argues that this is a result of the aggrandizing nature of the imagination, at this point in the 'Illustrations', it is due to the weakness of the poetic character, which is unable to resist a triumphant 'Legitimacy':

Their souls are effeminate, half man and half woman: they want fortitude, and are without principle... Poets, therefore, cannot do well without sympathy and flattery. It is, accordingly, very much against the grain that they remain long on the unpopular side of the question. They do not like to be shut out when laurels are to be given away at court – or places under government to be disposed of, in romantic situations in the country. They are happy to be reconciled on the first opportunity to prince and people, and to exchange their principles for a pension.

(VII, p. 144)[31]

Here 'sympathy', rather than being the mechanism of poetic genius (at least in the case of Shakespeare), is the cause of its debasement. Writing in the *London Magazine* (*LM*) in 1821, Hazlitt made this point more explicitly, stating that what Coleridge 'calls *sympathising with others* is their admiring him, and it must be admitted that he varies his battery pretty often, in order to accommodate himself to this sort of mutual understanding' (XVII, p. 23). If Rousseau, for Hazlitt, could resist political power due to the strength of his ego, here it seems that all poets are easy prey for 'Legitimacy' due to their lack of a strong sense of selfhood and consequent desire for the approbation of others.[32] The exception to this rule is Milton, who, Hazlitt suggests, was both 'a poet, and an honest man: he was Cromwell's secretary' (VII, p. 144). Unlike the Romantic apostates, Milton did not change sides when the republican cause seemed to have failed, a point that Hazlitt would make with heavy irony a few months later:

> Milton lived to be older than the present Poet-laureat, but he did not with increase of years acquire his wisdom, his *mildness*, or his place ... What a pity that Milton did not read the Courier and the Quarterly Review! He might then have been not only as great a poet as Mr. Coleridge and Mr. Southey was at twenty, but as honest, wise, and as virtuous, as those gentlemen are at forty.
>
> (XIX, p. 190)

We will return to the subject of Milton below, for Hazlitt's consideration of the relationship between literature and politics in 'My First Acquaintance with Poets' is informed by an engagement with *Paradise Lost* (*PL*).

Hazlitt's fourth article on the *Times* is offered as the partial fulfilment of a pledge he made, in a review of Robert Owen's *New View of Society* (VII, pp. 99–100), to explain 'some of the causes which impede the natural progress of liberty and human happiness'. He argues that in 1792, 'Mr. Burke became a pensioner by writing his book against the French Revolution, and Mr. Thomas Paine was outlawed for his *Rights of Man*'. Since then, 'the press has been the great enemy of freedom, the whole weight of that immense engine (for the purposes of good or ill) having a fatal bias given to it by the two main springs of fear and favour' (VII, p. 145). By exploiting the 'weak sides of the human intellect', power is able to maintain itself through its control of literary culture. Having described, in the previous article, the influence of 'fear' on the Lakers' apostasy, Hazlitt now emphasizes the lure of 'favour':

> they could not live without the smiles of the great (not they), nor provide for an increasing establishment without a loss of character; instead of going into some profitable business and exchanging their lyres for ledgers, their pens for the plough (the honest road to riches), they chose rather to prostitute their pens to the mock-heroic defence of the most bare-faced of all mummeries, the pretended alliance of kings and people!
>
> (VII, p. 147)

This accusation is close to the bone, particularly in the case of Wordsworth. In order to provide for his wife and four children, maintain a middle-class existence, and remain a poet, he had been forced to apply to Lord Lonsdale for patronage, which had resulted in his Distributorship of Stamps.[33] Southey's journalism, and his acceptance of the Laureateship, also resulted from his inability to earn enough from his poetry to support his family as he wished. Of course, this does not necessarily mean that, as Hazlitt argues, the Lakers' pro-Tory writing was the product of mercenary motives. But the important point here is that he shows an awareness that their loss of independence may be partly caused by the realities of the literary marketplace – unless they are willing to give up poetry, or their social aspirations, they are forced to accept patronage and to 'prostitute their pens'. Here Hazlitt recognizes that apostasy may not only have psychological causes but also economic ones.

Hazlitt's writings on poetic apostasy have a complex relationship with his ideas about poetic genius. As we have seen, he argues that poets are attracted to tyranny for a host of reasons: the nature of poetic language, the associative process of the imagination, the weakness of the poetic character, greed (or, more charitably, financial necessity) and the desire for sympathy. He offers these different explanations as a sort of catch-all argument, which will cover Coleridge, Southey and Wordsworth. In such a mood, he represents both self-assertion and sympathy as leading inevitably to compliance with power, and it often seems from the *Examiner* articles that poets are eternally fated to work against the cause of 'the people'. However, even at this time, Hazlitt occasionally suggests that apostasy might be a result of the particular, contingent relationship between literature and power in the Regency period, and, in the rest of this chapter, I will show how this notion developed later in his career.

'Mr Coleridge's Lay Sermon'

On 10 December 1816, Coleridge's much-delayed *Statesman's Manual*, 'a lay sermon addressed to the higher classes of society', was published by Gale and Fenner. This intervention in the 'Distresses of the Country' debate has been well discussed by Robert Lapp, who has also given a close analysis of Hazlitt's *Examiner* review of 29 December.[34] He shows that Hazlitt improvises 'a kind of Sunday counter-sermon from the lay pulpit of political dissent' in which he represents Coleridge's book as an attempt to justify repressive conservative ideology through a tendentious misreading of the Bible.[35] Two weeks later, directly after his final article on the *Times*, Hazlitt published a letter under the pseudonym 'SEMPER EGO AUDITOR' (entitled 'Mr Coleridge's Lay Sermon'), in which he responded to his own review.[36] In 1823, Hazlitt would take this text as the basis for 'My First Acquaintance with Poets', and thus it forms an important link between his writings on apostasy in the 1810s, and his more complex account of the relationship between literature and political power in the mid-1820s.

The letter begins with a description of going to see Coleridge preach to a Unitarian congregation in January 1798. He is compared to John the Baptist and, implicitly, to Milton: a prophet-like figure whose preaching then, it is suggested, was very different from his recent publication: '*That* sermon, like *this* sermon, was upon peace and war; upon church and state – not their alliance, but their separation – on the spirit of the world, and the spirit of Christianity, not as the same, but as opposed to one another' (VII, p. 128). Hazlitt describes how as a young man he was so delighted with Coleridge's performance that, on his return home, the world around him was imbued with his political dreams:

> Poetry and Philosophy had met together, Truth and Genius had embraced, under the eye and with the sanction of Religion. This was beyond even my hopes. I returned home well satisfied. The sun that was still labouring pale and wan through the sky, obscured by thick mists, seemed an emblem of the *good cause*: and the cold dank drops of dew that hung half melted on the beard of the

thistle, had something genial and refreshing in them; for there was a spirit of hope and youth in all nature, that turned every thing into good. The face of nature had not then the brand of JUS DIVINUM on it.

(VII, p. 129)

This passage celebrates Hazlitt's youthful idealism whilst showing an awareness of its limitations. The older Hazlitt sees 'the cold dank drops of dew' as no more than that, but at the same time recognizes, without mockery, that they once seemed 'genial and refreshing'. The 'good cause' is, of course, political reform and refers to the 'Good Old Cause' of the seventeenth-century Commonwealthmen. Coleridge's oratorical skills must have been extraordinary if he truly gave Hazlitt such optimism at a time when the radical movement in England was in total disarray after the government clamp-down of the mid-1790s.[37] But by the 1820s, Hazlitt's view of this period was rose-tinted, to say the least, and there is no way of knowing the extent to which this nostalgic libertarian rhetoric describes his true feelings in 1798.

The pathetic fallacy in the passage quoted from the *Examiner* letter – that is, the young Hazlitt's apparent confusion of his own feelings and associations with the 'spirit' of the world around him – is important. The letter is an ironic version of the 'Greater Romantic Lyric' practised by Wordsworth and Coleridge.[38] As in 'Frost at Midnight', or 'Tintern Abbey', the text describes a landscape associated with a youthful unity with nature, which has since been lost. However, unlike its poetic analogues, Hazlitt's lyrical meditation does not achieve any form of positive resolution and he remains in a state of alienation from the world. His 'Fall' into the realm of experience is in no sense a fortunate one. The reason for this alienation is the triumph of 'Legitimacy' – Church and State – and the apparent decline of dissenting republicanism; when he writes of 'the brand of JUS DIVINUM', which disfigures 'the face of nature', he is alluding to a passage in the *Statesman's Manual* in which Coleridge claimed that 'the *Jus divinum*, or direct Relation of the State and its Magistracy to the Supreme Being' was to be found in Scripture.[39] Hazlitt had singled out this argument for particular criticism in his review of Coleridge's tract (VII, p. 121). Whereas in 1798, according to the letter, Coleridge gave Hazlitt a vision of nature which made it consonant with the '*good cause*', now he and other apostates claim that the divine right of kings is part of the natural order, not the 'rights of man'. As a result, Hazlitt feels that he has lost the close relationship that he once had with the world: that, like Coleridge's genius, is located firmly in the past:

I begin to suspect that my notions formerly must have been little better than a deception: that my faith in Mr. Coleridge's great powers must have been a vision of my youth, that, like other such visions, must pass away from me; and that all his genius and eloquence is *vox et preterea nihil*: for otherwise how is it so lost to all common sense upon paper?

(VII, p. 129)

In the final paragraph of the letter, Hazlitt introduces a theme that is present, in a more implicit form, throughout 'My First Acquaintance with Poets'. It is not just that Hazlitt's faith in Coleridge's genius and the triumph of the *'good cause'* has been disappointed. It is that Coleridge has invited this faith, awoken his imagination, enabled him to see nature as imbued with 'a spirit of hope and youth', irrevocably changed him and shaped his aspirations – and then left him a solitary Jacobin with broken dreams:

> I am naturally, Sir, a man of plain, dull, dry understanding, without flights or fancies, and can just contrive to plod on, if left to myself: what right then has Mr. C., who is just going to ascend in a balloon, to offer me a seat in the parachute, only to throw me from the height of his career upon the ground, and dash me to pieces? Or again, what right has he to invite me to a feast of poets and philosophers, fruits and flowers intermixed – immortal fruits and amaranthine flowers – and then to tell me it is vapour, and, like *Timon*, to throw his empty dishes in my face?
>
> (VII, p. 129)

Lapp rightly points out the ironic contrast between Hazlitt's claim that he is 'a man of plain, dull, dry understanding [and] his obviously exuberant experiment in style, at once eclectic and rhetorically pointed'.[40] The key word here is 'naturally'; Hazlitt is saying that he was born as a certain type of person, but that due to Coleridge's influence he became capable of the 'flights' and 'fancies' of the imagination. Unfortunately, the publication of the *Statesman's Manual* has shown him that the imagination cannot be trusted, for whereas in 1798, Coleridge's 'flights' were those of 'an eagle dallying with the wind' (VII, p. 128), now, with black humour, the poet is revealed to be a murderous balloonist. The *Examiner* letter uses the Romantic trope of the imaginative identification of the self with the natural world in order to lament the failure of the Romantic imagination to resist political power. It also ironizes the Romantic appropriation of the theme of 'the fortunate fall' into adulthood and experience by suggesting that, for Hazlitt, the loss of the republican Eden of his youth has been an utterly destructive plummet. However, despite his claim that his vision of 1798 'must pass away', his poetic rhetoric suggests the impossibility of returning to an innocent state of 'plain, dull, dry understanding' – even though what was once a glorious gift has now become a painful burden.

Genius, literature and liberalism

During the six years between the publication of the *Examiner* letter, and that of 'My First Acquaintance with Poets' in the *Liberal*, Hazlitt's position within literary culture changed substantially. In early 1817, he was still a writer of apparently ephemeral newspaper journalism; by 1823, he had published a number of books of lectures and essays, and contributed many articles to prestigious organs such as the *LM*, the *NMM* and the *ER*. This success had its price; he had become a target for Tory critics, and their attacks further justified his gloomy view of the corruption of literary culture. In 'On the Aristocracy of Letters' (1822), he divides the literary world between professional authors and aristocratic dilettantes who can write as they wish without having to worry about reviews or sales. Hazlitt is particularly envious of Byron, whose success, he claims, is partly due to his rank:

> He towers above his fellows by all the height of the peerage. If the poet lends a grace to the nobleman, the nobleman pays it back to the poet with interest. What a fine addition is ten thousand a year and a title to the flaunting pretensions of a modern rhapsodist!... in fact, his Lordship's blaze of reputation culminates from his rank and place in society.
>
> (VIII, pp. 209–10)

Byron's charmed existence is bitterly contrasted with the life of the professional writer, who, without 'extrinsic advantages of birth, breeding, or fortune', is 'a helpless and despised animal' (VIII, p. 210). Hazlitt's complaint is that the rules that govern the way in which literary culture is structured are far too close to those that govern the worlds of politics and class: writers, publishers, critics and readers place too much value on wealth, social status and political affiliation, rather than on literary ability. Thus although he still despises those writers who seek the patronage and protection of 'Legitimacy', he also realizes that it is difficult for them to remain independent when their success or failure is largely dependent on its support. The fate of Keats is a grim warning of what awaits those who do not ally themselves with power, for 'when the mercenary servile crew approached him, he had no pedigree to show them, no rent-roll to hand out in reversion for their praise: he was not in any great man's train, nor the butt and puppet of a lord' (VIII, p. 211). Here, apostasy is not represented as the result of the peculiar nature of poetic imagination, but rather of the structure of literary culture at a particular historical moment.

In the light of these opinions, and of his dislike of aristocratic poets, it is interesting that in 1822, Hazlitt agreed to contribute to the *Liberal: Verse and Prose from the South*, the quarterly periodical founded by Byron, Shelley and Leigh Hunt. This magazine was an attempt to counter the influence of the Tory press through the establishment of a small 'republic of letters' where class divisions and political affiliations were to be transcended by shared literary interests. Its title probably referred principally to Spanish democrats – *liberales* – who had rebelled successfully against King Ferdinand in 1820 (although the return to the liberal Constitution of 1812 only lasted until 1823). At the same time, the term 'liberal' had also begun to be used in England, mainly by Tories who sought to connect British radicals with European revolutionaries.[41] In the journal's 'Preface', Hunt emphasizes that the *Liberal* is to be a *literary* magazine, which will be concerned with 'liberalities in the shape of poetry, Essays, Tales, and Translations', and remarks that 'the object of our work is not political, except inasmuch as all writing now-a-days must involve something to that effect.'[42] But he also states that 'we are advocates of every species of liberal knowledge and that ... we go the full length in matters of opinion with large bodies of men who are called Liberals'.[43] The *Liberal*, then, was not a violently partisan journal and did not really have a detailed political agenda. Its broad support for European liberalism was aided by its distance from the British literary culture, its independence from government influence and the mixed class composition of the Pisan Circle.

The history of the *Liberal* is complicated and I will only give a brief outline of it here.[44] From 1818 until his death, Shelley wrote a number of letters imploring friends such as Hunt, Peacock and Hogg to come and visit him in Italy. Writing to Peacock in February 1819, he lamented the power of the *QR* to work against 'the cause of improvement', and called for 'a band of staunch reformers', to unite 'in so close and constant a league as that in which interest and fanaticism have bound the members of that literary coalition'.[45] In December 1820, Byron wrote to Thomas Moore, suggesting that they start a newspaper, a proposal that was still floating around the following August, when Shelley visited Byron in Ravenna.[46] The idea of the *Liberal* was clearly formulated during this visit: at the end of the month, Shelley wrote to Hunt from Pisa, stating that Byron had proposed that 'you should come out and go shares with him and me in a periodical work'.[47] For various reasons, Hunt did not make it to Italy for over ten months, arriving on 3 July 1822. Five days later Shelley was dead. By this time the *Liberal* had already provoked a flurry of anticipatory attacks in the British press, and Byron's friends, such as Moore and Hobhouse, were trying to get him to extricate himself from this 'unholy alliance'. Even before the publication of the first number on 15 October 1822, Byron had written to his publisher John Murray claiming that he was only involved in the magazine as an act of charity to the Hunt brothers, and when a garbled version of the letter appeared in the *John Bull*, the personal tensions that already existed between Hunt and Byron were exacerbated.[48] Their relationship deteriorated further over the winter and in February 1823, after further pressure from his London friends, Byron decided to withdraw.

Only four issues of the *Liberal* were published but the violent reaction of the Tory press throughout 1822 suggests that at the time it seemed like a potentially dangerous rival. In particular, the alliance between Byron and Hunt represented a powerful symbol of the way in which political and literary interests could transcend class divisions. This union of middle-class radicalism and aristocratic Whiggism, Hunt's editorial flair and Byron's saleability, clearly worried government writers, and many of the attacks on the periodical focused on the difference between the two men in social class, in order to reassert the distinctions that their collaboration tended to occlude. Of course, the effacement of such divisive distinctions was important to the ideal behind the *Liberal*, Shelley's dream of 'a band of staunch reformers' of different backgrounds coming together to do battle with the *QR*. This was to be a meritocracy, not an aristocracy, of letters, an attempt to assert the autonomy of genius from political power, and thus Hunt, writing in the preface to the first volume of the magazine, stated that 'the demigods of liberal worship' were not the 'legitimatized' few, but could be found 'wherever . . . we see the mind of man exhibiting powers of its own, and at the same time helping to carry on the best interests of human nature'.[49]

Although Tory sensibilities were offended by the first number of the magazine – particularly Byron's mockery of George III in *The Vision of Judgment* and his epigrams on the recently deceased Castlereagh – its content turned out mainly to be inoffensive *belles-lettres* produced by Hunt under great pressure, and, as its sales quickly declined, the press hysteria subsided. Hazlitt seems to have been asked to contribute after Shelley's death (presumably by John Hunt, who edited the magazine from

London), and Leigh Hunt and Byron seem to have first known of his involvement in September 1822. The first number of the magazine contained nothing by the essayist; he had done little or no writing over the summer, completely distracted by getting his divorce through the Scottish courts, and his obsession with Sarah Walker. His two contributions to the second number, published on 1 January 1823, were probably written in October at Winterslow, his rural retreat. Both 'On the Scotch Character' and 'On the Spirit of Monarchy' seemed calculated further to enrage the magazine's Tory critics. The former essay is an entertaining rant in which the writers of Hazlitt's arch-enemy, *Blackwood's Magazine*, are described as 'a troop of Yahoos'. One of them, John Wilson, responded with an article entitled 'On the Scotch Character – by a Flunky' in March 1823, which begins, 'Lord Byron being a somewhat whimsical nobleman, has lately hired two or three Cockneys as menial servants. They are to do his dirty work, for which they are to receive his cast-off clothes, and, we believe, twenty pounds per annum'.[50] Class tensions among the *Liberal* group, though, did not exist purely in the imagination of its enemies – and 'On the Spirit of Monarchy' probably added to them.

This fine essay, which has been unduly neglected by modern critics, returns to Hazlitt's argument in the *Coriolanus* review about the inevitable complicity of the imagination with political power: the epigraph, taken from the poet William Shenstone, includes the phrase 'poets are *Tories* by nature'. Hazlitt claims that human beings have a natural love of monarchy that results from a projection of our own self-love; kings and lords represent what we would all like to be. Our poetical faculties allow us to make idols of others, to believe in the symbolism of the state, and to imagine ourselves in positions of power. The conclusion, clearly referring to the journal in which the essay appears, would not have been out of place in Hunt's preface:

> There is nothing truly liberal but that which postpones its own claims to those of propriety – or great, but that which looks out of itself to others. All power is but an unabated nuisance, a barbarous assumption, an aggravated injustice, that is not directed to the common good: all grandeur that has not something corresponding to it in personal merit and heroic acts, is a deliberate burlesque, and an insult on common sense and human nature.
>
> (XVII, p. 265)

'On the Spirit of Monarchy' is a good example of the ambivalence of Hazlitt's political views during the 1820s. In the above passage, he argues that power that is not altruistic, and based on merit, is an insult to 'common sense and human nature', but for most of the essay, the argument is that humans *naturally* sympathize with the show of 'power', the pomp and ceremony of state occasions, regardless of the worthlessness of those in charge. Thus liberalism, which entails disinterested sympathy with others, is undermined by humanity's selfish sympathy with power.[51] As we have seen, Hazlitt had always viewed sympathy as a double-edged sword – the mechanism of benevolence *and* self-love – but the presence of such ambivalence in 'On the Spirit of Monarchy' appears to weaken the ideal, which the *Liberal* was supposed to support, of a reformist consensus that could stand up to political and social hegemony.

Interestingly, Shelley's then-unpublished 'Defence of Poetry' was also supposed to appear in the second number of the *Liberal*, which would have created a fascinating juxtaposition.[52] Shelley argues that the imagination, because it enables us to sympathize with others, is 'the great instrument of moral good' and that this faculty is strengthened by poetry.[53] Thus the imagination is a wholly progressive force and the poet is at the cutting edge of liberty. 'On the Spirit of Monarchy' would have been an excellent substitute for Peacock's 'The Four Ages of Poetry', which the 'Defence' was originally intended to answer, for, as I have argued, both Hazlitt and Peacock link poetry with the support of an outmoded social system. Hazlitt's essay describes 'the dark side' of the imagination – its tendency to create false idols – and thus undercuts Shelley's rather facile link between poetry and political progress. It would also have been fitting for the two essays to have been published together, because, as we have seen, Shelley may have partly derived his ideas about sympathy from Hazlitt.

The writer of 'The Candid No. II' in *Blackwood's Magazine* used 'On the Spirit of Monarchy' as evidence that the authors of the *Liberal* were republicans, a description which might well have annoyed Byron.[54] He also suggested that it was a calculated dig at the poet: 'I think I perceive in it, a reproof to some friend or patron of the author, wrapped up in a mystical half-allegorical form ... and that its title may be translated, "The royal court at Pisa, a picture from life." '[55] This seems far-fetched, but it is noteworthy that Hazlitt saw fit to attack hereditary privilege in a periodical founded, and partly funded, by a nobleman known to be proud of his status. The essayist later claimed that the article must 'have operated like a bomb-shell' among the Whig coteries of London; there is no evidence for this hyperbolical statement, but he may have been right to believe that it inspired Moore to write to Byron imploring him to escape from the magazine (XII, p. 379). According to Hunt, writing in 1828, Byron himself responded badly to Hazlitt's contributions:

> Lord Byron was in truth afraid of Mr. Hazlitt; he admitted him like a courtier, for fear he should be treated by him as an enemy, but when he beheld such articles as the 'Spirit of Monarchy,' where the 'taint' of public corruption was to be exposed, and the 'First Acquaintance with Poets,' where Mr. Wordsworth was to be exalted above deprecation ... his Lordship could only wish him out again, and take pains to show his polite friends that he had nothing in common with so inconsiderate a plebeian.[56]

If this is true, then Byron failed the test that Hazlitt set up for him by placing 'On the Spirit of Monarchy' in the second number of the *Liberal*. The essay is best seen as a challenge to the poet: it is asking him to prove, by *not* reacting badly to it, that he is fully committed to the *Liberal* project, and that it is possible to contest the Tory dominance of literary culture. He is asking Byron to forget about his rank and tolerate Hazlitt's tirade in order to show that a lordly poet can become a truly liberal member of the republic of letters. Thus although parts of the essay seem alien to the ideology behind the periodical, its very publication in the *Liberal*, as well as the Hunt-like peroration, reveal Hazlitt's interest in the project.

The third number of the *Liberal* contains 'My First Acquaintance with Poets', probably Hazlitt's best-known essay. It is a vision of the kind of sympathetic intercourse between men of genius that the *Liberal* was supposed to promote, but locates this republic of letters in a seemingly distant, golden past. This essay, and the way in which it relates to its forebears – the *Examiner* letter on 'Mr Coleridge's Lay Sermon', the lecture 'On the Living Poets', and the essay 'On Going a Journey' – has been the subject of some critical interest in recent years.[57] However, only Robert Lapp has pointed out that 'an accurate reading' of the essay must 'take into account the embattled circumstances of its publication in the *Liberal*' – here he is referring to the continuing attacks on the periodical, the discord between Byron and Leigh Hunt, and the indictment of John Hunt for the publication of 'The Vision of Judgment' at the end of 1822.[58] This is certainly the case, but Lapp's claim that the essay is unequivocally about the failure of 1820s liberalism is more doubtful. In 1823, Hazlitt dispenses with the stark contrasts of the *Examiner* letter, and although the essay contains powerful passages in which he laments the failure of his personal and political hopes, the overall result is more a celebration of the past than a jeremiad directed against the present.

'My First Acquaintance with Poets' repeats the account of Coleridge's sermon from the *Examiner* letter, but this is now a small section of a much larger piece. In the early part of the essay, Hazlitt describes his first meeting with Coleridge at the house of Hazlitt's father in Wem and in the latter half, he recounts his visit to Coleridge at Nether Stowey and his impressions of Wordsworth, whom he also met there. Although the essay is wistful and elegiac, there is an absence of recrimination, and Hazlitt cut the final two paragraphs from the *Examiner* letter where he had attacked Coleridge and suggested that his genius was '*vox et preterea nihil*'. The emphasis is now more on Hazlitt's youthful belief in the signs of genius exhibited by Wordsworth and Coleridge. However, the central irony of the letter remains; it is Coleridge who has given Hazlitt the imagination and inspiration to write such a masterly prose–poem – about the ultimate failure of those attributes.

Hazlitt signposts the essay's concern with 'fallenness' in its opening sentence, where (quoting from *PL*) he says of '1798', 'the figures that compose that date are to me like the "dreaded name of Demogorgon"'.[59] Tom Paulin has noted that this links the late 1790s to the next three lines of Milton's poem: 'Rumour next and Chance,/ And Tumult and Confusion all embroiled,/ And Discord with a thousand various mouths' (*PL*, II, ll. 965–7). This refers, Paulin suggests, to the tense political situation in England, the Irish uprising of 1798, and to the French Revolution itself (this last point seems to me to be supported by Hazlitt's reference to the date's 'figures' rather than simply to the date itself).[60] But Hazlitt also represents 1798 as the crucial time in his own education and the quotation is significant in itself as well as for the following lines. For to dread something is not merely to be afraid of it, but 'to regard [it] with awe and reverence' (*Oxford English Dictionary* (*OED*)): his point is that he now recognizes the enormous significance of his meeting with Coleridge. The fall he is about to describe is personal as well as political, although for Hazlitt, of course, the two were deeply intertwined.

Like a number of Romantic poems, 'My First Acquaintance with Poets' makes a strong connection between post-lapsarian consciousness and creativity, with the added complication that, as Hazlitt describes it, he was only able to become aware of his paradisical state – and capable of representing it – through an awakening that would ultimately contribute to its end. As they walk between Wem and Shrewsbury, Coleridge's conversation has a tremendous effect on his youthful protégé:

> I had no notion then that I should ever be able to express my admiration to others in motley imagery or quaint allusion, till the light of his genius shone into my soul... I was at that time dumb, inarticulate, helpless, like a worm by the way-side, crushed, bleeding, lifeless; but now... my ideas float on winged words, and as they expand their plumes, catch the golden light of other years. My soul has indeed remained in its original bondage, dark, obscure, with long-ings infinite and unsatisfied; my heart, shut up in the prison-house of this rude clay, has never found, nor will it ever find, a heart to speak to; but that my understanding also did not remain dumb and brutish, or at length found a language to express itself, I owe to Coleridge.
>
> (XVII, p. 107)

Coleridge transcends the boundaries of selfhood, enters into Hazlitt's 'soul' and awakens his imagination. The young man is initially 'stunned, startled..., as from deep sleep' but almost immediately his relationship with the natural world is transformed – 'there was a spirit of hope and youth in all nature' (XVII, p. 109) – and this awakening even-tually enables him to become a writer. However, this new knowledge and imaginative outlook is double-edged; in 1798, it is a source of joy, but now, Hazlitt implies, it has become a source of pain, as he has discovered that he cannot rely on the vision of the future that Coleridge has given him. If Coleridge is at first the God who creates the republican Eden of Hazlitt's youth, he is also, ultimately, the Devil who takes it away.

Lucy Newlyn has argued that Hazlitt's suspicions about the relationship between poetry and power are evident in an aside in 'My First Acquaintance with Poets', when he suggests that the spell-like '*chaunt*' in the recitation of Wordsworth and Coleridge is an 'ambiguous accompaniment', which may have deceived both them and their audience and which (Hazlitt implies) adumbrates their later apostasy (XVII, p. 118). She shows that Hazlitt's description of himself as an 'inarticulate... worm by the way-side', and a similar passage in his essay 'On Effeminacy of Character', alludes to the encounter between Eve and Satan in Book IX of *PL*. Hazlitt imagines himself as the serpent, 'created mute to all articulate sound' (*PL*, IX, l. 557), who becomes elo-quent when he is possessed by Satan/Coleridge. A little later in *PL*, Satan is compared to an 'Athenian or noble orator, pleading a noble republican cause' (*PL*, IX, ll. 665–78) and Newlyn suggests that Hazlitt:

> identified with the aspiration towards reason, knowledge, freedom of speech, and access to power, which Satan voices so persuasively in his temptation of Eve. He also emerged from and claimed allegiance to the republican and Dissenting tra-ditions of oratory which Milton was here celebrating. But he nonetheless shared with Milton a wariness towards the performative component of the speech-act, and the seductive body language which was its ambiguous accompaniment.[61]

Newlyn's discussion is characteristically nuanced and acute, and there is no doubt that Hazlitt was suspicious of what he saw as Coleridge's emphasis on mystificatory orality. But if it is true that he accused the poet of 'a cowardly refusal to embrace the modernity and progress associated with print culture',[62] it is also the case that Hazlitt had his suspicions about the tendencies of 'print culture' itself.

For it is important to realize that in 'My First Acquaintance with Poets' Hazlitt associates the faculty for eloquence that Coleridge has awoken with the failure of his own aspirations, as well as the Lake Poets' apostasy. In 1798, he was struggling with the composition of his 'metaphysical choke-pear', the *Essay on the Principles of the Human Action*, whereas now he is an in-demand journalist: 'I can write fast enough now'. However, this facility for periodical writing is not something to be celebrated: 'Am I better than I then was? Oh no! One truth discovered, one pang of regret at not being able to express it, is better than all the fluency and flippancy in the world. Would that I could go back to what I then was!' (XVII, p. 114). In 1798, Hazlitt, Wordsworth and Coleridge exist in a rural republic of letters made up of sympathetic relationships, where individual genius is encouraged, and, at least in the case of Coleridge, associated with civil and religious liberty: 'Truth and Genius has embraced, under the eye and with the sanction of Religion' (XVII, p. 108). One of the narratives underlying 'My First Acquaintance with Poets' is the story of how these young writers have moved from an ideal rural existence in which ideas flow freely and 'Legitimacy' is about to be defeated, to engage with an urban literary marketplace in which 'Legitimacy' triumphs by exploiting the self-interest of its members. This situation is compared implicitly to the 1790s, which 'was not a time when *nothing was given for nothing*. The mind opened, and a softness might be perceived coming over the hearts of individuals, beneath "the scales that fence" our self-interest' (XVII, p. 116).[63] In the narrative of Hazlitt's own life, this was a time of leisured contemplation, long before he had become a journalist working in London. The contrast between the rural idyll of his youth and the harsh realities of the literary marketplace must have been very much in his mind during the composition of 'My First Acquaintance with Poets', for at that time (February 1823) he was confined under house arrest for debt.[64]

We can get a better sense of Hazlitt's nostalgia for his rural life by glancing at the essay 'On Living to One's Self', from the first volume of *Table-Talk* (1821):

> For many years of my life I did nothing but think. I had nothing else to do but solve some knotty point, or dip in some abstruse author, or look at the sky, or wander by the pebbled sea-side . . . I cared for nothing, I wanted nothing. I took my time to consider whatever occurred to me, and was in no hurry to give a sophistical answer to a question – there was no printer's devil waiting for me.
>
> (VIII, p. 92)

Hazlitt not only associates the late 1790s with dreams of republicanism, but with an ideal of liberated literary production, in which he was not prey to the demands of the reading public, that 'mean, stupid, dastardly, pitiful, selfish, spiteful, envious, ungrateful animal', which is led through the nose by malicious critics (VIII, pp. 97–9).

But while 'My First Acquaintance with Poets' describes an earthly paradise inhabited by idealistic men of letters, the literary world of the 1820s is a hell where writers are tormented by devils, in the guise of errand boys, who constantly demand 'sophistical answer[s]' to feed a ravenous public.

One of Hazlitt's favourite passages from *PL* was Milton's description of his Satan:

> . . . his form had not yet lost
> All her Original brightness, nor appear'd
> Less than Arch Angel ruin'd and th'excess
> Of Glory obscured.
>   (*PL*, I, ll. 591–4)

This is applied to Coleridge in Hazlitt's proleptic review of *The Statesman's Manual* of September 1816 (VII, p. 118) and it also informs the virtuoso account of the poet's fall into conservatism in *The Spirit of the Age* (XI, pp. 32–4). In both cases the allusion is significant more for its 'sense of irreparable loss' (V, p. 53) than the link between Coleridge and Satan itself. But in 'My First Acquaintance with Poets', Hazlitt does not use Satanic allusion merely for its elegiac qualities but as a way of trying to understand the gap between 1798 and 1823. As Newlyn has remarked, 'Satanic allusion is not the register of ideological certitude, but of moral and political *angst*: the Romantics turn to Milton when they are themselves preoccupied, as he had been, by the problematic relation of earthly politics to religious or moral truth'.[65] Engaging with *PL* allows Hazlitt to address two pressing questions. Why has literature become a prop for 'Legitimacy'? And can this process be reversed?

It does not seem to have been noted by any critic that the next few lines of Milton's description of Satan lie behind Hazlitt's account of his walk home after Coleridge's sermon, when he suggests that 'the sun that was still labouring pale and wan through the sky, obscured by thick mists, seemed an emblem of the *good cause*':

> As when the Sun new-ris'n
> Looks through the Horizontal misty Air
> Shorn of his Beams, or from behind the Moon
> In dim Eclipse disastrous twilight sheds
> On half the Nations, and with fear of change
> Perplexes Monarchs.
>   (*PL*, I, ll. 594–9)

Hazlitt conflates Milton's first simile – straightforwardly descriptive of Satan's damaged glory – with his second, which emphasizes, rather ominously, Satan's role as a challenger of monarchical authority. The 'labouring' sun represents the republican cause for the youthful Hazlitt because he has been inspired by Coleridge's Satanic sermon, which challenges the Pitt administration and its policy of war with France. And just as Satan represents, for Milton, both republican ideals and their corruption and failure, Coleridge's sermon in 1798 is haunted by the entirely opposed views of his future self: 'the sermon was upon peace and war; upon church and state – not their alliance, but their separation – on the spirit of the world and the spirit of Christianity, not as the same, but as opposed to one another' (XVII, p. 108). Something similar happens later in the essay, when Hazlitt describes Coleridge speaking 'Of Providence, foreknowledge, will, and fate,/ Fix'd fate, free-will, foreknowledge absolute' (XVII, p. 117; *PL*, II, ll. 559–60). This quotation, taken from Milton's description of the discussions of some of the fallen angels, emphasizes Coleridge's status as a philosophical talker. The allusion omits, but simultaneously evokes, the next line of the poem: 'And found no end, in wand'ring mazes lost' (*PL*, II, l. 561). Hazlitt believed that Coleridge had stumbled away from his true vocation as a republican poet: in *The Spirit of the Age* he describes how he 'wandered into Germany and lost himself in the labyrinths of the Hartz Forest and of the Kantean philosophy' (XI, p. 34). And in 'My First Acquaintance with Poets', Hazlitt observes that Coleridge cannot walk in a straight line:

> he continually crossed me on the way by shifting from one side of the footpath to the other. This struck me as an odd movement, but I did not at that time connect it with any instability of purpose or involuntary change of principle as I have done since.
>
> (XVII, p. 113)

Looking back on 1798 from the perspective of 1823, Coleridge's brilliant conversation, his sermon and his wandering walk, all carry the implication of his fall into mysticism and conservatism.

The question of 'free-will' goes right to the heart of Hazlitt's writings on genius and power. Is there something inherently bad about the poetic imagination, or has it been the victim of bad circumstances? Did the apostates fall, or were they pushed? Like *PL*, 'My First Acquaintance with Poets' gives a highly equivocal answer. In Milton's poem, the Fall of Man, like the failure of the Commonwealth, is something that is both pre-ordained and freely chosen: at this stage in his career, Hazlitt understands the 'degradation' of genius in similar terms. Newlyn points out that Satan cannot be pigeonholed either as hero or villain, and that Milton's poem suggests that 'if what is good may be the origin of what is evil, then what is evil may none the less have access to what is good'. Therefore, 'the moral ambiguity of Satan allows Milton to go on believing that, however far the Commonwealth has failed, there was still the chance of a political outcome which might genuinely implement the divine plan'. This was, of course, of great relevance to Romantic writers who sought to understand the causes of 'the miscarriage of revolutionary ideals'.[66] Now 'moral ambiguity' has no place in most of Hazlitt's writings on apostasy, which offer a linear narrative of good men turned bad due to the nature of the literary imagination. But the version of Coleridge produced by 'My First Acquaintance with Poets' *is* morally ambiguous: he is both Miltonic ideologue and Tory apologist. This ambiguity is made possible by focusing on the optimism of 1798 while hinting at the very different perspective of 1823: the effect is not only that the two periods are contrasted but, to some extent, that they are *elided*.

There is no doubt that Hazlitt's essay is, in part, meant to show that contemporary literary culture is corrupt. But its use of Miltonic allusion – and its appearance within a progressive publication like the *Liberal* – serves to suggest that the spirit of the 1790s can be recovered, for Hazlitt's depiction of the republic of letters is clearly a representation of the Utopian ideal of the magazine: literary genius is shown to be a locus of resistance to 'Legitimacy'. Milton was not only a hero to early nineteenth-century radicals and liberal Whigs, but, significantly, one of the 'Spirits' who Hunt invokes in the journal's 'Preface': 'be present, not ye miserable tyrants, slaves, bigots, or turncoats of any party... but ye MILTONS and ye MARVELLS'.[67] Like the *Liberal* itself, 'My First Acquaintance with Poets' suggests that creative writers like Milton and Hazlitt *can* stay true to their early ideals despite the apparent failure of their political hopes and, furthermore, that the fall of those who have, like Coleridge (and, in a different way, Byron), become too close to power can be reversed. Read in the context of its initial publication, and Hazlitt's writings on poetic apostasy, the essay's account of the link between independent genius and political radicalism seems much less nostalgic than if it is read in an anthology or his collected works. It is still deeply ambivalent, but offers at least the possibility that through the alliance of Byron, Hunt and Hazlitt, its vision might be renewed.[68]

The failure of the *Liberal*

'Arguing in a Circle', one of Hazlitt's two contributions to the fourth and final number of the *Liberal* (the other was 'Pulpit Oratory – Dr. Chalmers and Mr. Irving'), also sends out a somewhat mixed message. He begins by rejoicing in 'the progress that has been made in public opinion and political liberty, and that may be still farther made' (XVII, p. 268), but this optimistic beginning is vitiated by the bulk of the essay which is spent attacking Burke and the Lake poets as political apostates. Hazlitt's ambivalence is even more strongly apparent in his essay 'The Periodical Press', written in the same period and published in the May 1823 number of the *ER*, which starts by accepting, even celebrating, the rise of periodical literature, but ends by bitterly lamenting the way in which it has been hijacked by power.

This essay is a notable contribution to contemporary debates about the relationship between genius and literary culture, appearing in the pages of a journal that, if no longer the dominant force it had once been, was still powerful and widely read. In the first half of the essay, Hazlitt argues that the contemporary deluge of periodical criticism is a *symptom* of a lack of original genius, rather than its *cause*. As in the *Examiner* essay 'Why the Arts are not Progressive' of 1814 (IV, pp. 160–4), he argues that, in all arts, the greatest geniuses appear at their beginning. The modern world suffers from an anxiety of influence which prevents writers and artists from reaching the heights of creativity achieved by their forebears. Hazlitt counsels that this situation should be accepted – 'there is a change in the world, and we must conform to it... Let us be contented to serve as priests at the shrine of ancient genius' (XVI, p. 218) – and even embraces the rise of the periodicals: 'Therefore, let Reviews flourish – let Magazines increase and multiply – let the Daily and Weekly Newspapers live for ever! We are optimists in literature, and hold, with certain limitations, that, in this respect, whatever is, is right!' (XVI, p. 220). He also apparently dismisses the 'objection' that periodical criticism is an 'engine of party-spirit and personal invective', by noting that that this simply proves the Press's power and importance (XVI, p. 220).

Towards the end of the essay there is a sudden shift in tone. 'The illiberality of the Periodical Press', Hazlitt proclaims,

> is 'the sin that most easily besets it.' We have already accounted for this from the rank and importance it has assumed, which have made it a necessary engine in the hands of party. The abuse, however, has grown to a height that renders it desirable that it should be crushed, if it cannot be corrected; for it threatens to overlay, not only criticism and letters, but to root out all common honesty and common sense from works of the greatest excellence, upon large classes of society. All character, all decency, the plainest matters of fact, or deductions of reason, are made the sport of a nickname, an inuendo [*sic*], or a bold and direct falsehood.
>
> (XVI, pp. 232–3)

Here the relaxed, *laissez-faire* attitude that characterizes the early part of 'The Periodical Press' gives way to an interventionist zeal as Hazlitt demands that the partisanship of the press must be 'crushed' as a threat to society. Note the accusation of 'illiberality'; the press is not only base or bigoted, but it is opposed to political liberalism, and therefore to the *Liberal*. It should be an instrument of progress, but has been hijacked by the government and forced to 'act in a retrograde direction to its natural one' (XVI, p. 234). Ever since the *Anti-Jacobin*, opposition writers have been exposed to 'reckless slander and vulgar abuse', and in such a climate the apostasy of the Lake Poets seems almost inevitable:

> Who, indeed, was likely to stand, for any length of time, 'the pelting of this pitiless storm' – the precipitation of nicknames from such a height, the thundering down of huge volumes of dirt and rubbish, the ugly blows at character, the flickering jests on personal defects – with the complacent smiles of the great, and the angry shouts of the mob, to say nothing of the Attorney-General's informations, filed *ex officio*, and the well-paid depositions of spies and informers?
>
> (XVI, pp. 234–5)

This may seem to be Hazlitt at his most pessimistic, but is actually a more positive view of the relationship between literature and power than he expresses in the *Coriolanus* review or the articles on the *Times*. Here it is not the nature of the imagination that leads poetic genius into the arms of power, but the way in which the British government has learnt to manipulate the periodical press: the fallenness of literary culture is due to circumstances rather to the innately bad motivation of its members. Hazlitt was aware that the increasing power and extent of periodical writing (and other 'popular' forms) tended to weaken aristocratic control over literary production, as authors became increasingly dependent on the approbation of large numbers of readers, rather than rich patrons. Thus at times he could view the political repression of literary culture in his lifetime as a contingent situation, which might one day change.

Peter George Patmore noted in 1853 that Hazlitt had believed that the *Liberal* was 'an undertaking which, had it been cordially taken up by Byron and his friends, might...have produced great results'.[69] For a short time, the journal seemed like a beacon lighting the way for the redirection of the great engine of the periodical press towards progress. However, the magazine's failure confirmed Hazlitt's fears that genius was inevitably degraded in the early nineteenth century. There is no doubt that he blamed the demise of the journal on the intervention of Murray, Moore and Hobhouse, and his lordship's cowardice. In *The Spirit of the Age*, he remarks that Byron

> patronizes men of letters out of vanity, and deserts them from caprice or from the advice of his friends. He embarks in an obnoxious publication to provoke censure, and leaves it to shift for itself for fear of scandal. We do not like Sir Walter's gratuitous servility: we like Lord Byron's preposterous *liberalism* little better. He may affect the principles of equality, but he resumes his privileges of peerage, upon occasion.
>
> (XI, p. 77)

Byron, then, had failed Hazlitt's test: he had been unable to disregard his rank and engage in the republic of letters. However, more disturbing for Hazlitt was the behaviour of the poet's supposedly 'liberal' friends, which he describes in 'On Jealousy and Spleen of Party', the superb final essay in the *Plain Speaker* (1826):

> Who would have supposed that Mr. Thomas Moore and Mr. Hobhouse, those staunch friends and partisans of the people, should also be thrown into almost hysterical agonies of well-bred horror at the coalition between their noble and ignoble acquaintance, between the Patrician and 'the Newspaper-Man?' Mr. Moore darted backwards and forwards from Cold-Bath-Fields' Prison to the Examiner-Office, from Mr. Longman's to Mr. Murray's shop, in a state of ridiculous trepidation, to see what was to be done to prevent this degradation of the aristocracy of letters, this indecent encroachment of plebeian pretensions, this undue extension of patronage and compromise of privilege.
>
> (XII, p. 378)[70]

Such actions, and of course the failure of the *Liberal*, simply served to confirm Hazlitt's fatalism: in the current political climate, he claims in this essay, the dreams of the 1790s are no longer viable (XII, p. 373). Now, all political parties seek to distance themselves from the idea of 'liberty' due to its associations with Jacobinism; neither Whigs nor Reformers will have anything to do with the popular radicalism propagated by '[Henry] Hunt, Carlisle, or Cobbett' (XII, p. 376). He represents himself as a political pariah: disliked by the sycophantic Whigs because of his antagonism towards power, and dismissed by the cold-hearted Utilitarians due to his literary inclinations.

Pierre Bourdieu has argued that as literature becomes more autonomous from the State, writers are more able to make decisive political interventions. 'The intellectual', a cultural figure that he believes was invented towards the end of the nineteenth century with Zola's intervention in the Dreyfus affair, can assert the values of an autonomous cultural field against the field of power:

> Enclosed within his own order, with his back against his own values of freedom, disinterestedness and justice, precluded by them from abdicating his specific authority and responsibility in exchange for necessarily devalued profits or temporal powers, the intellectual asserts himself against the specific laws of politics (those of *Realpolitik* and reasons of state) as defender of universal principles which are in fact the universalisation of the specific principles of his own universe.[71]

We do not necessarily have to accept Bourdieu's wildly optimistic account of 'autonomisation', or even his assumption that the values of an autonomous literary field are inevitably liberal ones, to see how well his description of the late nineteenth-century 'intellectual' fits Hazlitt. The proviso – and it is a big one – is that living in an earlier period, the essayist's cultural authority was severely limited by the weakness of the literary field vis-à-vis the field of power and as a result he paid a heavy personal cost for attempting to use his role as a writer and critic to assert the 'values of freedom, disinterestedness and justice' against 'Legitimacy'. By the mid-1820s, his sense of marginality and failure had made him a bitter and disappointed man, although it is cheering to note that he lived long enough to hear news of the July Revolution of 1830 and the overthrow of the Bourbons. In recent years, there has been increased critical and journalistic interest in Hazlitt's work, but his status as a pathbreaking and influential figure in the history of British culture has still fully to be registered and explored. Hazlitt had his limitations, but no British writer has expressed more powerfully than him the belief that it is the duty of literature to resist compromise with power, or has faced with more courage and clear-sightedness its failures to do so.

6   'The Quack Artist'

Benjamin Robert Haydon and
the dangers of publicity

When a great Genius appeared in Italy or Greece, it was instantly a question what shall we do to afford him peace & security that he may give vent to his conceptions undisturbed by necessity or harrassed by want. When a great Genius appears in England, it is what shall [we] do to bring him down (curse him) to our own level, that by his success in high efforts he may not cast reflections indirectly on the grovelling practice of the Trade.[1]

Benjamin Robert Haydon's career was spent trying to bully the world into accepting that he was the great artist who was to lead the 'British School' of art to victory over its Continental rivals. He campaigned tirelessly for public patronage of history painting and, especially in his later years, often represented himself as a persecuted, suffering genius who was traduced by the press, plotted against by the Royal Academy ('the Trade'), and ignored by the aristocracy and the public. At the same time, he also liked to show himself to be a powerful masculine hero who was destined for great renown due to his God-given artistic ability. 'Genius', he wrote in such a mood, 'will arise and make its way, if born at the bottom of the Indian Ocean' (I, p. 241). But since his suicide in 1846, Haydon has attracted far more attention from literary critics and biographers than from art historians, who have generally considered his neo-classical history paintings to be of little value.[2] He is now known, if at all, for his tragicomic life story, recounted with enormous verve in his *Diary*, and his acquaintance with Romantic luminaries such as Hazlitt, Hunt, Keats and Wordsworth.[3]

In the late 1810s and early 1820s, however, Haydon received more press attention than any other British artist and was widely fêted as a man capable of emulating the great Italian painters of the Renaissance. This fame was partly a result of his artistic choices: although landscape and genre paintings were becoming more valued during the early nineteenth century, most critics still paid at least lip service to the Academic hierarchy of genres which put history painting – and history painters – at the top.[4] Furthermore, Haydon's rise coincided with a period of post-Napoleonic triumphalism in which people were particularly receptive to signs of greatness in British artists. Also, his battles with the Royal Academy and the British Institution meant that he tended to exhibit in one-man shows; thus his paintings were noticed in separate articles rather than being lumped together with those of most other artists in reviews of the summer exhibitions. But the main reason for Haydon's fame was that due to a lack of patronage he was forced to adopt a campaign of relentless self-promotion in order to sell his works: this led one caricaturist to dub him 'The Quack Artist'.[5] During the first half of his career, he had many friends and contacts in the press, and they, for the most part, supported him and his views on the future of British art. He was also a prolific author, producing a large number of pamphlets, exhibition catalogues and articles.[6] The effect of all this writing by and about Haydon was to focus the public's attention more on the artist himself than on the paintings he produced: thus although his art was deeply backward-looking, his celebrity should be understood as essentially modern in its emphasis on personality over product.

Throughout this book, we have seen that Romantic claims about the transcendent nature of genius were undercut or problematized by their subordination to ideological, financial or psychological ends. The case of Haydon brings this tension into stark relief. Although he courageously struggled to reconcile an ideal of disinterested genius with the demands of artistic production in a commercial society, his constant self-promotion tended to make him appear anything but public-spirited. Magazine writers often celebrated his genius at the same time as deprecating his hunger for publicity. But this chapter will show that both Haydon and his critics were so thoroughly imbricated in the commercialized construction and consumption of genius that these efforts to separate culture and commerce proved very difficult to sustain.

Haydon on genius, high art and the public

Haydon's views on genius did not change substantially after his formulation of them early in his career, but they are described most fully in the *Lectures on Painting and Design* (1844–6). The key thing to understand, he argued, was that genius was an *innate* characteristic, and he took issue with Joshua Reynolds's claim, in the second of his *Discourses*, that its effects could be produced by imitation and hard work.[7] Instead, he stated that 'if you have great genius, industry only can prove it; but if you have not, industry . . . will certainly never supply the original deficiency of nature'.[8] He also disagreed with Samuel Johnson's argument that genius was 'accidentally determined to some particular direction', although he followed Johnson's basic description of it as 'a mind of large general powers'.[9] Haydon thought that such a mind would have a particular susceptibility to certain sense impressions, which would determine whether the genius became a poet, artist, warrior or whatever.[10] This distinction was important to him, because it meant that the role that a man of genius took in society was not haphazard, but a matter of design. It allowed him to believe that his career as a history painter had been chosen for him by God.

Haydon sometimes represented genius as an intensely powerful, almost unstoppable, force, but he generally argued that it needed the aid of circumstances to bring it to full fruition: 'genius must exist, patronage *can't create it*; but genius may exist, and die without full development for want of patronage'.[11] However, the notion that genius might lie undiscovered was, at least in the early part of his career, utterly unacceptable to him, as is apparent in his response to Shelley's claim, in *Queen Mab*, that poverty and tyranny could prevent genius from expressing itself: 'How many a rustic Milton has passed by,/ Stifling the speechless longings of his heart,/ In unremitting drudgery and care!'[12] Haydon described this as 'the commonest of all common trash', for a genius would never be concealed, regardless of his lowly station (II, p. 154). This, he believed, was because such people had been singled out by God for the performance of a great task, although he accepted that this fulfilment would be limited and imperfect without the aid of the right circumstances.

We have to understand that for Haydon reviving British history painting was a task of the utmost importance. As John Barrell has put it, his classical republican concept of art 'was based on the conviction that a state which has lost a sense of the civic and patriotic values inherent in High Art is a state which has lost everything worth having'.[13] But the emphasis in his writings on the importance of innate genius undermines his adherence to a discourse of classical republicanism, which emphasizes the public function of art, for

> his insistence on the primacy of genius makes it hard for him to insist, with any great conviction, on the reciprocity of the relations between art and society ...
> The relations between the political republic and the republic of taste are reduced by Haydon almost entirely to relations of patronage, and, as far as form is concerned, the responsibility of the artist to paint public pictures seems reduced to the responsibility to paint in a public *style* – a responsibility which is argued for in a sternly moral language, but which seems to be in no particular moral relation with the society which welcomes or ignores it, beyond the fact that the production of works in that style reflects some kind of moral credit on the society which patronises and welcomes it.[14]

Barrell goes on to suggest that Haydon 'has no clear theory' of the way that public art contributes to the public sphere, and, as a result, genius becomes not only the primary cause of art, but its major justification. History painting is principally to be valued as a sign of individual and national genius, rather than for its actual effects on the public: thus in 1812, Haydon claimed that it was the only sort of painting 'which can give rank to "this England in art," and which only wants rank in such matters to be the greatest nation the world has ever seen yet'.[15] His frequent analogies between England's/Britain's artistic and military glory and his view of himself as the type of masculine hero so often depicted in his paintings may seem utterly strange to modern readers, but that is because we assume a gap between art and politics, which simply does not exist within the discourse of classical republicanism. Haydon's contradiction was that he sought to promote himself as a civic hero – a public man – using all the advertising paraphernalia available in a commercial society, in order to appeal to an audience which had 'come to regard art as an essentially private thing'.[16]

As Haydon became increasingly frustrated with the lack of interest in high art exhibited by the aristocracy, and the failure of the Royal Academy to reform itself, the idea that there might be an inevitable antipathy between genius and power became a recurring theme of the *Diary*. Although he tended towards 'Church & King' Toryism, Haydon's actual politics were complex and his allegiances shifted during his lifetime. He was certainly not a democrat, but had some sympathy with the reform movement of the late 1810s (II, p. 249) and was a strong supporter of the

Reform Bill of 1832. There is an interesting oscillation in his later writings between assertions that he is a loyalist whose desire to reform the Academy, and to paint in the 'Grand Style', has been misinterpreted as dangerous to Church and State,[17] and angry denunciations which represent genius in rebellion against a *status quo* comprising an enervated aristocracy and a self-interested Royal Academy. For example, in November 1823 he wrote:

> Perhaps the reason that the Legitimate of the day don't like great works & heroic subjects & prefer small pictures & the actions of the peasantry is that the actions of the heroes makes them feel their own insignificance, whereas the Dutch boors & English paupers are a continual assurance of their own superiority. There is something radical in heroism & Genius they can't be taught, but are independent of birth & hereditary succession.

> (II, p. 435)

Haydon, then, was quite willing to play on the radical possibilities of classical republicanism when it suited him by using the aristocracy's preference for genre painting over history painting as evidence for their lack of heroic virtue and, by implication, their unsuitability for government. Here, this claim is conflated with a 'Romantic' emphasis on innate genius as an unpredictable gift which has nothing to do with 'birth' and which therefore encourages a meritocratic society rather than one based on inherited rank (Haydon was himself the son of a bookseller).[18]

In the final years of his life, Haydon's personal bitterness led to further 'radical' outbursts. In 1843, he entered two paintings in the Cartoon Competition to decorate the new Palace of Westminster (the old one had burnt down in 1834). Haydon believed that the holding of the Competition was a result of his vociferous campaign for state patronage of history painting, and the failure of his two entries – *Adam and Eve* and *Edward the Black Prince* – gave him a shock from which he never really recovered.[19] A few weeks later, he wrote a passage in his *Diary* lamenting the dislike of 'High Art' evinced by the Royal Academy and the aristocracy, and then exclaimed, with revolutionary vigour, that 'the fact is, the energy of this great Country is struggling to split the superincumbent pressure of Aristocracy, which burks its vigor, and it will earthquake its weight bye [and] bye with an explosion which will mingle all in confusion, & clear the Sky' (V, p. 299). As usual, Haydon is principally talking about himself here and there is a considerable sexual charge to his imagery. The effeminate aristocracy is like a succubus that straddles the heroic genius and saps his energy – but such is his masculine power that his ejaculation will vanquish the demon.

Haydon was forced to blame the aristocracy, the Royal Academy and Parliament for the failure of high art, because to blame 'the people' would have meant accepting that the art could not be reformed on his terms. Thus in his hands the theory of innate genius became, at times, a radical principle, mainly because he attached it to a classical republican theory of art which made history painting central to a healthy society. Haydon's attempt to link genius with public art led to severe contradictions, but, almost until the end of his life, he managed to maintain his belief that ordinary people – once purified of the corrupt principles inculcated by patrons, connoisseurs and the Royal Academy – would be affected by history painting on a basic emotional level. So the recent suggestion that Haydon was an artistic elitist who had no desire 'to bring the elevated art of painting to broader consumer markets' is inaccurate.[20] He was opposed to the commercial realities of his day and continually asserted that the production of art should not simply be determined by market forces: but this is not necessarily an elitist position. In fact, he wanted history painting, especially his own, to be seen by as many people as possible and therefore campaigned for state patronage and for the opening up of exhibitions to individuals of all ranks. Haydon fought constantly, with brush and pen, for a public art that could be appreciated, potentially, by *every* member of British society. It was only in April 1846, when his exhibition at the Egyptian Hall was ignored by crowds who had come to see the midget Tom Thumb in the same building, that Haydon's faith in the public was shattered. 'They rush by thousands to see Thumb', he lamented, 'It is an insanity, a Rabies, a madness, a Furor, a dream. I would not have believed it of the English people!' (V, p. 531). Two months later, he killed himself.

Haydon in the press, 1814–20

The golden period of Haydon's relationship with the press was from the exhibition of *The Judgment of Solomon* in 1814, to that of *The Raising of Lazarus* in 1823, which was shortly followed by his first imprisonment for debt. During this time he had a tremendous network of support among critics and editors. *Solomon* was widely praised, often at great length: in an enormous review in the *Examiner*, Robert Hunt presented the painting as an answer to 'the impugners of British talent', stating that 'the unity and richness of the colour, light, and shade, resemble and indeed equal the lustre of the Venetian School', and that 'not even RAFAEL has surpassed him in the grand object of Art – the portraiture of the heart, or, as it is commonly termed, expression'.[21] The critic in the patriotic *New Monthly Magazine* (*NMM*) saw it as 'a powerful auxiliary to the well-founded claims that Great Britain now possesses the first school of historical painting in the world'.[22] John Scott, editor of the liberal *Champion*, gave the picture almost an entire page of his newspaper and praised Haydon as a heroic genius who would revive the arts in Britain. A year later, Scott wrote that the picture was to be 'regarded as one of the earliest achievements of a genius that belongs to our country, and promises to exalt the characteristics of the period to a high pitch of estimation'.[23] The reviewers' emphasis on Haydon's contribution to national greatness was, of course, exactly what the painter himself continually asserted in his diary.

After *Solomon*, it was to be six years before Haydon would again exhibit a substantial work, and yet during this period he constantly appeared in the press. As Colbert Kearney has shown, he used the *Examiner* as a mouthpiece for asserting his own genius and his ideas on art, both through his own anonymous reviews and letters, and the continual puffing of Robert Hunt's 'Fine Arts' column, where 'readers are kept informed of his progress with *Christ's Entry* [*into Jerusalem*], and there are times when it is clear that Hunt is writing with Haydon, literally or metaphorically, beside him'.[24] It was in the *Examiner* that the painter printed the attacks on Richard Payne

Knight and the Royal Academy in 1812 that were to have such an influence on his career.[25] Haydon had even closer links with the *Annals of the Fine Arts* (*AFA*) (1816–20), edited by his friend, the architect James Elmes, the *raison d'etre* of which was to promote Haydon as a great genius and propound his plans for British art.[26] The *Annals* campaigned for the government purchase of the Elgin Marbles and for the reformation of the Royal Academy, claiming that it was run by portrait painters who cared nothing for the historical art that it was originally designed to support.

Although, as we shall see, the critic William Carey described the *Annals* as 'Anti-British', it is too simplistic to argue, as Paul Magnuson does, that the quarterly was 'radical' due to its interest in 'Grecian subjects' and its attacks on the Royal Academy.[27] His suggestion that the 'esthetics of classical art' which it promoted 'outraged the conservative social order' is overstated; the social order had enough to be 'outraged' about in the years after Waterloo without worrying too much about relatively esoteric artistic debates. However, there was clearly a tension in the position of the magazine, the politics of which, as Andrew Hemingway has pointed out, 'were if anything conservative'.[28] During the late 1810s, any organ or person seeking the reform of public institutions could potentially be seen as radical and there is limited evidence that Haydon, at least, was tarred with this brush. But this tension between conservatism and reform was not really felt by the painter himself until the 1820s.

The *Annals* did a massive amount of work to promote Haydon as a heroic genius who was destined to overcome the conspiracy against him. To take a few examples, in its first number, he is described as 'a young historical painter of the greatest promise'[29]; in the second, Elmes notes 'his high feeling for his great calling' (*AFA*, I, p. 155); in the sixth, it is asked 'Did Rafaelle at twenty put forth a more powerful picture than Dentatus?' (*AFA*, II, p. 407).[30] The writer, possibly Elmes, goes on to state that 'Haydon is a spirit born for his times and I sincerely believe that nothing but the firmness with which he has so successfully kept his ground, in spite of all attempts to calumniate and crush him, could have produced the effects he has produced, and is producing' (*AFA*, II, p. 409). Later numbers contained similar comments. It also printed a number of letters and articles by the painter, some pseudonymous, the most self-adulatory of which were the 'Dreams of Somniator', two bizarre fantasies describing the defeat and humiliation of the Royal Academicians. In the first, 'The River of Time', most of them are drowned – only Fuseli, West, Flaxman, Wilkie, Turner and Callcott survive, led by the triumphant Haydon, who is crowned with laurels (*AFA*, II, pp. 461–74). In the second, the ghost of 'Michel Angelo' appears in the council chamber at the Royal Academy, and punishes the Academicians for their crimes against art by transmogrifying them into suitable objects: Lawrence becomes 'sweet oil', Shee 'a magpie', West 'a chamelion' and so on. Fuseli, despite his ignorance of 'nature', is rewarded for his 'fiery fancy' by being sent to Hell, which to him is heaven. Only Turner and Wilkie are unpunished: the latter is told to 'join your friend H-yd-n, with my best wishes to him; tell him he will succeed in all his noble views and plans' (*AFA*, III, p. 16). Although these articles are interesting as examples of Haydon's desire to present himself as a heroic figure who deserves adoration, ultimately they are little more than schoolboy squibs, and it is hard to believe, as Elmes claimed, that the Royal Academy lived in dread of 'Somniator' (*AFA*, IV, p. i).[31]

The fifth and final volume of the *Annals*, published in 1820, has a valedictory feel. It is dedicated to 'the Royal Academy of London, in respect of its recent Symptoms of Improvement' and in the 'Preface', Elmes states that the magazine's objectives have been achieved. Most importantly, its puffing of Haydon has been vindicated by the success of *Christ's Entry into Jerusalem*: 'our readers will recollect how we were taunted for mentioning his name in conjunction with the great men of other ages, whereas the public journals have joined his name with almost every one of them in succession' (*AFA*, V, pp. 128–9). Its last number contained the most notable piece of myth-making to appear in the *Annals*: Elmes's 'Memoirs of Benjamin Robert Haydon' (*AFA*, V, pp. 335–78). This lengthy article, which might as well have been written by the artist himself, contains all the themes and claims which later appear in his *Autobiography*: the conspiracy of the Royal Academy, who were jealous of his genius and hated history painting; his discovery of the Elgin Marbles *before* Benjamin West; his heroic attacks on Richard Payne Knight, which led to the purchase of the Marbles; his self-sacrifice for the public good; his triumph with *Christ's Entry*. The article represents as fact a highly tendentious version of the painter's life history which attempts, predictably, to show him in the best possible light. One example will suffice: Haydon's attack on Knight at the beginning of 1812 is presented as an act of 'less prudence than courage and firmness' (*AFA*, V, p. 356), for the connoisseur was a member of the British Institution, and Haydon's *Macbeth* was being exhibited there at the time with the possibility of being awarded a premium. However, as William Carey argued in 1819 – and the evidence of the *Diary* bears this out – Haydon did not know that Knight was the anonymous writer whom he was attacking.[32] In fact, the articles were, although sincere, also an attempt to ingratiate himself with the British Institution by attacking the Royal Academy – an attempt which totally backfired. Rather than being an example of Haydon's courage in speaking of the truth regardless of his self-interest, they tell us more about how his attempts to manage his career could go disastrously wrong.

In the 1820s, as we have seen, Haydon would claim that his attacks on Knight and the Royal Academy in the *Examiner* and the *Annals* had caused him to be labelled as a dangerous radical, thus leading to the alienation of his aristocratic patrons. This was of course a convenient excuse for his financial woes, and one which perhaps says more about the difficulties in Haydon's political position than it does about the way in which he was represented by others. But Haydon did experience some criticism in the late 1810s that had political resonances, and it should be said that all of the major attacks he received during his career were in Tory periodicals.[33] As a friend of Hunt, it is not surprising that he makes four guest appearances in Lockhart's 'Cockney School' articles. In the first, he is merely mentioned in passing; in the fourth, he is 'that clever, but most affected artist, who as little resembles Raphael in genius as he does in person'; in the fifth he is used as an example of Cockney 'egotism':

> Why is it that they seem to think the world has no right to hear one single word about any other person than Hunt, the Cockney Homer, Hazlitt, the Cockney Aristotle, and Haydon, the Cockney Raphael? They are all very eminent men in their own eyes, and in the eyes of the staring and listening groupes whom it is their ambition to astonish.

Lockhart went on to describe Haydon as having 'his own greasy hair combed loosly [*sic*] over his collar, after the manner of Raphael', and a few months later, mockingly exhorted the artist to paint a heroic picture of Hunt and Hazlitt having tea with Jupiter.[34]

Haydon, like the other Cockneys, is depicted as a pretentious *parvenu* with delusions of grandeur, who is able to deceive his lower middle-class audience of apprentices and clerks into accepting his grandiose claims. But he got off very lightly compared with Hazlitt, Hunt and Keats, possibly because *Blackwood's* was not very interested in painting. In 1820, however, the magazine reviewed *Christ's Entry into Jerusalem*. In the meantime, Haydon had descended on Edinburgh, sweeping all before him, and met Lockhart and Wilson. The *Blackwood's* critic declared that 'Mr Haydon is already by far the greatest historical painter that England has yet produced. *In time*, those that have observed this masterpiece, can have no doubt he may take his place by the side of the very greatest painters of Italy'.[35] A year later, 'A Letter Concerning Haydon's Paintings' argued that as they clearly manifested 'the power of dramatic expression', the artist ought not 'to be seriously blamed for using copious means to draw the notice of the public . . . A manly self-confidence is not only becoming, but necessary'.[36] Haydon's power, both as artist and man, to overawe his critics can be seen in the transformation he undergoes in *Blackwood's*: from an ignorant, self-aggrandizing coxcomb to a genius of 'manly self-confidence' who could truly be described as a 'Cockney Raphael'.

The most serious attacks on Haydon appeared in the *NMM*. As we have seen, its critic praised *Solomon* in 1814, and the magazine continued to support the artist up until 1818, when it described him as 'decidedly one of the most promising of the present race'.[37] In 1819, however, William Carey became art critic for the magazine. Earlier in the 1810s, Carey had staunchly supported Haydon, praising him in the *Champion*, the *Examiner*, the *Literary Gazette* and his *Critical Description of [Benjamin West's] 'Death on a Pale Horse'*. This latter work prompted a churlish review by Elmes in the *Annals*, which trumpeted Haydon, denigrated West and accused Carey of writing under the latter's instruction (*AFA*, III, pp. 79–90). In his hysterical response, a 350 page book called *Desultory Exposition of an Anti-British System of Incendiary Publication* (1819 – the full title is over fifty words long), Carey attacked Haydon and Elmes, accusing them of seeking to elevate the painter by denigrating other artists, the Royal Academy, the British Institution and the 'British School' as a whole.

Despite its frenzied and repetitive prose, the *Exposition* makes some acute points. Through a close reading of the *Annals*, Carey shows how Haydon sought to manipulate public opinion in his favour by constructing an image of himself as a heroic, persecuted genius. While continuing to praise the artist's works, he also notes that the rival history painter William Hilton, barely mentioned by the *Annals*, had managed to produce fifteen paintings in the time it had taken Haydon to produce four.[38] The following passage is typical of the *Exposition*, and contains the two most interesting aspects of Carey's attack – the construction of Haydon and Elmes as charlatans, and the implication that such quackery is unpatriotic, perhaps even politically dangerous:

> Mr. Haydon is to be praised and extolled and puffed; he is to be always honored with *laudations*, (p. 523 v. 2 AFA) and kept 'WHOLLY and SOLELY' before the public as the MUNCHAUSEN of the *palette* and *pencil*, a sort of *pictorial*

Mountebank on a stage; with his *anonymous Bill-sticker, Hornblower* and *Merry Andrew*, placarding the walls, sounding his blasts of astonishment, or playing a solo on the salt-box to attract the eyes and ears of the amazed Multitude. *All freedom of opinion is to be abolished.* Every public writer is to lay down his pen, or become a slave to the *Anti-academical* and *unitarian System*: a Creature, a Parasite, and a defamatory Instrument in the hands of this odious Anti-British Confederacy. The Press is to be converted into an engine for Disappointed Vanity and Envy, to work their unholy purposes, and all contemporary merit, every living British Artist, is to be thrown out of sight, or only brought forward as a mere background and inferior figure to Mr. Haydon; or this scribling Jack-pudding, his Trumpeter, Showman, and Puff-master General is to be let loose upon us.[39]

Haydon and Elmes are not merely quacks who are trying to hoodwink the multitude for personal gain, but demagogues engaged in an 'Anti-British confederacy' who seek to use the press to abolish 'freedom of opinion' and work 'their unholy purposes' against the Royal Academy in particular; thus Carey seeks to play on contemporary fears of populist politics.[40] Later in the *Exposition*, in another passage which comes close to accusing Haydon and Elmes of radicalism, he describes the *Annals* as manifesting an 'arrogant disrespect for rank and dignity of the highest order', including the King and the Prince Regent.[41]

Although the *Desultory Exposition* is known to writers on Haydon, it does not seem to have been noticed that Carey made similar points in the *NMM* during 1819. These articles are bound to have had a much wider circulation than his privately printed book. In the first of his 'Fine Arts' columns, Carey states that

> our sincere and constant efforts shall, therefore, be diverted to create a national pride in BRITISH GENIUS, and a national love of BRITISH ART; to unite the whole body of our native artists and their PATRONS, the ROYAL ACADEMY and THE BRITISH INSTITUTION, more clearly; and to establish the glory of England in the Fine Arts as triumphantly as our victorious fleet and armies have established her fame in arms.[42]

This type of patriotic rhetoric, with its comparison of English/British artistic and military glory is exactly the language that Haydon uses throughout his life, but in further articles Carey makes it clear that he thinks that it is Haydon who has sought to destroy this glory by celebrating himself and denigrating all other British artists, as well as the Royal Academy and the British Institution.[43] Within the pages of the *New Monthly*, Carey's assertion that Haydon and Elmes were 'anti-British' had an extra edge, for the staunchly Tory periodical loudly and continually proclaimed itself to be a supporter of 'Loyalty and Religion' and enemy of 'Jacobinism'. Ironically, Haydon, a Francophobic nationalist, was thus implicitly linked with 'Buonaparte's adulators', to whom the magazine, of course, was firmly opposed.[44] It is clear then that Haydon's attacks on national institutions such as the Royal Academy and the British Institution *could* be interpreted as radical, particularly during a period of political instability.[45] However, despite the impression that one gets from Haydon's diary, and the comments of some of his defenders, it is *not* the case that he was continually attacked as a radical in the 1810s and 1820.

As in the case of *Blackwood's*, the *New Monthly* changed its tune in 1820. Carey seems to have stopped writing for the magazine early in that year; he is unlikely to have produced the unsigned review in July which praised *Christ's Entry*, and anticipated from Haydon's 'future labours...works which may equal the productions of the most auspicious times'.[46] The leading article in December 1820 was a 'Memoir of Benjamin Robert Haydon, esq.' which is similar in tone to its analogue in the *Annals*, although much shorter. Here Haydon is a heroic genius who has triumphed over all obstacles, motivated only by a 'disinterested ardour' for history painting which justifies his slightly excessive attacks on his opponents. The article ends with something like an apology for Carey's articles:

> The private character of this artist has not been spared in the acrimonious contests which have been alluded to in the previous pages. Unable to resist the proof of his talent as a painter, some adversaries have called him a radical reformer, and others a deist... We have reason to know that he is sincerely attached to the British constitution, and considers the principal reform of which it is capable to be an extension of national encouragement to historical painting. So much for his politics. His religion may be discovered in his pictures.[47]

I have found no evidence of direct references to Haydon as either a 'radical reformer' or a 'deist' in the periodical press, although it may be that the *New Monthly's* writer is referring to rumours circulating in the art world, or perhaps some of the anonymous letters that Haydon received throughout his life. On the other hand, it is quite possible that his information is from the painter himself and simply reveals Haydon's paranoid fear that he had become branded as a radical.

Although some reviewers expressed reservations about the Christ figure in Haydon's new painting, the glowing comments in the *New Monthly* were fairly typical.[48] For most critics, the triumph was not only Haydon's, but also Britain's. Robert Hunt, in the *Examiner*, claimed that he had given the country 'additional celebrity' and had proved 'that high capability of Genius in Art is not confined to the more felicitous latitudes of Greece and Italy'.[49] Elmes, unsurprisingly, felt enabled by the success of the painting to state that Haydon

> is a man of undoubted genius, that he is the first painter in the country, that his works have raised the reputation of the English school; and that he has constantly devoted himself, disregarding all emolument, to the highest walk of art, through every species of want, ill-treatment and difficulty.

> (*AFA*, V, p. 373)

The most interesting review of *Christ's Entry* was by John Scott in the *London Magazine* (*LM*). It begins with a familiar lament about the lack of government patronage for history painting, which means that a painter like West or Haydon is forced 'to advertise himself like a quack doctor, to squeeze that support from the shillings of the people, which he has vainly hoped to obtain from public patronage respectably manifested'.[50] Scott sees the civic values enshrined by high art as inevitably degraded by commercialism. And although he describes *Christ's Entry* as 'the greatest effort of the English School of painting', he spends most of the article lamenting Haydon's own quack-like practices. One-man shows, Scott argues, are bad for 'an artist's character'. Not only are catalogues and advertisements 'dangerous stimulants' but the artist is also likely to be tempted 'unduly to consider the popular taste in the selection of a subject, and to introduce accessaries calculated to gratify popular prejudice in the mode of treating it'.[51] An artist who pandered to the populace could not, of course, be described as engaged 'in a gallant struggle for the triumph of his art', but rather as being 'resolved in *distinguishing* himself...by a dexterity of management, not exactly reconcileable to that dignity with which the public display of genius should always be invested'.[52] So the distinction here is between the heroic, disinterested genius, and the quack artist, who seeks to manipulate public opinion in order to increase his own fame (the term 'management', in this context, has overtones of deceit or trickery). This, one might think, is meant to be a description of Haydon, but Scott is careful to point out that the latter 'is animated by the most ardent devotion to the cause of fine art', and that his writings have greatly improved 'public opinion', and also led to a greater number of good exhibitions, as well as the purchase of the Elgin Marbles. However, he also criticizes, at some length, two aspects of *Christ's Entry* as being particularly sensationalist: Haydon's claim, in the advertisements, that it had been 'six years at the easel', and his portrayal of Voltaire in the painting, who is scoffing at Christ. Taken as a whole, the review is strongly supportive of the artist, but the suggestion is clearly that he is in danger of degrading himself and his pictures by attempting to 'manage' public opinion by the wrong methods.

In three letters published in the *Examiner*, John Landseer, one of Haydon's pupils, took strong exception to Scott's remarks.[53] Landseer denied that that there was anything 'reprehensibly improper' about advertising a public exhibition and charging a shilling for entry. This was much better, he claimed, than putting artists at the mercy of the Hanging Committee at the Royal Academy. In 'The Lion's Head' for July 1820, Scott was keen to emphasize that he had not meant to attack Haydon, and the next month he printed an article which contained a short piece by the artist entitled 'On the Relative Encouragement of Sculpture and of Painting in England', and some additional remarks by Scott.[54] He repeated his claim that Haydon had a tendency to seek celebrity by unworthy means, but emphasized that this was entirely unnecessary due to his 'great talents and noble resolution'. It seems strange that Scott, after attacking the artist's puffing, was willing to introduce Haydon's 'address' as 'equally manly and called for'; for, apart from pleading for more patronage for history painting, the artist also exhorts patrons to purchase *Christ's Entry* for 3000 guineas. Although he is careful not to make any direct assertions about his own genius, Haydon effectively does so through a series of rhetorical questions: 'have I, or have I not, displayed talents to justify my pretensions? Is my pursuit worthy [of] encouragement, or is it not? Do I, or do I not, deserve to be encouraged? The public must decide'.[55] Of course, by then the exhibition of *Christ's Entry* had been extremely successful, and nearly everybody agreed about Haydon's artistic abilities: so what he is actually saying is that 'the public *have* decided – and would you like to buy my painting for three thousand guineas?' Once again, a periodical that had criticized the painter's publicity-seeking had become a vehicle for his self-promotion.

Haydon in the press, 1820–46

William Hazlitt, despite being Haydon's friend, was more dubious than most about *Christ's Entry*, describing it, in the *Edinburgh Review* (*ER*), as 'a masterly sketch' rather than the finished product, in an article in which he also asserted that the fine arts were not natural to the English character.[56] Years earlier, Haydon had believed that he could manipulate Hazlitt in order to disseminate his own views (II, p. 65), but this had proved impossible: one of the few constants in Hazlitt's art criticism is his theory that any art will inevitably decline after its first glorious period, a view that was of course anathema to Haydon.[57] The final straw came in 1824 when, in a review of Lady Morgan's *Life of Salvator Rosa*, Hazlitt discussed Salvator and James Barry as irritable geniuses who lacked true greatness: 'Those who are at war with others, are not at peace with themselves. It is the uneasiness, the turbulence, the acrimony within that recoils upon external objects. Barry abused the Academy, because he could not paint himself'.[58] Haydon, predictably, took these remarks to be aimed at him (which they probably were) and denounced Hazlitt in his diary as an apostate who had gone over to the 'courtier like side' (II, pp. 493–6).

But despite Haydon's claims that Hazlitt had once been his 'furious defender', the essayist had always expressed doubts about the painter's ability, though none about his strength of character – 'I also know an artist who has at least the ambition and the boldness of genius', he wrote in the *LM* in 1820.[59] In his review of *Christ's Agony in the Garden*, also in the *London*, he described it as 'a comparative failure' and took issue with Robert Hunt in the *Examiner* for supposedly declaring that 'the shades of Raphael, Michael Angelo, and Coreggio, can find no better employment than to descend again upon the earth...and stand with hands crossed, and eyes uplifted in mute wonder, before Mr. Haydon's picture'.[60] The painter, argued Hazlitt, had reached the point when he 'should fling himself boldly and fairly into the huge stream of popularity...instead of buoying himself up with borrowed bloated bladders, and flimsy newspaper paragraphs'.[61] These comments, of course, continued Scott's remarks in the same magazine a year earlier. However, just like Scott, Hazlitt was unable to maintain the attack. For having tried to undercut the puffing of Haydon, he came up with some hyperbole of his own:

> One great merit of Mr. Haydon's pictures is their size...His genius is gigantic. He is of the race of Brobdignag, and not of Lilliput...He bestrides his art like a Colossus. The more you give him to do, the better he does it. Ardour, energy, boundless ambition, are the categories of his mind, the springs of his enterprise...Vastness does not confound him, difficulty arouses him, impossibility is the element in which he glories.[62]

Even Hazlitt, it seems, could not avoid being sucked into the vortex of publicity surrounding Haydon. This description makes the artist out to be one of his own heroic figures and seems calculated to feed his egotism. It is literally a *puff*, inflating Haydon to gigantic size: no wonder that the final phrase of the quotation – 'impossibility is the element in which he glories' – became an occasional mantra to the painter later in life.

Having built Haydon up in 1821, at the end of the decade Hazlitt seemed to want to knock him down. In the twelfth of the *Conversations of Northcote*, first published in the *London Weekly Review* in 1829, he strongly criticized the painter's attempts to bully the public (though he only names him as 'X-'): 'he had no real love of his art, and therefore did not apply or give his whole mind sedulously to it; and was more spent on bespeaking notoriety beforehand by puffs and announcements of his works, than on giving them that degree of perfection which would ensure lasting reputation'.[63] A further attack which was meant to appear in the *NMM* was not published until 1853:

> I never heard him speak with enthusiasm of any painter or work of merit, nor show any love of art, except as a puffing-machine for him to get up into and blow a trumpet in his own praise. Instead of falling down and worshipping such names as Raphael and Michael Angelo, he is only considering how he may, by storm or strategem, place himself beside them, on the loftiest seats of Parnassus, as ignorant country squires affect to sit with judges on the bench... Haydon should have been the boatswain of a man of war; he has no other ideas of glory than those which belong to a naval victory, or to vulgar noise and insolence; not at all as something in which the whole world may participate alike.[64]

The final sentence sums up perfectly Haydon's own confusion between art and war; the way in which he saw other painters, art institutions and the public as opponents who had to be loudly beaten into submission.

It was probably easier to emphasize Haydon's inferiority to the Old Masters in 1829 than it had been in 1820, because, although the artist continued to gain much attention and praise during the intervening years, critical responses were more muted than they had been earlier in his career. The *Annals* was now defunct; Leigh Hunt was in Italy (although Robert Hunt continued to write for the *Examiner* until the end of 1828); John Scott was dead; and Hazlitt, as we have seen, was proving impossible to manipulate.[65] *The Raising of Lazarus* (1823) was well received, by both the public and the press, but Haydon's imprisonment for debt, and appearance in advertisements as a charity case, tarnished his image as an invincible hero. After 1823, a combination of poor eyesight and the pressures produced by the horrendous state of his finances meant that the quality of his paintings deteriorated, and although they still tended to gain positive reviews, there were very few further comparisons with Raphael or Titian. His comic paintings of everyday life – the *Mock Election*, *Chairing the Member*, and *Punch* – were widely praised for their Hogarthian manner, but these productions, of course, meant relatively little either to Haydon (apart from financially), or to those critics who still subscribed to the old hierarchy of genres.

Accusations of charlatanism continued to bedevil the painter, and became more frequent as critics and the public became bored with his attempts to raise his profile and his endless hectoring on the subject of public patronage. The *Magazine of the Fine Arts*, reviewing his Pall Mall exhibition in 1821, criticized the catalogue and noted 'the disgust with which mankind regard self-adulation and puffing' – months later it alluded to him as 'a conceited imposter'.[66] In 1825, the *John Bull* mocked his portraits at the Society of British Artists as 'gigantic absurdities' that proved his 'lunacy'. The reviewer noted, with some irritation, that Haydon 'had left his impudence upon record by asking Parliament for money because he was a *great artist*', and proclaimed that 'such evidence of self-conceit when coupled with these abominable productions, is, perhaps, hardly to be equalled'.[67] The *Literary Gazette* normally praised Haydon's paintings, but deplored his 'puff' of *The Mock Election* as 'the most ill-advised' of his 'absurd and offensive' writings.[68] In April 1832, the *Gentleman's Magazine* lambasted the 'quackery, conceit, and bombast' of his exhibition catalogue for *Eucles*.[69]

The most serious attack on Haydon appeared in 1834. *Fraser's Magazine* (*FM*), which rarely paid attention to the fine arts, printed an eight-page article ridiculing him and his picture of the Reform Banquet. The reviewer, probably William Maginn, began by remarking on Haydon's notoriety, 'inasmuch as, besides being a great painter, he is a very considerable writer on painting, a violent declaimer against the Royal Academy, a vituperator of the public taste, and an insufferable coxcomb'.[70] What follows is a short biography of the artist, which should be read as a parody of the eulogistic 'memoirs' of Haydon that appeared earlier in his career.[71] We are told of his arrogance in his youth, how he aped Raphael and 'at the same time he puffed himself and was patronised by others' – these remarks clearly echo the 'Cockney School' attacks of fifteen years earlier. The painting of *Christ's Entry* is described as 'spoil[ing] a very considerable piece of canvas, by smearing over it'. After mocking Haydon's portraits as 'colossal caricatures', in similar terms to the *John Bull* attacks, Maginn gives some praise for the *Mock Election*, but then states that after this 'lucid interval',

> he relapsed into his old habits of inefficiency; and his time was spent in daubing hideous objects, and writing pamphlets and statements about himself and his art, and his debts and his duns; till at last he sunk into an oblivion dark and deep.[72]

The rest of the article is spent attacking Reform, and laughing at Haydon's exhibition catalogue.

Clearly the main motivation for *Fraser's* attack was political – describing Haydon's painting allowed the magazine to mock Whig politicians like Brougham and Grey – but the way in which Haydon is represented is revealing. If he was not quite in 'oblivion dark and deep' during the 1830s, he was beginning to seem more and more like a faintly comic, marginal figure.[73] He had his victories in the last decade of his life – his popular lecture tours, the establishment of Schools of Design, and his commission to paint the Worldwide Anti-Slavery Convention (although the resulting picture was a failure) – but his public profile declined steadily. In January 1842, he lamented that 'in the Press, now, I have hardly a Friend . . . I have only to shew a work to set the whole Press in an uproar of abuse' (V, p. 121). This is something of an exaggeration, but reveals Haydon's sense that he had become yesterday's man, whose artistic principles were increasingly remote from those of either the critics or the public.[74] Even his martyrdom in 1846 could only temporarily slow down the slump in his reputation that continued into the twentieth century.

Cruikshank on Haydon: two caricatures

During the 1840s, George Cruikshank published two caricatures in the *Comic Almanack*, which, if they do not depict Haydon directly, can certainly be read as making references to his career. The first, 'Guy Fawkes Treated Classically – An Unexhibited Cartoon' (Plate 3), appeared in 1844, and the second, 'Born a Genius and Born a Dwarf' (Plate 4), appeared in 1847, a few months after his suicide. What is interesting about both images is that they simultaneously celebrate the painter – his ambition, his showmanship, his suffering, perhaps even his artistic ability – and satirize him. Cruikshank succeeds in encapsulating the dualistic response that Haydon so often provoked, representing him as neither genius, nor quack, but a strange mixture of both.

David Blayney Brown has assumed that the 'Guy Fawkes' caricature is directed at Haydon, but both Robert L. Patten and William Feaver have described it aimed at 'vasty' history painting in general.[75] Although Cruikshank's fantasy of a painting so enormous that it cannot be got through the doorway to Westminster Hall was based on the travails of a different artist, the most apt proponent of the 'Grand Style' for his satirical purposes was clearly Haydon.[76] However, to see the image as simply 'a satire on Haydon's pictorial giganticism and on his submissions to the Westminster Cartoon Competition' is to understate its complexity.[77] For when reading the caricature alongside the accompanying text, the huge and grotesque figure of Guy Fawkes becomes a symbol not just of Haydon's art, but of the painter's image of himself as a powerfully masculine heroic genius, and his attempt to force this image on to the public. The text plays with images of size and compression, making them refer both to the physical dimensions of the painting, and the artist's personality – 'though I had cramped my genius already to suit the views of the Commissioners, and the size of the door, I found I must have stooped much lower if I had resolved on finding admittance for my work'.[78] As we have seen, this trope, in which a description of Haydon's heroic style of painting is also applied to his character or genius, was also used by other writers. The two most notable instances are Hazlitt's comment that 'his genius is gigantic ... He bestrides his art like a Colossus', and Thackeray's review of the Royal Academy exhibition of 1845, where he describes the painter's *Uriel and Satan* as 'a broad-shouldered, swaggering, hulking archangel', and states that 'there is something burly and bold in this resolute genius which will attack only enormous subjects'.[79] Both these writers share Cruikshank's ambivalence towards their subject; the grand magnitude of Haydon's art, ambition, and personality is both sublime *and* ridiculous.[80]

'Guy Fawkes Treated Classically' actually contains two images of Haydon, for if the figure of Guy Fawkes represents him as heroic genius, the tiny figure of the artist

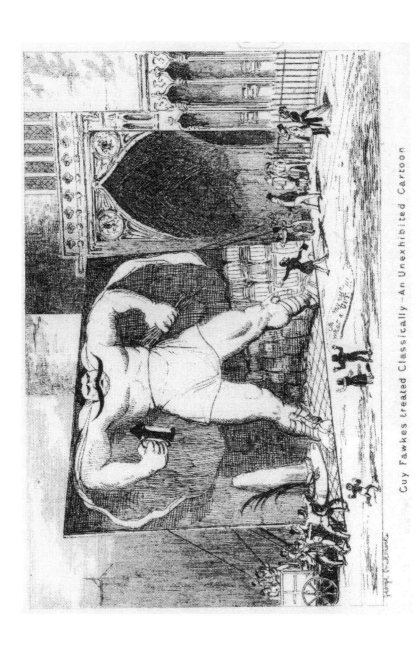

Guy Fawkes treated Classically - An Unexhibited Cartoon

Plate 3 George Cruikshank, 'Guy Fawkes Treated Classically – An Unexhibited Cartoon', *Comic Almanack*, 1844. Reproduced by permission of the Syndics of Cambridge University Library.

BORN A GENIUS   AND   BORN A DWARF.

Plate 4 George Cruikshank, 'Born a Genius and Born a Dwarf', *Comic Almanack*, 1847. Reproduced by permission of the Syndics of Cambridge University Library.

who is so dwarfed by his painting represents him as a quack touting his marvel to the watching public. This alludes to the painful irony of Haydon's career: that, as an artist who sought to inculcate public, heroic virtue, he was forced to use ever more desperate, showman-like measures to sell his paintings to a culture in which art was increasingly a matter of private consumption. In Cruikshank's caricature, both the showman and the hero he purveys, are, like Haydon, ultimately excluded by the authorities of art, but they do get public recognition, if not exactly approbation: 'as it was carried through the streets, it seemed to be generally understood and appreciated, every one, even children, exclaiming as it passed, "Oh! there's a Guy!" '[81] However, the painting in 'the grand style' that was supposed to adorn a public building is reduced to no more than a travelling freak show in which the Barnum-like artist (Haydon as charlatan) touts his Belzoni-like strongman (Haydon as heroic genius) to the gaping multitude.

'Born a Genius and Born a Dwarf' is described by Brown as 'no less vicious' than the Guy Fawkes caricature, again implying that the image is directed solely at Haydon.[82] Although it seems cruel of Cruikshank to use Haydon's sufferings as a vehicle for satire so soon after his suicide, the caricature itself is certainly much more than an attack on the artist. Patten has described its different targets very well:

> the satire cuts in all directions, at the public for preferring miniature to heroic, at life for promoting deformity over genius... It also cuts at Haydon for his romantic excesses and thundering prophets and at all the other entrants in the Westminster competition whose vacuous cartoons beat out Haydon's submission. And it alludes complexly to Cruikshank's own situation: he is both Haydon, humiliated by the public's rejection, and Tom Thumb, master of miniatures, though his own art can be distinguished from the blowsy rhetoric of romantic prophecy on one side and the diminutive trumpery of modern amusements on the other.[83]

The image is remarkable in that it both affirms and explodes the idea of Haydon as a neglected genius. If one reads 'genius' ironically, then the satire is on the artist's ridiculous overestimation of his own abilities: he is not really a genius and that is why he is in such a bad state. On the other hand, if genius is read as straightforwardly descriptive, like 'dwarf', then the picture becomes a satire on a society which rewards physical freakishness rather than creative ability. In that case, the picture supports Haydon's own arguments about the ill-treatment he has suffered throughout his career.

The text accompanying the image has the effect of fixing its meaning to the latter interpretation. Entitled 'Jupiter and the Mother: An Idyll', it describes the complaints of a mother, who, having prayed to Jupiter that her unborn child will be 'the most admired of all thy Children – the richest – the happiest of Men', discovers, a few years later, that she has given birth to a dwarf. She lambasts Jupiter for having failed to bless the child 'with a form of Power, and a mind of Genius', but the deity tells her, 'had I conferred on him the Genius thou sighest after, he would have felt but Want and Neglect in the world... For know that Mind alone can sympathize with Mind; and mindless Man enriches those who minister rather to the luxury of his Senses, than to the refinement of his intellect'.[84] This passage, with its theme of neglected genius and concomitant indictment of an ignorant mass audience who care only for sensual pleasure is remarkably similar to sentiments recorded in Haydon's journal a few years earlier:

> The greatest curse that can befall a Father in England is to have a Son gifted with a passion & a genius for High Art. Thank God with all my Soul & all my nature, my Children have witnessed the harrassing agonies under which I have ever painted, that the very name of Painting, the very name of High Art, the very thought of Pictures, gives them a hideous & disgusting taste in their mouths. Thank God, there is not one of my boys, or a Girl, who can draw a straight line, even with a ruler, much less without one, & I pray God on my knees, with my forehead bent to the Earth, my lips in the Dust, that they [*sic* for *he*] will, in his mercy, inflict them with every other passion, appetite, misery, wretchedness, disease, insanity, or gabbling Idiotism, rather than a longing for Painting – this scorned, miserable Art, this greater imposture than the human species it imitates – a greater delusion than a painted whore.
>
> (V, p. 179)

The almost comic hyperbole of this extract reveals the disgust that Haydon sometimes felt towards his own life in his final years, especially the incessant haggling with his creditors that was necessary in order to avoid imprisonment for debt. 'Jupiter and the Mother', then, supports and uphold the self-image of a scorned martyr that Haydon projected in his dark moments.

But 'Born a Genius and Born a Dwarf' goes beyond its accompanying text to provoke a variety of possible meanings. Like the earlier caricature, it is partly about freakishness: whereas in the Guy Fawkes image, Haydon was compared with a circus strongman, here he is contrasted with a circus midget. Again, Cruikshank registers the link with showmanship which is so crucial to understanding Haydon's career. It is possible that the caricaturist may have been partly inspired by a passage in Goldsmith's *Citizen of the World*, in which the partiality of the London crowd for strange sights and monstrosities is attacked: 'a man, though in his person faultless as an aerial genius, might starve; but if stuck over with hideous warts like a porcupine, his fortune is made for ever'.[85] With that in mind, what is ostensibly a contrast between 'Genius' and 'Dwarf' can be interpreted as placing them on the same level. Both are freaks of nature, born not made, who seek to profit by their difference from the norm. Tom Thumb lives in luxury because his particular variety of freakishness is more to the public taste than that exhibited (the pun is intended) by Haydon. So even if the caricature accepts the painter's claims about his genius, it can take the gloss off those claims by denying him the right to special treatment due to his abilities. He has tried his best to promote himself, but has come up against a greater freak – Thumb – and a greater showman – Barnum – than he is.

Cruikshank's two caricatures brilliantly explore the ambiguities and anxieties surrounding the relationship between genius and the public sphere in the first half of the nineteenth century. How can you recognize a true genius? Can you promote genius without debasing it? Is genius doomed to be neglected by society? Tom Thumb is clearly dwarfish (although technically he was a midget), but the Haydon image requires that the viewer decide whether or not 'genius' is meant ironically. This is, of course, a difficult decision: Haydon's poverty and alienation can be read as a sign of his lack of artistic ability, but it can equally be read as a sign of the public's inevitable lack of taste. What is remarkable about the painter's career is the extent to which, despite his bitterness and sense of martyrdom – and while continuing to believe himself to be a great genius – he tried to resist the latter interpretation of his own life. Like some of his literary contemporaries, he paraded his own alienation and sought solace in it, but, most of the time, Haydon refused the consolations of posterity and sought to engage with the public rather than to dismiss it as inherently debased.

Conclusion

On 22 June 1846, Haydon's professional disappointments and financial problems finally overcame him. He got up early, bought a pistol, returned home and locked himself in his painting room. There he wrote his will, letters to his wife and three children, his final diary entry, and then, just before shooting himself, the following lines:

> No man should use certain evil for probable good, however great the object. Evil is the prerogative of the Deity.
>
> I create good, I create, *I* the Lord do these things.
>
> Wellington never used evil, if the good was not certain; Napoleon had no such scruples & I fear the Glitter of his Genius rather dazzled me – but had I been encouraged, nothing but good would have come from me; because when I was encouraged, I paid every body. God Forgive the evil for the sake of the good. Amen.[1]

The 'certain evil' refers, in Haydon's case, to the accrual of debts in the pursuit of his artistic ambitions, debts that he was often unable to pay. As in so much of his autobiographical writing, here the painter is both guilt-ridden and self-exculpatory, caught uneasily between acknowledging his errors and blaming other people for forcing him into committing them. For Haydon, debt was much more than a practical problem. Not only did it lead to considerable pressures and embarrassments, but it also emphasized his alienation from acceptable society and therefore the improbability of reconciling genius and the public. Writing in 1843 of his stepson's attendance at 'a grand meeting of the Art Union distribution', he stated that 'I never go, because a Man who has not paid his debts in a Commercial Country, where faith with Creditor is the basis of moral Virtue, ought to be diffident in appearing'.[2]

Haydon's comparison between his lifestyle and the actions of Wellington and Napoleon may seem absurd but, even at the very end, he had little doubt that he was cut from the same cloth as the greatest figures of his time. Despite his vigorous nationalism, he had an obsessive interest in Napoleon and had painted twenty-three versions of *Napoleon Musing at St Helena*. He also hero-worshipped Wellington and, after attending Church with the Duke in 1839, had described him as 'the greatest hero of his age, who had conquered the greatest genius'.[3] This distinction between 'hero' and 'genius' is telling; Haydon believed himself to be both, but seems to have sensed that, towards the middle of the nineteenth century, the two categories might be in tension. Heroes follow the rules, pay their debts, prostrate themselves before God; geniuses recognize no laws beyond the necessity of their own self-assertion. If Haydon was caught between a civic humanist account of the public function of art, and a Romantic emphasis on the importance of individual genius in artistic creation, he was also caught between different conceptions of how greatness should conduct itself. On occasion, he behaved and wrote as if he believed that the true artist was and should be absolved from following social norms, but his final piece of writing suggested otherwise.

It is well known that Harold Skimpole, the amoral aesthete in *Bleak House* (1852–3), is partly based on Leigh Hunt, but Dickens also had Haydon in mind when creating this character – an artistic dilettante who selfishly refuses to abide by the rules and duties that govern the rest of society (including paying his debts and helping the unfortunate). We are told that after his death Skimpole 'left a diary behind him, with letters and other materials towards his Life; which was published, and which showed him to have been the victim of a combination on the part of mankind against an amiable child'.[4] Haydon also appears in Thackeray's novel *The Newcomes* (1853–5) as the comically self-promoting history painter Mr Gandish. Both these portrayals evince the Victorian challenge to the aestheticism, egotism and disdain for propriety that was associated (rightly or wrongly) with the Romantics. The story of the Victorian reaction to Romanticism is one of changing attitudes to art, genius and morality, and perhaps some simple generalizations about these attitudes are useful at this stage.[5] On the one hand, we might identify three claims as 'Romantic': (a) art and literature is principally a matter of self-expression, (b) great art and literature is often incomprehensible to normal people and (c) the behaviour of geniuses should not be judged by the same criteria as that of normal people. The 'Victorian' counter-claims are: (a) art and literature is principally a matter of the expression of shared experience, (b) great art and literature is, or should strive to be, comprehensible to normal people and (c) the possession of genius does not constitute an excuse for impropriety or immorality.

The reality, of course, was much more complicated than this simple opposition suggests. As we have seen, 'Romantic' arguments about the autonomy of genius were highly contested in the Romantic period itself, and were put under pressure by the combined forces of Evangelicalism and the professionalisation of literature. Furthermore, despite their distrust of the individualism that they associated with the literature of the early nineteenth century, genius was still an important concept for Victorian writers and readers. Great authors were supposed to work hard, submit to prevalent moral and social codes and communicate effectively with the public, but they were also expected to be original and, in some way, inspired. And there was also a strong counter-current of 'post-Romantic' writing throughout the nineteenth century that continued to emphasize the separation of genius and true art from normal society: this is evident in, for example, the work of the 'Spasmodic' poets, the Pre-Raphaelites and the proto-Modernist aesthetes of the 1890s. The influence of Thomas Carlyle and other sage figures reveals the continued desire of readers and critics to put their trust in cultural figures who seemed to stand above the worlds of politics and commerce, and who could offer spiritual solace at a time when the foundations of Christianity appeared to be crumbling. As is well known, Carlyle exalted the role of poets and men of letters as visionaries whose task was to communicate the spiritual nature of reality to humanity. However, it is significant that he strongly criticized the English Romantics; argued that good literature should be forceful, strong and sincere; used the word 'heroism' more often than 'genius' and preached the 'gospel of work'. It is also notable that the literary heroes in his early writings, such as Burns and Goethe, were later replaced, to a large degree, by strong men of action such as Cromwell and Frederick the Great – perhaps reflecting his doubts about the extent to which writers could affect society.

By the middle of the nineteenth century, the Romantic debate about the transgressive nature of genius had broadened out into the wider question of the role of the exceptional individual in an increasingly democratic society. For Carlyle, the great man is to be applauded for imposing his vision on the rest of humanity, regardless of their opinions or desires. His increasingly strident declamations on this topic contributed to the decline of his cultural authority after 1850. The most trenchant criticism of Carlylean hero-worship came from Russia, in Dostoevsky's *Crime and Punishment* (1866): its central character, Raskolnikov, is a murderous *reductio ad absurdum* of Carlyle's 'great man'. Unlike Carlyle, John Stuart Mill did not believe that the liberty of the many should be sacrificed to any individual, however brilliant or heroic, but *On Liberty* (1859) expressed his fears that individual genius was threatened by the development of a conformist, democratic society. Although he had been an early enthusiast for the positivist philosophy of Auguste Comte, Mill believed that the 'social system' put forward in Comte's *Systeme De Politique Positive* (1851–4) sought to establish 'a despotism of society over the individual'.[6] Mill was also dubious about the conclusions of one of Comte's disciples, Henry Thomas Buckle, who argued in his popular *History of Civilisation in England* (1857–61) that historical change was due to general causes rather than the influence of great men.[7]

The tension between genius and the public that came into being in the Romantic period also lay behind the arguments about 'degeneration' that reverberated around Europe towards the end of the nineteenth century.[8] Persistent anxieties about the transgressive nature of genius were given new power by its association with criminality in the writings of Lombroso and Nordau. At the same time, we find the development of a self-consciously 'degenerate' art and literature that predicated itself on a rejection of normal society. A key figure here is Nietzsche. In *Twilight of the Idols* (1889), he notes that 'the English have only two ways of accommodating the genius and the "great man": either *democratically*, after the manner of Buckle, or *religiously*, after the manner of Carlyle'.[9] Whereas for positivists, genius was produced by society, and for transcendentalists, it was produced by God, Nietzsche argued that it was produced by neither, thereby suggesting that it was entirely free of the conventional morality of 'the herd'. 'Evil' (assuming the term retained any meaning) would no longer be, as Haydon had claimed, 'the prerogative of the Deity' – and the painter's anxieties about the social transgression represented by debt should be compared with Nietzsche's assertion that 'the genius – in his works, in his deeds – is necessarily a squanderer: his greatness lies in his *expenditure*'. Genius is the result of an explosion of energy accumulated over a long period of time and therefore 'the relationship between a genius and his age is like that between strong and weak, or old and young'.[10] Nietzsche's ideas had a considerable influence on the self-consciously elitist anathematization of mass culture by the Modernist writers of the early twentieth century.[11]

We seem to have come a long way from Romantic literary magazines: but it was through them that, in Britain at least, genius first became widely discussed and represented. Although it was often imagined to be a force that transcended a 'debased' literary culture, arguments about genius, and biographical accounts of figures like Wordsworth, Shelley and Scott, played an important role in commercial and ideological conflicts within that culture. In fact, I would want to argue that Romantic genius was, to a large degree, *produced* by those conflicts. I hope that this book has also shown that early nineteenth-century writing contained a range of different claims about genius and that whereas some authors represented it as a conservative force, or located it in the realm of the purely aesthetic, others, such as Hazlitt, Hunt and even Bulwer, could argue that it was, or should be, on the side of the people against arbitrary power. Such arguments were possible because in the Romantic period the battle lines between genius and mass culture were still being drawn up.

Notes

Introduction

1 The two main sources for the idea of genius in the context of the history of aesthetics are M. H. Abrams, *The Mirror and the Lamp*, London: Oxford University Press, 1953 and James Engell, *The Creative Imagination*, Cambridge, MA: Harvard University Press, 1985. See also Jonathan Bate, *The Genius of Shakespeare*, London: Macmillan, 1997, chapter 6; Christine Battersby, *Gender and Genius*, London: The Women's Press, 1989; Herbert Dieckmann, 'Diderot's Conception of Genius', *Journal of the History of Ideas* 2, 1941, pp. 151–82; Bernhard Fabian, introduction to Alexander Gerard, *An Essay on Genius*, London: W. Strahan, 1774; repr. Munich: Wilhelm Fink, 1966; Penelope Murray (ed.) *Genius: The History of an Idea*, Oxford: Basil Blackwell, 1989; Giorgio Tonelli, 'Genius from the Renaissance to 1770' and Rudolf Wittkower, 'Genius: Individualism in Art and Artists', both in Philip P. Wiener (ed.) *The Dictionary of the History of Ideas*, New York: Charles Scribner's Sons, 1973, pp. 293–7, 297–312.

2 See Roy Pascal, *The German Sturm und Drang*, Manchester: Manchester University Press, 1953, pp. 233–99.

3 From Lavater's *Physiognomical Fragments*; quoted in Pascal, p. 138.

4 'Genius versus Capital: Eighteenth-Century Theories of Genius and Adam Smith's *Wealth of Nations*', *MLQ* 55, 1994, pp. 169–89 (p. 170).

5 For scientific genius in the Romantic period, see Jan Golinski, *Science as Public Culture: Chemistry and Enlightenment in Britain, 1760–1820*, Cambridge: Cambridge University Press, 1992, chapter 7; Trevor H. Levere, 'Humphry Davy, "The Sons of Genius", and the Idea of Glory', in Sophie Forgan (ed.) *Science and the Sons of Genius: Studies on Humphry Davy*, London: Science Reviews, 1980, pp. 33–58; Simon Schaffer, 'Genius in Romantic Natural Philosophy', in Andrew Cunningham and Nicholas Jardine (eds) *Romanticism and the Sciences*, Cambridge: Cambridge University Press, 1990, pp. 82–98. For 'political' genius, see especially Simon Bainbridge, *Napoleon and English Romanticism*, Cambridge: Cambridge University Press, 1995.

6 All, except Heraud, are discussed in Rosemary Ashton, *The German Idea: Four English Writers and the Reception of German Thought 1800–1860*, Cambridge: Cambridge University Press, 1980.

7 Engell, *Creative Imagination*, pp. 308–9.

8 Samuel Taylor Coleridge, *Biographia Literaria*, ed. James Engell and Walter Jackson Bate, 2 vols, vol. 1, p. 304, in *The Collected Works of Samuel Taylor Coleridge*, 7, ed. Kathleen Coburn, London: Routledge & Kegan Paul, 1983.

9 Engell, *Creative Imagination*, p. 342.

10 Leo Braudy, *The Frenzy of Renown: Fame and its History*, New York: Vintage, 1997, p. 13.

11 Ibid., p. 401.

12 Ibid., p. 425.

13 Raymond Williams, *Culture and Society*, London: The Hogarth Press, 1993, p. 36.

14 Pierre Bourdieu, 'Intellectual Field and Creative Project', trans. Sian France, in M. F. D. Young (ed.) *Knowledge and Control*, London: Collier-Macmillan, 1971, pp. 161–88 (p. 163).

15 This is more suggestive than Bourdieu's later claim that the idea of genius was purely a response to 'the pressures of an anonymous market' for literature, thereby reducing it to a species of false consciousness; see Pierre Bourdieu, *The Field of Cultural Production*, ed. Randal Johnson, Cambridge: Polity Press, 1993, p. 114.

16 Mark Rose, *Authors and Owners: The Invention of Copyright*, Cambridge, MA: Harvard University Press, 1993, chapter 7, and Martha Woodmansee, 'The Genius and the Copyright: Economic and Legal Conditions of the Emergence of the Author', *Eighteenth-Century Studies* 17, 1984, pp. 425–48.

17 Jerome J. McGann, *The Romantic Ideology: A Critical Investigation*, Chicago, IL: The University of Chicago Press, 1983, p. 13. In 1974, Robert Currie described genius as a pernicious 'ideology' which was 'used most often in reaction to the mass power mobilised through spread of education, growth of cities, capitalism, liberalism, constitutionalism and democracy'; *Genius: An Ideology in Literature*, London: Chatto & Windus, 1974, p. 10.

18 Robert Keith Lapp, *Contest for Cultural Authority: Hazlitt, Coleridge, and the Distresses of the Regency*, Detroit, MI: Wayne State University Press, 1999, p. 12.

19 Williams, *Culture and Society*, p. 47.

20 I do not mean to suggest here that there was a simple opposition between Romanticism and utilitarianism (or political economy). Philip Connell has shown, in an excellent monograph, that their relationship was highly complex and equivocal; see *Romanticism, Economics and the Question of 'Culture'*, Oxford: Oxford University Press, 2001.

21 For a brief account of the conservative reaction to the political implications of genius, see Andrew Elfenbein, *Romantic Genius: The Prehistory of a Homosexual Role*, New York: Columbia University Press, 1999, pp. 35–8.

22 Paul Bénichou, *The Consecration of the Writer, 1750–1830*, trans. Mark K. Jensen, Lincoln, NB: University of Nebraska Press, 1999.

23 Robert M. Ryan, *The Romantic Reformation: Religious Politics in English Literature, 1789–1824*, Cambridge: Cambridge University Press, 1997, p. 224.

24 For the Romantic poets as religious reformers see Stephen Prickett, *Romanticism and Religion: The Tradition of Wordsworth and Coleridge in the Victorian Church*, Cambridge: Cambridge University Press, 1976 and Ryan, *Romantic Reformation*.

25 Marlon B. Ross, *The Contours of Masculine Desire: Romanticism and the Rise of Women's Poetry*, New York: Oxford University Press, 1989. See also Sonia Hofkosh, *Sexual Politics and the Romantic Author*, Cambridge: Cambridge University Press, 1998.

26 For detailed accounts of the complex relationship between writing on genius and ideas about gender and sexuality, see Battersby, *Gender and Genius*, and Elfenbein, *Romantic Genius*.

27 Lee Erickson, *The Economy of Literary Form: English Literature and the Industrialization of Publishing, 1800–1850*, Baltimore, MD: The Johns Hopkins University Press, 1996, chapter 3.

28 Mark Parker, *Literary Magazines and British Romanticism*, Cambridge: Cambridge University Press, 2000.

29 Ibid., p. 3.

30 David S. Hogsette, 'Coleridge as Victorian Heirloom: Nostalgic Rhetoric in the Early Victorian Reviews of *Poetical Works*', *Studies in Romanticism* 37, 1998, pp. 63–75 (p. 63).

31 Ibid., p. 67. I would add that Coleridge was not always represented as a 'secular' figure.

32 Jon P. Klancher, *The Making of English Reading Audiences, 1790–1832*, Madison, WI: The University of Wisconsin Press, 1987, p. 51.

33 Ibid., pp. 51–60.

34 Ibid., pp. 52–73.

35 See Lee Erickson, *The Economy of Literary Form*, pp. 26–9.

36 Ashley J. Cross, 'From Lyrical Ballads to Lyrical Tales: Mary Robinson's Reputation and the Problem of Literary Debt', *Studies in Romanticism* 40, 2001, pp. 571–605 (p. 572).

37 An important recent work on the fraught relationship between Romantic poetry and periodical writing is Lucy Newlyn's *Reading, Writing, and Romanticism: The Anxiety of Reception*, Oxford: Oxford University Press, 2000.

38 David E. Latané, 'The Birth of the Author in the Victorian Archive', *VPR* 22, 1989, pp. 109–17. Klancher also emphasizes the 'transauthorial' discourse produced by periodicals; see *The Making of English Reading Audiences*, p. 52.

39 I should add that, despite my caveats, Latané's discussion of writing on genius in the late Romantic periodical press in relation to modern attempts to deconstruct the idea of authorship is extremely acute and suggestive.

40 For a good account of this view, see Tia DeNora and Hugh Mehan, 'Genius: A Social Construction: the Case of Beethoven's Initial Recognition', in Theodore R. Sarbin and John I. Kitsuse (eds) *Constructing the Social*, London: Sage Publications, 1994, pp. 157–73. See also DeNora's excellent study *Beethoven and the Construction of Genius*, Berkeley, CA: University of California Press, 1995, and Michael Howe's *Genius Explained*, Cambridge: Cambridge University Press, 1999, although Howe takes a much less rigorous constructivist perspective than DeNora and Mehan.

41 See Andrew Bennett, *Romantic Poets and the Culture of Posterity*, Cambridge: Cambridge University Press, 1999, especially chapter 2.

42 Pierre Bourdieu, *The Field of Cultural Production*, and *The Rules of Art*, trans. Susan Emanuel, Cambridge: Polity Press, 1992.

43 Bourdieu, *Rules of Art*, p. 190.

44 Toril Moi also makes this point, and notes that Bourdieu 'mobilized a huge team of researchers' for his analysis of Flaubert's *L'Education sentimentale*; see 'The Challenge of the Particular Case: Bourdieu's Sociology of Culture and Literary Criticism', *MLQ* 58, 1997, pp. 497–508 (p. 505).

1 Literary genius, transgression and society in the early nineteenth century

1 Isaac D'Israeli, *An Essay on the Manners and Genius of the Literary Character*, London: Cadell and Davies, 1795, p. vii.

2 Ibid., p. xv. For a detailed discussion of D'Israeli's response to the commercialization of literature, see Philip Connell, 'Bibliomania: Book Collecting, Cultural Politics, and the Rise of Literary Heritage in Romantic Britain', *Representations* 71, 2000, pp. 24–47 (pp. 33–43).

3 As James Ogden has noted, although D'Israeli uses 'genius' to mean 'characteristic disposition' in the book's title, in the text it is frequently used to mean 'native intellectual power of an exalted type'; *Isaac D'Israeli*, Oxford: Clarendon Press, 1969, p. 34. In later editions the title was changed to *The Literary Character, Illustrated by the History of Men of Genius, Drawn from their own Feelings and Confessions*.

4 Examples of this genre include the anonymous 'On the Neglect of Genius', *Imperial Magazine*, October 1821, pp. 938–46; W. H. Ireland, *Neglected Genius*, London: George Cowie, 1812; Isaac D'Israeli, *Calamities of Authors*, 2 vols, London: John Murray, 1812; 'Sylvaticus' [J. F. Pennie], *The Tale of a Modern Genius; or, The Miseries of Parnassus*, 3 vols, London: J. Andrews, 1827.

5 D'Israeli, *Literary Character*, p. 113.

6 Samuel Taylor Coleridge, *Biographia Literaria*, ed. James Engell and Walter Jackson Bate, 2 vols, vol. 1, pp. 30–47, in *The Collected Works of Samuel Taylor Coleridge*, 7, ed. Kathleen Coburn, London: Routledge & Kegan Paul, 1983. For an interesting discussion of genius and literary production in the *Biographia*, see John Whale, *Imagination under Pressure, 1789–1832*, Cambridge: Cambridge University Press, 2000, pp. 172–6.

7 Coleridge, *Biographia*, vol. 1, pp. 31–3.

8 Coleridge, *Biographia*, vol. 1, pp. 38–41.

9 Ibid., p. 224.

10 General scholarly accounts of the *Edinburgh* and the *Quarterly* include Marilyn Butler, 'Culture's Medium: the Role of the Review', in Stuart Curran (ed.) *The Cambridge Companion to British Romanticism*, Cambridge: Cambridge University Press, 1993, pp. 120–47; John O. Hayden, *The Romantic Reviewers 1802–1824*, London: Routledge & Kegan Paul, 1969, chapter 1; Joanne Shattock, *Politics and Reviewers: The 'Edinburgh' and the 'Quarterly' in the Early Victorian Age*, London: Leicester University Press, 1989. For the *Edinburgh* in particular, see John Clive, *Scotch Reviewers: The 'Edinburgh Review', 1802–1815*, London: Faber & Faber, 1957; Massimiliano Demata and Duncan Wu (eds) *British Romanticism and the Edinburgh Review: Bicentenary Essays*, Basingstoke: Palgrave, 2002; Ina Ferris, *The Achievement of Literary Authority*, Ithaca, NY: Cornell University Press, 1991, especially pp. 19–32; Biancamaria Fontana, *Rethinking the Politics of Commercial Society: The 'Edinburgh Review' 1802–1832*, Cambridge: Cambridge University Press, 1985; Dickie A. Spurgeon, 'The Edinburgh Review', in *BLM*, pp. 139–44. The *Quarterly* has been less well served by modern scholars and at the time of writing (July 2004), Jonathan Cutmore's excellent website *The Quarterly Review Project* does not seem to be available online. See, however, Hill Shine and Helen Shine, *The Quarterly Review Under Gifford*, Chapel Hill, NC: The University of North Carolina Press, 1949, and Roger P. Wallins, 'The Quarterly Review', in *BLM*, pp. 359–67.

11 For Jeffrey's critical principles, see Peter F. Morgan, *Literary Critics and Reviewers in Early Nineteenth-Century Britain*, London: Croom Helm, 1983, chapter 1.

12 Butler, 'Culture's Medium', p. 141.

13 The *Quarterly* generally praised Byron, partly because they shared publishers until almost the very end of his career. But in his positive review of Byron's 'Dramas', the churchman Reginald Heber strongly criticised *Don Juan* in passing, lamenting that in the past Byron's readers had witnessed 'the systematic and increasing prostitution of those splendid talents to the expression of feelings, and the promulgation of opinions, which, as Christians, as Englishmen, and even as men, we were constrained to regard with abhorrence'. See *QR*, July 1822, p. 476.

14 *'Reliques of Burns'*, *ER*, January 1809, p. 255.

15 Ibid., p. 252.

16 Ibid., p. 253.

17 Ibid., p. 254.

18 'The Vision', in *The Poems and Songs of Robert Burns*, ed. James Kinsley, 3 vols, Oxford: Clarendon Press, 1968, vol. 1, p. 162. There are a number of Romantic-period discussions of Burns and the 'irregularities' of genius reprinted in *Robert Burns: The Critical Heritage*, ed. Donald A. Low, London: Routledge & Kegan Paul, 1974. For a suggestive account of Burns's posthumous reputation, see Nicholas Roe, 'Authenticating Robert Burns', in Robert Crawford (ed.) *Robert Burns and Cultural Authority*, Edinburgh: Polygon, 1999, pp. 159–79.

19 See his review of Southey's *Thalaba*, *ER*, October 1802, p. 419.

20 The effect of *Die Räuber* on German students is also mentioned in the *Anti-Jacobin's* parody of German drama, *The Rovers*, published in June 1798; see Graeme Stones and John Strachan (eds) *Parodies of the Romantic Age*, 5 vols, London: Pickering and Chatto, 1998, vol. 1, ed. Graeme Stones, p. 220.

21 Perhaps responding to Coleridge, D'Israeli gave a classic formulation of this view in the 1818 edition of the *Literary Character*, in a chapter entitled 'On the Irritability of Genius'.

22 Lee Erickson, *The Economy of Literary Form*, Baltimore, MD: The Johns Hopkins University Press, 1996, pp. 47–8.

23 See Walter Jackson Bate, *John Keats*, Cambridge, MA: Harvard University Press, 1963, pp. 608–9. It is interesting to note that around this time both Coleridge and De Quincey were driven by financial need to become writers for *Blackwood's*; see Robert Morrison, 'Opium-Eaters and Magazine Wars: De Quincey and Coleridge in 1821', *VPR* 30, 1997, pp. 27–40 (p. 29).

24 For the founding of *Blackwood's*, see Margaret Oliphant, *Annals of a Publishing House: William Blackwood and his Sons*, 3 vols, Edinburgh: William Blackwood, 1899, vol. 1, chapters 1 to 3.

25 Wilson claimed that the October 1817 issue sold 10,000 copies, and that in 1820 the magazine was selling at 'SOMEWHERE BELOW 17000!' Clearly these figures need to be treated with circumspection; see 'An Hour's Tete-a-Tete [*sic*] with the Public', *BEM*, October 1820, pp. 80–1.

26 'Baron von Lauerwinkel' [John Gibson Lockhart], 'Remarks on the Periodical Criticism of England', *BEM*, March 1818, p. 671.

27 Ibid., pp. 673–4.

28 Ibid., pp. 677–9.

29 See Andrew Bennett, *Romantic Poets and the Culture of Posterity*, Cambridge: Cambridge University Press, 1999.

30 I agree with J. H. Alexander that *Blackwood's* often used to Jeffrey to 'epitomise all that they were reacting against', but they also pitched themselves against the *Quarterly* and, indeed, contemporary literary culture as a whole. Alexander's article, '*Blackwood's*: Magazine as Romantic Form', has been very helpful in stimulating my ideas about the journal; *Wordsworth Circle* 15, 1984, pp. 57–68.

31 [William Maginn and possibly John Wilson], 'Preface', *BEM*, 1826, pp. xxii–xxiii. Wilson makes similar claims in 'An Hour's Tete-a-Tete [*sic*] with the Public', p. 93.

32 'Z.' [John Gibson Lockhart], 'On Cockney School of Poetry No. IV' and 'An Old Friend with a New Face' [Lockhart], 'Hazlitt Cross-Questioned', both in *BEM*, August 1818, pp. 524, 550–2.

33 Robert Morrison, ' "Abuse Wickedness, but Acknowledge Wit": *Blackwood's* and the Shelley Circle', *VPR* 34, 2001, pp. 147–64 (p. 149). Some time after writing this chapter, I came across Kim Wheatley's discussion of the *Blackwood's* reviews of Shelley in *Shelley and his Readers: Beyond Paranoid Politics*, Columbia, MO: University of Missouri Press, 1999. Wheatley also focuses on the aestheticising rhetoric of these articles and contrasts it interestingly with the 'paranoid style' of much early nineteenth-century reviewing.

34 [Lockhart, De Quincey and possibly Wilson], 'Observations on *The Revolt of Islam*', *BEM*, January 1819, pp. 475–6. Strout originally attributed the Shelley reviews to John Wilson: see '*Maga*, Champion of Shelley', *Studies in Philology* 29, 1932, pp. 95–119. Later he found good evidence for Lockhart's authorship: see 'Lockhart, Champion of Shelley', *Times Literary Supplement*, 12 August 1955, p. 468. However, Robert Morrison has argued that 'credit for the review [of *The Revolt of Islam*] belongs primarily to De Quincey': see 'De Quincey, Champion of Shelley', *Keats–Shelley Journal* 41, 1992, pp. 36–41 (p. 41).

35 [Lockhart, De Quincey and possibly Wilson], 'Observations', p. 476.

36 Morrison, '*Blackwood's* and the Shelley Circle', p. 154.

37 [John Wilson], 'On Literary Censorship', *BEM*, November 1818, p. 176.

38 Ibid., p. 177.

39 [John Wilson], 'On the Analogy Between the Growth of Individual and National Genius', *BEM*, January 1820, p. 379.

40 Ibid., p. 380.

41 [John Gibson Lockhart], 'Rosalind and Helen, a Modern Ecologue', *BEM*, June 1819, p. 274.

42 [John Taylor Coleridge], 'Shelley's *Revolt of Islam*', *QR*, April 1819, p. 471. Coleridge knew Shelley at Eton.

43 [Lockhart], 'Rosalind and Helen', p. 273.

44 [John Gibson Lockhart], '*Alastor; or, the Spirit of Solitude*', *BEM*, November 1819, p. 153.

45 Ibid., p. 154.

46 Terry Eagleton, *The Function of Criticism: From 'The Spectator' to Post-Structuralism*, London: Verso, 1984, p. 38.

47 William Hazlitt, 'On the Qualifications Necessary for Success in Life', *CWH*, vol. 12, p. 208. First published in the *LM* in June 1820.

48 *BEM*, September 1820, pp. 686–7.

49 See especially Jeffrey N. Cox, *Poetry and Politics in the Cockney School*, Cambridge: Cambridge University Press, 1998, chapter 1.

50 [Lockhart, De Quincey and possibly Wilson], 'Observations', p. 482.

51 Letter to Charles Ollier, December 15 [or 25], 1819 in *CWS*, vol. 10, p. 134.

52 'Portraits of the Metropolitan Poets, No. III, Mr Percy Bysshe Shelley', *The Honeycomb*, 12 August 1820, pp. 65–72; quoted in Percy Bysshe Shelley, *Poems and Prose*, ed. Timothy Webb, London: J. M. Dent, 1995, p. 496.

53 'Percy Bysshe Shelley, Charles Ollier, and William Blackwood: The Contexts of Early Nineteenth-Century Publishing', in Kelvin Everest (ed.) *Shelley Revalued: Essays from the Gregynog Conference*, Leicester: Leicester University Press, 1983, pp. 183–226 (p. 198).

54 [John Gibson Lockhart], 'Sir Egerton Brydges's Recollections', *BEM*, May 1825, p. 506. Lockhart's complaint about the 'prostitution' of genius was not a new one: see 'No Genius', letter to Mr Urban, *Gentleman's Magazine*, March 1799, pp. 199–200.

55 [John Wilson], 'Noctes Ambrosianae No. XLII', *BEM*, April 1829, p. 536.

56 Ibid., p. 537.

57 For 'domestic ideology', see Leonore Davidoff and Catherine Hall, *Family Fortunes: Men and Women of the English Middle Class, 1780–1850*, London: Routledge, 1992, especially chapter 3.

58 Hofland's follow-up novel, *The Daughter of a Genius*, which also went through many editions, was first published in 1823.

59 Barbara Hofland, *The Son of a Genius: A Tale for the Use of Youth*, London: J. Harris, 1812, p. 88.

60 Ibid., pp. 4–5.

61 A similar Evangelically tinged suspicion of the claims of genius can be found in Jane Austen's unfinished novel, *Sanditon* (written in 1817), where the foolish would-be seducer Sir Edward Denham states, in the course of a discussion of Burns, that 'it were Pseudo-philosophy to expect from the soul of high toned Genius, the grovellings of a common mind. – The Coruscations of Talent, elicited by impassioned feeling in the breast of Man, are perhaps incompatible with some of the prosaic Decencies of Life'. See *The Works of Jane Austen*, ed. R. W. Chapman, 6 vols, London: Oxford University Press, 1923–54, vol. 6, p. 398.

62 Hofland, *Son of a Genius*, p. 62.

63 Ibid., pp. 5–6.

64 'Preface', *SMA*, vol. 1, p. vi.

65 Samuel Carter Hall, *Retrospect of a Long Life: From 1815 to 1883*, 2 vols, London: Richard Bentley, 1883, vol. 1, p. 314. Hall probably edited *SMA* from 1826 to 1828, although this is not clear from his account. There is a short account of the *British Magazine* by Lance Schacterle in *BLM*, pp. 66–8. Schacterle mentions *SMA* in passing – this is the only reference to the periodical that I have found in modern criticism.

66 'Sketches of Biography and Character No. I: Sheridan', *SMA*, 21 January 1826, p. 39.

67 'N.', 'Sketches of Biography and Character No. V: Robert Burns', *SMA*, 20 May 1826, pp. 317–18.

68 *SMA*, 17 June 1826, p. 372.

69 'Lord Byron and his Writings', *SMA*, 24 June 1826, p. 384.

70 Ibid., p. 390.

71 'Literary Men often the Patrons and Apologists of Vice', *SMA*, 21 October 1826, pp. 241–2.

72 Ibid., p. 241.

73 Ibid., p. 242. Burns's argument is also criticised as 'a gross impiety' in the Preface to the third volume of *SMA*.

74 Ibid., p. 243.

75 Eagleton, *Function of Criticism*, p. 37. For more helpful assessments of the periodical, see Miriam J. Thrall's *Rebellious Fraser's*, New York: Columbia University Press, 1934 and J. Van Dann, 'Fraser's Magazine', in *BLM*, pp. 171–5.

76 See, for example, [William Maginn], 'L'Envoy', *FM*, January 1831, p. 745. Although *Fraser's* tended to represent itself as conducting a lonely campaign against puffing, the *Athenaeum's* campaign started earlier, and was conducted with more fairness and rigour; see Leslie A. Marchand, *The Athenaeum: A Mirror of Victorian Culture*, New York: Octagon Books, 1971, chapter 2.

77 For an acute analysis of the journal's treatment of the novel in general and Bulwer's work in particular, see Rebecca Edwards Newman, ' "Prosecuting the Onus Criminus": Early Criticism of the Novel in *Fraser's Magazine*', *VPR* 35, 2002, pp. 401–19.

78 [William Maginn, perhaps with John Abraham Heraud], 'Fashionable Novels', *FM*, April 1830, p. 321.

79 'Ned Culpepper, the Tomahawk' [William Maginn, perhaps with John Abraham Heraud], 'Mr Edward Lytton Bulwer's Novels; and Remarks on Novel-Writing', *FM*, June 1830, p. 512.

80 Ibid., p. 514.

81 There is still very little work on the literary culture of the 1830s; one good modern account is Kathryn Chittick's *Dickens and the 1830s*, Cambridge: Cambridge University Press, 1990, especially chapter 2. For an examination of some of the ways in which writers of this period assimilated the work of their Romantic forebears, see Richard Cronin, *Romantic Victorians: English Literature, 1824–1840*, Basingstoke: Palgrave, 2002.

82 See H. B. de Groot, 'The Status of the Poet in an Age of Brass: Isaac D'Israeli, Peacock, W. J. Fox and Others', *Victorian Periodicals Newsletter* 10, 1977, pp. 106–29 and Andrew Hemingway, 'Genius, Gender and Progress: Benthamism and the Arts in the 1820s', *Art History* 16, 1992, pp. 619–46.

83 Nigel Cross, *The Common Writer*, Cambridge: Cambridge University Press, 1985, pp. 90–1.

84 Patrick Leary, '*Fraser's Magazine* and the Literary Life, 1830–1847', *VPR* 27, 1994, pp. 105–26 (p. 106).

85 Ibid.

86 [Thomas Carlyle], 'Count Cagliostro: in Two Flights. Flight First', *FM*, July 1833, p. 25. Reprinted in *WTC*, vol. 28, p. 264.

87 Lord George Gordon Byron and Thomas Moore, *The Works of Lord Byron: With his Letters and Journals and his Life*, 17 vols, London: John Murray, 1833, vol. 3, pp. 125–36.

88 *The Infirmities of Genius*, 2 vols, London: Saunders & Otley, 1833, vol. 1, pp. 157–9. For later scientific debates about genius, see George Becker, *The Mad Genius Controversy*, Beverly Hills: Sage Publications, 1978.

89 [Christian Johnstone], 'The Infirmities of Genius Illustrated', *TEM*, October 1833, p. 49.

90 There is a detailed discussion of Moore's account of Byron as genius in Joseph Reed, *English Biography in the Early Nineteenth Century: 1801–1838*, New Haven, CT: Yale University Press, 1966, chapter 6. For a good account of Byronism in the 1830s, see Andrew Elfenbein, *Byron and the Victorians*, Cambridge: Cambridge University Press, 1995, chapter 2.

91 [John Abraham Heraud], 'On Poetic Genius, Considered as a Creative Power', *FM*, February 1830, p. 57.

92 Thrall notes that Heraud's view that genius had innate qualities that led it to a certain vocation is the opposite of Carlyle's theory of genius, in which the path that a great man takes depends on the demands of his age rather than his particular bent. She also shows that by December 1834, Heraud was voicing Carlyle's theory; see *Rebellious Fraser's*, pp. 88–91, 264.

93 [John Abraham Heraud], 'The Last of the Supernaturalists', *FM*, March 1830, p. 217.

94 The claim that great poets are necessarily virtuous is made most powerfully by Shelley in the *Defence of Poetry* (*CWS*, vol. 7, p. 118). But it is also strongly implied in Wordsworth's Preface to *Lyrical Ballads* (*PWW*, vol. 1, p. 138), and, as we have seen, in Coleridge's *Biographia Literaria*. In a letter to John Scott written in 1816, Wordsworth claimed that 'all men of *first* rate genius have been as distinguished for dignity, beauty, and propriety of moral conduct': see William Wordsworth and Dorothy Wordsworth, *The Letters*

of William and Dorothy Wordsworth, ed. Ernest de Selincourt, 2nd edn, rev. Mary Moorman and Alan G. Hill, 8 vols, Oxford: Clarendon Press, 1967–93, vol. 3, p. 322.

95 John Abraham Heraud, *Substance of a Lecture on Poetic Genius as a Moral Power*, London: James Fraser, 1837, p. 36.

96 Ibid., p. 44.

97 [John Abraham Heraud and William Maginn], 'Galt's Life of Byron', *FM*, October 1830, pp. 347–70. Assuming that Thrall is right about the authors of this article, I suspect that Maginn wrote the first three pages of the review, but am fairly certain that the passages on Byron's genius are by Heraud.

98 Ibid., pp. 367–8.

99 Ibid., p. 370.

100 See Samuel Chew, *Byron in England*, London: John Murray, 1924, chapter 12.

101 David S. Hogsette has argued that early Victorian critics represented Coleridge 'as a poetic and intellectual saint around whom a stable cultural history could be established'; 'Coleridge as Victorian Heirloom: Nostalgic Rhetoric in the Early Victorian Reviews of *Poetical Works*', *Studies in Romanticism* 37, 1998, pp. 63–75 (p. 63). However, as Robert Lapp has shown, Coleridge was a much more equivocal figure than Hogsette suggests, for in *Fraser's* he was also depicted as an anarchic *bon-vivant*; 'Romanticism Repackaged: The New Faces of "Old Man" Coleridge in *Fraser's Magazine*, 1830–35', *European Romantic Review* 11, 2000, pp. 235–47. I would suggest that Hogsette's description is much more applicable to representations of the notoriously clean-living Wordsworth than to those of his fellow Lake Poet.

102 [John Abraham Heraud], 'Wordsworth's *Poetical Works*', *FM*, November 1832, p. 619.

103 [Probably John Abraham Heraud], 'Wordsworth's New Volume of Poetry', *FM*, June 1835, p. 702.

104 Brydges seems to have been forced into periodical writing in old age due to the legal expenses incurred by his failed attempts to prove that he had a legitimate claim to the baronetcy of Chandos; see Leary, '*Fraser's Magazine* and the Literary Life', p. 117.

105 Sir Samuel Egerton Brydges, 'On Intellectual Endowments', *FM*, September 1833, p. 291. Further references to this article are in the text.

106 See John Barrell, *English Literature in History 1730–80: An Equal, Wide Survey*, London: Hutchinson, 1983, introduction.

107 Brydges would not have read *A Defence of Poetry*, which was not published until 1840.

108 Sir Samuel Egerton Brydges, 'On the Charge that Men of Genius and High Talents want Judgment and Practical Sense', *FM*, June 1836, p. 674. Further references to this article are in the text.

109 Sir Samuel Egerton Brydges, 'An Essay on Originality of Mind, Illustrated by a Few Notices of Those Eminent Men who have been Distinguished by it, Especially Poets', *FM*, May 1837, p. 583.

110 Ibid., p. 584.

111 In 1825 Brydges published a defence of Byron in which he argued that the poet's genius acted as 'a magical antidote' to his 'strange propensities to evil'; see *An Impartial Portrait of Lord Byron, as a Poet and a Man*, Paris: Galignani, 1825, p. 17.

112 [William Maginn], 'Gallery of Illustrious Literary Characters XLV: Sir Egerton Brydges', *FM*, February 1834, p. 146. This is a notably generous account of Brydges in a series that is sometimes waspish about its subjects.

113 For example, 'On Intellectual Endowments', *FM*, September 1833, p. 297.

114 [Edward Lytton Bulwer], 'Sir Egerton Brydges's *Autobiography*', *ER*, July 1834, p. 439.

115 Ibid., p. 144.

116 It is noteworthy that in his novel *Paul Clifford* (1830), Bulwer takes issue in two lengthy footnotes with Thomas Moore's account of the 'poetical character' in his *Life of Byron*. Bulwer argues that Byron's errors and eccentricities were due to his character and lifestyle and had nothing to do with the fact that he was a poet. See *Paul Clifford*, London: George Routledge, 1896, pp. 163–5, 242–3.

117 In particular, see his articles 'Literature Considered as a Profession', *NMM*, 1831, pp. 227–32, 'Aristocracy', *NMM*, August 1832, p. 167 and 'Proposals for a Literary Union', *NMM*, November 1832, pp. 418–21. For the nineteenth-century controversy about the gentlemanly status of authors, see K. J. Fielding, 'Thackeray and the "Dignity of Literature"', *TLS*, 19 September 1958, p. 536 and 26 September 1958, p. 552; T. W. Heyck, *The Transformation of Intellectual Life in Victorian England*, London: Croom Helm, 1982, chapter 2; Michael Lund, *Reading Thackeray*, Detroit, MI: Wayne State University Press, 1988, chapter 3.

118 Edward Lytton Bulwer, *England and the English*, 2 vols, London: Richard Bentley, 1833, vol. 1, p. 148.

119 [Bulwer], 'Sir Egerton Brydges's *Autobiography*', p. 445.

120 Ibid.

121 I am not, of course, suggesting that the Reform Act of 1832 created a 'popular' parliamentary government. But to conservatives like Brydges it seemed like the beginning of a slippery slope towards democracy, whereas enthusiastic reformers like Bulwer believed it to be the start of a new epoch in which government would be carried out for the benefit of the entire nation rather than a small aristocratic minority.

122 Sir Samuel Egerton Brydges, 'Sir Egerton Brydges' Reply to the "Edinburgh Review"', *FM*, December 1834, pp. 729–30.

123 Isaac D'Israeli, *The Literary Character, Illustrated by the History of Men of Genius*, London: John Murray, 1822, p. 10.

124 *WTC*, vol. 27, pp. 69–70.

125 *WTC*, vol. 28, p. 24.

126 The classic account of the *MR* is Francis E. Mineka's *The Dissidence of Dissent*, New York: Octagon Books, 1972. As Jason Evan Camlot has pointed out, Mill chose to write for the journal because he felt that it was exceptional in the periodical marketplace in that its readers did not read it for 'amusement' and had 'open improvable minds'; see 'Character of the Periodical Press: John Stuart Mill and Junius Redivivus', *VPR* 32, 1999, pp. 166–76 (p. 170).

127 *Victorian Poetry: Poetry, Poetics and Politics*, London: Routledge, 1993, p. 29.

128 'The True Spirit of Reform', *MR*, January 1835, p. 8.

129 'Some Considerations Respecting the Comparative Influences of Ancient and Modern Times on the Development of Genius', *MR*, August 1832, p. 556.

130 Ibid., p. 563.

131 Ibid., p. 564. See also the same writer's 'On the Intellectual Influences of Christianity', *MR*, September 1832, pp. 627–34. The claim that the progress of science and that of poetry went hand in hand was also made by Fox in 1831; see 'Tennyson's *Poems*', *Westminster Review*, January 1831, pp. 210–22.

132 'Antiquus.' [John Stuart Mill], 'On Genius', in the *Collected Works of John Stuart Mill*, ed. John M. Robson, 33 vols, Toronto: University of Toronto Press, 1981–91, vol. 1, ed. John M. Robson and Jack Stillinger, pp. 334–5. First published in the *MR*, October 1832.

133 [Mill], *Collected Works*, vol. 1, p. 334.

134 [John Stuart Mill], 'Writings of Junius Redivivus', in *Collected Works*, vol. 1, p. 370. First published in the *MR*, April 1833.

135 For a more detailed discussion of Mill's essays on 'Junius Redivivus' 'as documents expressing a liberal conception of effective authorship' (p. 166), see Camlot, 'Character of the Periodical Press'.

136 Mill, *Collected Works*, vol. 1, p. 373.

137 Allan Cunningham, *Biographical and Critical History of the British Literature of the Last Fifty Years*, Paris: Baudry's Foreign Library, 1834, p. 325. This was first published a series of articles in the *Athenaeum* in 1833.

138 [William Maginn?], 'Allan Cunningham's *Fifty Years*', *FM*, February 1834, p. 240.

139 Unfortunately, neither Thrall's *Rebellious Fraser's* nor the *Wellesley Index* give an author for this important essay. Maginn's editorship had ended in 1836 under the pressures of debt,

estrangement from his wife, and the savage beating of James Fraser by the aggrieved novelist Grantley Berkeley (which led to a duel between him and Maginn), although he still occasionally contributed to the magazine. Heraud does not seem to have contributed anything after volume sixteen, the volume before this article appeared. Francis Mahony ('Father Prout') had taken over the editorship for a short time after Maginn's departure, but there is no information as to who edited the periodical from 1838 to 1842. The article's continual sniping at Bulwer makes it probable that it was by one of these three *Fraser's* 'old boys', and the use of 'Cockney School' rhetoric, particularly the claim that Keats died of 'weakness, probably consequent on thin potations', seems to make Maginn's authorship the more likely, although it could well have been a joint effort. Thackeray was contributing to the magazine at this time and it is also possible that he may have had something to do with the article. Its sentiments on genius are similar to those he expresses in *Pendennis* (see below).

140 Horne was to return to the subject of genius ten years later in *A New Spirit of the Age* (1844).
141 Ann Blainey, *The Farthing Poet*, London: Longman, 1968, chapter 2.
142 [Richard Henry Horne], *Exposition of the False Medium and Barriers Excluding Men of Genius from the Public*, London: Effingham Wilson, 1833, p. 117.
143 Ibid., pp. 118–19.
144 [William Maginn?], 'Genius and the Public', *FM*, October 1838, p. 383.
145 Ibid., pp. 383–4.
146 [Horne], *Exposition*, pp. 127–30.
147 Quoted in Leary, '*Fraser's Magazine* and the Literary Life', p. 118.
148 Ibid., p. 114.
149 The best account I have read of the controversy caused by *Pendennis*, and Thackeray's response, is in Lund, *Reading Thackeray*, chapter 3.
150 William Makepeace Thackeray, *The History of Pendennis*, ed. John Sutherland, Oxford: Oxford University Press, 1999, p. 415.
151 Ibid., p. 450.
152 Gordon N. Ray, *Thackeray: The Age of Wisdom: 1847–1863*, London: Oxford University Press, 1958, p. 137.
153 Heyck, *Transformation of Intellectual Life*, p. 30.
154 'A Most Talented Family', *FM*, August 1836, p. 164.
155 'A Most Talented Family', *FM*, July 1836, p. 104.
156 Ibid.

2 Literary biography and its discontents

1 Samuel Taylor Coleridge, 'On The Errors of Party Spirit: or Extremes Meet', *The Friend*, ed. Barbara E. Rooke, 2 vols, vol. 2, p. 138, in *The Collected Works of Samuel Taylor Coleridge*, 4, ed. Kathleen Coburn, London: Routledge & Kegan Paul, 1969.
2 'A Prefatory Observation on Modern Biography', *The Friend*, ed. Rooke, vol. 2, pp. 286–7, in *The Collected Works of Samuel Taylor Coleridge*, 4.
3 For the importance of the home and family at this time, see Clara Tuite, 'Domesticity', in Iain McCalman (ed.) *An Oxford Companion to the Romantic Age*, Oxford: Oxford University Press, 1999, pp. 125–33.
4 While in the final stages of editing this book, I came across Julian North's excellent essay 'Self-Possession and Gender in Romantic Literary Biography', in Arthur Bradley and Alan Rawes (eds) *Romantic Biography*, Aldershot: Ashgate, 2003. North shows that Wordsworth and Coleridge perceive literary biography as a feminine form which threatens the masculine self-possession of the poet, and that this conception of genius is indeed challenged by biographers like Thomas De Quincey and Marguerite Blessington.
5 'A Letter to a Friend of Robert Burns', in *PWW*, vol. 3, p. 119. All further references are within the text.

6 Thomas Carlyle, 'Burns', in *WTC*, vol. 26, p. 291.

7 *WTC*, vol. 27, p. 101.

8 *WTC*, vol. 26, p. 264.

9 Ibid., p. 266.

10 Ibid., p. 291.

11 Carlyle makes a similar claim in a long passage in 'Jean Paul Friedrich Richter'; *WTC*, vol. 27, pp. 100–1.

12 *WTC*, vol. 26, p. 316.

13 *WTC*, vol. 5, p. 157.

14 F. R. Hart, *Lockhart as Romantic Biographer*, Edinburgh: Edinburgh University Press, 1971, chapter 3.

15 *CWH*, vol. 16, p. 153.

16 Ibid., pp. 153–4.

17 *The Yale Edition of the Complete Works of Samuel Johnson*, 16 vols, New Haven, CT: Yale University Press, 1969–89, vol. 3, ed. W. J. Bate and Albrecht B. Strauss, p. 74.

18 *CWH*, vol. 16, p. 153.

19 Quoted in Grevel Lindop, *The Opium-Eater: A Life of Thomas De Quincey*, Oxford: Oxford University Press, 1985, pp. 315–16.

20 Wordsworthian arguments against literary biography remained viable for at least twenty years after his remarks on Burns: for example, William Empson, in his 1838 review of Prior's *Life of Goldsmith*, argued that knowing the sordid reality of the author's life destroyed the pleasure one could find in the ideal world of his texts; 'Prior's *Life of Goldsmith*', *ER*, April 1837, p. 210.

21 *WDQ*, vol. 11, p. 61.

22 Ibid.

23 Ibid., p. 62.

24 *CWH*, vol. 17, pp. 109–13.

25 For 'inspiration' in nineteenth-century literature, see Timothy Clark, *The Theory of Inspiration*, Manchester: Manchester University Press, 1997.

26 Isaac D'Israeli, *The Literary Character, Illustrated by the History of Men of Genius, Drawn from their own Feelings and Confessions*, London: John Murray, 1818, p. 287.

27 Ibid., p. 291.

28 Ibid., p. 292.

29 Similar claims were made by John Wilson in an article apparently influenced by D'Israeli: 'On the Influence of the Love of Fame on Genius', *BEM*, September 1818, p. 703.

30 'Sir Walter Scott', in *WTC*, vol. 29, p. 26.

31 [John Scott], 'Blackwood's Magazine', *LM*, November 1820, pp. 509–21; 'The Mohock Magazine', *LM*, December 1820, pp. 666–85; 'The Mohocks', *LM*, January 1821, pp. 76–7.

32 See Patrick O'Leary, *Regency Editor: The Life of John Scott*, Aberdeen: Aberdeen University Press, 1983, chapters 8 and 9.

33 Peter T. Murphy, 'Impersonation and Authorship in Romantic Britain', *ELH* 59, 1992, pp. 625–49 (p. 626).

34 Ibid., p. 636.

35 'Z.' [John Gibson Lockhart], 'On the Cockney School of Poetry No. I', *BEM*, October 1817, p. 39.

36 Quoted in Leigh Hunt, 'To Z.', *Examiner*, 16 November 1817, p. 729.

37 Kim Wheatley has pointed out that Lockhart's comments 'imply that Hunt's own sexual proclivities cannot be differentiated from those of the characters in his story. Rather than exposing Hunt's private life, they confuse reality with fiction in a way that actually makes Hunt far more compelling than he would have otherwise been'. See 'The *Blackwood's* Attacks on Leigh Hunt', *Nineteenth-Century Literature* 47, 1992, pp. 1–37 (p. 2).

38 Hunt, 'To Z.', p. 729.

39 'Z.' [John Gibson Lockhart], 'Letter from Z. to Mr Leigh Hunt', *BEM*, January 1818, p. 416.

40 Leigh Hunt, 'Attack on the Editor in a Magazine', *Examiner*, 13 April 1818, p. 233.

41 'On the Cockney School of Poetry No. III', *BEM*, July 1818, p. 454. As Wheatley suggest, this passage reveals Lockhart's 'double standard, in that his anonymity preserves the "radical distinction" between private and public where his own life is concerned'; 'The *Blackwood's* Attacks on Leigh Hunt', p. 19.

42 See Robert Morrison, 'John Wilson and the Editorship of *Blackwood's Magazine*', *Notes and Queries* n.s. 46, 1999, pp. 48–50.

43 Samuel Halkett and John Laing, *Dictionary of Anonymous and Pseudonymous English Literature*, new edn by James Kennedy, W. A. Smith and A. F. Johnson, 9 vols, Edinburgh: Oliver and Boyd, 1928, vol. 3, p. 126.

44 [Macvey Napier?], *Hypocrisy Unveiled and Calumny Detected in a Review of Blackwood's Magazine*, Edinburgh: Francis Pillans, 1818, p. 8.

45 Ibid., p. 21.

46 Ibid., p. 52.

47 Ibid., p. 54.

48 'A' [Edward Lytton Bulwer], 'Upon the Spirit of True Criticism', *NMM*, April 1832, p. 356. See also his unsigned 'To our Friends, on Preserving the Anonymous in Periodicals', *NMM*, November 1832, pp. 385–9.

49 Edward Lytton Bulwer, *England and the English*, 2 vols, London: Richard Bentley, 1833, vol. 2, p. 25.

50 [William Maginn], 'Letters of Timothy Tickler, esq. to Eminent Literary Characters. No. IX', *BEM*, September 1823, p. 311.

51 For more on 'pimpled Hazlitt', see Alan Lang Strout, 'Hunt, Hazlitt, and *Maga*', *ELH* 4, 1937, pp. 151–9.

52 'It has always seemed to us that works of this description are peculiarly suited to those short sketches, which either give new or brief views of the characters of celebrated men, or embrace such anecdotes and descriptions, as a more elaborate work, obliged to condense its materials, would omit'; [Bulwer], 'To Our Friends, on Preserving the Anonymous in Periodicals', p. 389. It is also noteworthy that the early instalments of Marguerite Blessington's controversial 'Journal of Conversations of Lord Byron' were published in the *NMM* during Bulwer's editorship.

3 Magazine biography in the late Romantic period

1 Annette Wheeler Cafarelli, *Prose in the Age of Poets*, Philadelphia, PA: University of Philadelphia Press, 1990. Other useful accounts of early nineteenth-century biography include Richard D. Altick, *Lives and Letters: A History of Literary Biography in England and America*, New York: Alfred A. Knopf, 1965; Arthur Bradley and Alan Rawes (eds) *Romantic Biography*, Aldershot: Ashgate, 2003; Richard Cronin, *Romantic Victorians: English Literature, 1824–1840*, Basingstoke: Palgrave, 2002, chapter 1; Francis R. Hart, *Lockhart as Romantic Biographer*, Edinburgh: Edinburgh University Press, 1971; Joseph Reed, *English Biography in the Early Nineteenth Century: 1801–1838*, New Haven, CT: Yale University Press, 1966; Jonah Siegel, *Desire and Excess: The Nineteenth-Century Culture of Art*, Princeton, NJ: Princeton University Press, 2000, chapter 4.

2 Leo Braudy also points out that the ways in which authors presented themselves to their audiences is not really an issue for Johnson, whereas it clearly is for Romantic writers like Hazlitt: *The Frenzy of Renown: Fame and its History*, New York: Vintage, 1997, p. 392.

3 M. H. Abrams, *The Mirror and the Lamp*, London: Oxford University Press, 1971, p. 226.

4 Henry Colburn, publisher of the *NMM* and the *Literary Gazette*, was notorious for this sort of 'puffing'. See, for example, the 'review' of Leigh Hunt's *Lord Byron and Some of his Contemporaries* in the *NMM*, January 1828, pp. 84–96. Cafarelli quotes from this article in order to show that Hunt had his supporters, and seems unaware that it was no more than an extended advertisement for one of Colburn's publications; Cafarelli, *Prose*, p. 145.

5 [John Scott], 'Portraits of Authors', *Champion*, 2 January 1814, p. 414.
6 There is the need for more research on 'canonizing' during the Romantic period and
  I have found nothing at all on the role of literary galleries in this process. However, there
  has been recent interest in literary anthologies: see Greg Kucich, 'Gendering the Canons
  of Romanticism: Past and Present', *Wordsworth Circle* 27, 1996, pp. 95–102 and Laura
  Mandell, *Romantic Canons: A Bibliography and an Argument*, 1998. Online available
  http://www.orgs.muohio.edu/anthologies/canon.htm (accessed 6 July 2004).
7 Notable examples of galleries not discussed here include [John Scott], 'Portraits of
  Authors', *Champion*, 1814; 'Contemporary Authors', *Monthly Magazine*, 1817–20; 'On
  Living Novelists', *NMM*, 1820; [John Scott], 'Sketches of Living Authors', *LM*, 1820–1;
  [Leigh Hunt], 'Sketches of the Living Poets', *Examiner*, 1821; [F. D. Maurice], 'Sketches
  of Contemporary Authors', *Athenaeum*, 1828; 'Living Literary Characters', *NMM*, 1831;
  Allan Cunningham, 'Biographical and Critical History of the Literature of the Last Fifty
  Years', *Athenaeum*, 1833 (published in book form in 1834); George Gilfillan, *A Gallery of
  Literary Portraits*, Edinburgh: William Tait, 1845, first published in the *Dumfries Herald*,
  1842–4; and [Richard Henry Horne] (ed.) *A New Spirit of the Age*, 2 vols, London: Smith,
  Elder and Co., 1844. For an account of the latter, see Ann Blainey, *The Farthing Poet*,
  London: Longman, 1968, chapter 13.
8 Mark Parker, *Literary Magazines and British Romanticism*, Cambridge: Cambridge
  University Press, 2000, pp. 153–5. Useful discussions of *The Spirit of the Age* include
  Cafarelli, *Prose*, chapter 4; Gregory Dart, 'Hazlitt and Biography', *Cambridge Quarterly* 29,
  2000, pp. 338–48; John Kinnaird, *William Hazlitt: Critic of Power*, New York: Columbia
  University Press, 1978, chapter 9; James Mulvihill, 'Character and Culture in Hazlitt's
  Spirit of the Age', *Nineteenth-Century Literature* 45, 1990, pp. 281–99; Patrick Story,
  'Hazlitt's Definition of the Spirit of the Age', *Wordsworth Circle* 6, 1975, pp. 97–108 and,
  also by Story, 'Emblems of Infirmity: Contemporary Portraits in Hazlitt's *The Spirit of the
  Age*', *Wordsworth Circle* 10, 1979, pp. 81–90.
9 Parker, *Literary Magazines*, chapter 4, and Marilyn Butler, 'Culture's Medium: The Role
  of the Review', in *The Cambridge Companion to British Romanticism*, ed. Stuart Curran,
  Cambridge: Cambridge University Press, 1993, pp. 120–47 (p. 143).
10 See Nanora Sweet, 'The *New Monthly Magazine* and the Liberalism of the 1820s', *Prose
   Studies* 25, 2002, pp. 147–62.
11 'Y. I.' [Cyrus Redding], 'The Good Old Times', *NMM*, November 1823, p. 428.
12 Ibid.
13 Ibid., p. 433.
14 Ibid., p. 430.
15 *CWH*, vol. 12, pp. 128–9. All further references to *CWH* are in the text in the form
   (vol. number, page number).
16 Story, 'Hazlitt's Definition of the Spirit of the Age', p. 99.
17 Parker, *Literary Magazines*, p. 155.
18 Walter Scott, *Ivanhoe*, ed. Graham Tulloch, Edinburgh: Edinburgh University Press,
   1998, p. 382.
19 Kinnaird, *William Hazlitt*, p. 302.
20 Maginn wrote all but five of the seventy-nine portraits. The others were by [Lockhart],
   'The Doctor' [i.e. Maginn himself], January 1831; [Carlyle], 'Baron Von Goethe', March
   1832 and [Francis Mahony], who did three: 'Miss Landon', October 1833; 'Pierre-Jean de
   Béranger', March 1835; 'Henry O'Brien', August 1835.
21 Maginn's victims were: The Opium Eater (July 1824); Dr Kitchener (August 1824);
   Sir Humphry Davy (September 1824); Bishop the Composer (October 1824).
22 [William Maginn], 'Gallery of Illustrious Literary Characters IV: Samuel Rogers', *FM*,
   September 1830, p. 237, and 'Gallery of Illustrious Literary Characters V: Thomas
   Moore', *FM*, October 1830, p. 266.
23 It is interesting to compare Maginn's 'Gallery' with the series of 'Living Literary
   Characters' that ran in the *New Monthly* in 1831. These were much longer articles, by

different authors, which contained an account of the subject's biography, works and
appearance, and were accompanied by engravings of formal portraits and busts. But the
judiciousness and sobriety of these articles makes them boring, and this may have been
why they stopped when Bulwer became editor of the magazine at the end of 1831.

24 Patrick Leary, 'Fraser's Magazine and the Literary Life, 1830–1847', VPR 27, 1994,
pp. 105–26 (p. 111).

25 [William Maginn], 'The Election of Editor for Fraser's Magazine', FM, May 1830,
pp. 496–508 (p. 497); July 1830, pp. 738–57; September 1830, pp. 238–50. For a good
analysis of the magazine's use of Coleridge, see Robert Lapp, 'Romanticism Repackaged:
The New Faces of "Old Man" Coleridge in Fraser's Magazine, 1830–35', European Romantic
Review 11, 2000, pp. 235–47.

26 Leary, 'Fraser's Magazine and the Literary Life', p. 112.

27 Lapp, 'Romanticism Repackaged', p. 246.

28 Perhaps it is not surprising that there are no women in The Spirit of the Age, given
Hazlitt's treatment of women writers in his Lectures on the English Poets (1818): for an
interesting discussion of this, see Marlon B. Ross, The Contours of Masculine Desire:
Romanticism and the Rise of Women's Poetry, New York: Oxford University Press, 1989,
pp. 256–9.

29 [Maginn and Lockhart], 'ODoherty's Maxims. Part One', BEM, May 1824, p. 603.

30 'A' [Edward Lytton Bulwer], 'On the Influence and Education of Women', NMM, March
1832, pp. 228–9.

31 [Edward Lytton Bulwer], 'Romance and Reality. By L. E. L.', NMM, December 1831,
p. 546.

32 Ibid., p. 545.

33 For a detailed discussion of More's arguments, see Ross, Contours of Masculine Desire,
pp. 204–9.

34 'The Female Character', FM, May 1833, p. 595.

35 Ibid., p. 599.

36 Ibid., p. 600.

37 [Francis Mahony], 'Gallery of Illustrious Literary Characters XLI. Miss Landon', FM,
October 1833, p. 433. In 1824, Maginn contrasted Landon's 'brilliant' love poetry with
the unpalatable works of Baillie, Hemans and Porden: 'For what can a woman well write
on but love?'; 'The Rhyming Review', John Bull Magazine, August 1824, p. 77.

38 For an interesting discussion of Landon's relationship to the category of the 'poetess', see
Glennis Stephenson, Letitia Landon: The Woman Behind L.E.L., Manchester: Manchester
University Press, 1995, especially chapter 1.

39 Anne K. Mellor, Romanticism and Gender, London: Routledge, 1993, p. 114.

40 [William Maginn], 'Regina's Maids of Honour', FM, January 1836, p. 80.

41 Mellor, Romanticism and Gender, p. 122.

42 For Landon's life history, see Stephenson, Letitia Landon, chapter 2.

43 [William Maginn], 'Gallery of Illustrious Literary Characters XXVII. E. L. Bulwer', FM,
August 1832, p. 112.

44 Michael Sadleir, Bulwer and His Wife: A Panorama, London: Constable, 1931, pp. 422–6.
Westmacott was the editor of the scurrilous newspaper The Age. Sadleir's claim is also
mentioned as a strong possibility in Angela Leighton, Victorian Women Poets: Writing
Against the Heart, Hemel Hempstead: Harvester Wheatsheaf, 1992, p. 54.

45 I am very grateful to David Latané, who is writing a monograph on Maginn, for pointing
out to me some of the flaws in Sadleir's theory.

46 Malcolm Elwin, Victorian Wallflowers, London: Jonathan Cape, 1934, p. 120.

47 Quoted in Stephenson, Letitia Landon, p. 49.

48 Elwin, Victorian Wallflowers, p. 117.

49 Mellor, Romanticism and Gender, p. 123.

50 [Maginn], 'Regina's Maids of Honour', p. 80.

51 Nathaniel Willis, Pencillings by the Way, London: T. Werner Laurie, 1942, pp. 407–8.

52 For a detailed account of Willis and Blessington, see Michael Sadleir, *Blessington-D'Orsay: A Masquerade*, London: Constable, 1933, chapter 2.

53 [Maginn], 'Regina's Maids of Honour', p. 80.

54 I am grateful to Kiera Chapman for her helpful comments on Maginn's account of Blessington.

55 I focus in this book on what seem to me to be the most interesting magazine reminiscences, but there were a great many others, including: [John Mitford?], 'Extract of a Letter from Geneva, with Anecdotes of Lord Byron, &c.', *NMM*, April 1819 (this preceded Polidori's story 'The Vampyre', which was published in the magazine as Byron's work); 'Elia' [Charles Lamb], 'Christ's Hospital Five-and-Thirty Years Ago', *LM*, November 1820; 'J. B.' [B. W. Proctor], 'My Recollections of the Late William Hazlitt', *NMM*, November 1830; Thomas Medwin, 'Memoir of Shelley', *Athenaeum*, July and August 1832; Marguerite Blessington, 'Journal of Conversations with Lord Byron', *NMM*, intermittently from August 1832 to December 1833; 'S. Y.' [Sarah Flower Adams], 'An Evening with Charles Lamb and Coleridge', *MR*, March 1834, pp. 162–8; [Richard Henry Horne], 'Dies sub Coelo', *MR*, June 1834, pp. 365–92 (includes ten pages of reminiscences of W. H. Ireland); [John Abraham Heraud], 'Reminiscences of Coleridge, Biographical, Philosophical, Poetical, and Political', *FM*, October 1834; Charles Le Grice, 'College Reminiscences of Mr. Coleridge', *Gentleman's Magazine*, December 1834; Barry Cornwall, 'Recollections of Charles Lamb', *Athenaeum*, 24 January and 7 February, 1835. Other book-length reminiscences were made available to the readers of magazines through lengthy quotations in reviews and advertisements.

56 Leigh Hunt, *Lord Byron and Some of his Contemporaries*, London: Henry Colburn, 1828, p. v.

57 Ibid., p. 143.

58 [John Gibson Lockhart], '*Lord Byron and Some of his Contemporaries*', *QR*, March 1828, p. 404.

59 Cafarelli, *Prose*, p. 139.

60 Hunt, *Lord Byron*, p. 92.

61 Ibid., p. vi.

62 This appeared in six parts: January 1832, pp. 90–6; February 1832, pp. 136–44; April 1832, pp. 343–52; July 1832, pp. 65–73; October 1832, pp. 321–30; December 1832, pp. 505–13. Another article by Hogg, 'The History of Percy Bysshe Shelley's Expulsion from Oxford', was published in the *NMM* in May 1833, pp. 17–29.

63 Neil Fraistat, 'Illegitimate Shelley: Radical Piracy and the Textual Edition as Cultural Performance', *PMLA* 10, 1994, pp. 409–23.

64 [F. D. Maurice], 'Sketches of Contemporary Authors. No. VIII. – Percy Bysshe Shelley', *Athenaeum*, 7 March 1828, p. 194.

65 Richard Cronin, 'Shelley, Tennyson, and the Apostles, 1828–1832', *Keats–Shelley Review* 5, 1990, pp. 14–40. For a general account of the Apostles in this period, see Peter Allen, *The Cambridge Apostles: The Early Years*, Cambridge: Cambridge University Press, 1978.

66 For Shelley's reputation in the nineteenth century, see Roland A. Duerksen, *Shelleyan Ideas in Victorian Literature*, The Hague: Mouton, 1966, pp. 22–8; Karsten Klejs Engelberg, *The Making of the Shelley Myth*, London: Mansell Publishing, 1988, especially chapter 3; John Mullan, Chris Hart and Peter Swaab (eds) *Lives of the Great Romantics by their Contemporaries I*, 3 vols, London: Pickering and Chatto, 1996, vol. 1, ed. John Mullan, introduction.

67 *NMM*, January 1832, p. 93.

68 *NMM*, January 1832, pp. 94–5.

69 *NMM*, December 1832, p. 513.

70 Ibid.

71 Bulwer's editorship lasted for just under two years, after which Hall returned to the helm and the magazine lost its political edge.

72 Edward Lytton Bulwer, *Paul Clifford*, London: George Routledge, 1896, p. 23. Bulwer's motivation for the attack was the paper's criticism of his novel *Pelham* in 1829.

73 Thomas Jefferson Hogg, *The Life of Percy Bysshe Shelley*, 2 vols, London: Edward Moxon, 1858, vol. 1, p. xiv.

74 Ibid., pp. xv–xvi.

75 Ibid., p. xvi.

76 Ibid., p. xvii.

77 [John Abraham Heraud], 'New Poem. – By Percy Bysshe Shelley: The Wandering Jew: Introduction', *FM*, June 1831, pp. 529–36.

78 'A' [Edward Lytton Bulwer], 'The Knowledge of the World in Men and Books', *NMM*, December 1831, p. 525.

79 *NMM*, October 1832, pp. 321–2.

80 Richard Holmes, *Shelley: The Pursuit*, Harmondsworth: Penguin, 1987, p. 43.

81 [Hogg], 'Percy Bysshe Shelley at Oxford', *NMM*, October 1832, pp. 324–5.

82 Ibid., p. 325.

83 For more on the circumstances of the publication of Hunt's volume, and reproductions of the corrected proofs, see *The Manuscripts of the Younger Romantics: Percy Bysshe Shelley*, ed. Donald H. Reiman, 3 vols, New York: Garland, 1985, vol. 2: *The Mask of Anarchy*.

84 *CWS*, vol. 3, p. 226.

85 Ibid., p. 229.

86 Ibid., p. 230.

87 Ibid., pp. 232–3.

88 [Edward Lytton Bulwer], 'The Faults of Recent Poets: Poems by Alfred Tennyson', *NMM*, January 1833, p. 69. Later that year, Bulwer described Shelley's poetry as being 'of a remarkably ethereal and spiritualising cast': *England and the English*, 2 vols, London: Bentley, 1833, vol. 2, p. 102.

89 [Edward Lytton Bulwer], 'Sir Egerton Brydges's *Autobiography*', *ER*, July 1834, p. 445.

90 See Bouthaina Shaaban, 'Shelley in the Chartist Press', *Keats–Shelley Memorial Bulletin* 34, 1983, pp. 41–60.

91 'The Author of *Eugene Aram*' [Edward Lytton Bulwer], 'Death of Sir Walter Scott', *NMM*, October 1832, p. 303.

92 Harriet Martineau, 'The Achievements of the Genius of Scott', *TEM*, January 1833, pp. 445–60. See also her article 'The Characteristics of the Genius of Scott' in the previous issue, pp. 301–14. W. J. Fox was also unwilling to consider Scott as a man of the people, see [W. J. Fox], 'On the Intellectual Character of Sir Walter Scott', *MR*, November 1832, pp. 721–8.

93 [Bulwer], 'Death of Sir Walter Scott', p. 300.

94 Harriet Martineau, 'The Achievements of the Genius of Scott', p. 459.

95 *WTC*, vol. 29, p. 35.

96 Ibid., p. 38.

97 R. P. Gillies, *Recollections of Sir Walter Scott, Bart.*, London: James Fraser, 1837.

98 [William Maginn], 'Domestic Manners of Sir Walter Scott', *FM*, August 1834, p. 125.

99 Ibid.

100 Ibid., p. 127.

101 Ibid., p. 135.

102 [R. P. Gillies], 'Recollections of Sir Walter Scott. I. – His Boyhood and Youth', *FM*, October 1835, p. 251.

103 Ibid., p. 252.

104 Sir Samuel Egerton Brydges, 'On the Charge that Men of Genius and High Talents want Judgment and Practical Sense', *FM*, June 1836, p. 675.

105 [Gillies], 'Recollections of Sir Walter Scott. I.', pp. 252–3.

106 Ibid., p. 253.

107 [R. P. Gillies], 'Recollections of Sir Walter Scott. "The Sere and Yellow Leaf"', *FM*, January 1836, p. 106.

108 [Fox], 'On the Intellectual Character of Sir Walter Scott', p. 728.

109 [Gillies], '"The Sere and Yellow Leaf"', p. 106.

110 Ibid., p. 112.
111 Ibid., p. 120.
112 For helpful discussions of these articles, see Cafarelli, chapter 5; John E. Jordan, *De Quincey to Wordsworth: A Biography of a Relationship*, Berkeley, CA: University of California Press, 1962, chapter 5; Julian North, 'Self-Possession and Gender in Romantic Biography', in Arthur Bradley and Alan Rawes (eds) *Romantic Biography*, pp. 109–38; Margaret Russett, *De Quincey's Romanticism*, Cambridge: Cambridge University Press, 1997, chapter 5. My ideas on the 'Lake Reminiscences' have also been stimulated by an unpublished paper by Mirga Nekvedavicius, which was delivered at the Thomas De Quincey conference at the University of Bristol, May 2001.
113 [Leigh Hunt], 'The Wishing Cap No. III', *TEM*, May 1833, p. 142.
114 Ibid.
115 Grevel Lindop, *The Opium-Eater: A Life of Thomas De Quincey*, Oxford: Oxford University Press, 1985, p. 304.
116 Mark A. Weinstein, 'Tait's Edinburgh Magazine', in *BLM*, pp. 401–5 (p. 402).
117 Robert Morrison, 'Red De Quincey', *Wordsworth Circle* 29, 1998, pp. 131–6.
118 *WDQ*, vol. 10, p. 318.
119 Ibid., pp. 333–4.
120 Ibid., pp. 338–9.
121 Quoted in Barry Symonds, ' "Do not suppose that I am underwriting myself": The Labyrinth of De Quincey's Manuscripts', *Wordsworth Circle* 29, 1998, pp. 137–40 (p. 137).
122 *WDQ*, vol. 10, p. 339.
123 Ibid.
124 Ibid., pp. 340–1.
125 Ibid., p. 347.
126 Lapp, 'Romanticism Repackaged', p. 236.
127 *WDQ*, vol. 11, pp. 98–102.
128 *WDQ*, vol. 10, pp. 336–7.
129 *WDQ*, vol. 15, p. 303.

4 *Blackwood's Edinburgh Magazine* and the construction of Wordsworth's genius

1 *WDQ*, vol. 10, pp. 145–6.
2 Carl Woodring, 'Wordsworth and the Victorians', in Kenneth R. Johnston and Gene W. Ruoff (eds) *The Age of William Wordsworth*, New Brunswick, NJ: Rutgers University Press, 1987, pp. 261–75 (p. 262).
3 Andrew Bennett, *Romantic Poets and the Culture of Posterity*, Cambridge: Cambridge University Press, 1999, pp. 44–50; Lee Erickson, *The Economy of Literary Form*, Baltimore, MD: The Johns Hopkins University Press, 1996, chapter 3; Lucy Newlyn, *Reading, Writing, and Romanticism*, Oxford: Oxford University Press, 2000, chapter 3; Thomas Pfau, *Wordsworth's Profession*, Stanford, CA: Stanford University Press, 1997; Mark Schoenfield, *The Professional Wordsworth*, Athens, GA: University of Georgia Press, 1996.
4 John L. Mahoney, *Wordsworth and the Critics*, Rochester, NY: Camden House, 2001, chapter 1; Thomas M. Raysor, 'The Establishment of Wordsworth's Reputation', *Journal of English and German Philology* 54, 1955, pp. 61–71; William S. Ward, 'Wordsworth, the "Lake" Poets, and their Contemporary Magazine Critics, 1798–1820', *Studies in Philology* 42, 1945, pp. 87–113.
5 See, however, Stephen Gill, *Wordsworth and the Victorians*, Oxford: Clarendon Press, 1998 and John Mullan, Chris Hart and Peter Swaab (eds) *Lives of the Great Romantics by their Contemporaries I*, 3 vols, London: William Pickering and Chatto, 1996, vol. 3, ed. Peter Swaab, pp. xi–xxvii.
6 W. J. B. Owen, 'Costs, Sales, and Profits of Longman's Editions of Wordsworth', *The Library* n.s. 12, 1956, pp. 93–107 (pp. 93–5).
7 Ward, 'Wordsworth', p. 88.

8 Ward, 'Wordsworth', p. 89; Owen, 'Costs', pp. 95–6.
9 For the *Edinburgh's* circulation, see Richard D. Altick, *The English Common Reader*, Chicago, IL: University of Chicago Press, 1963, p. 392.
10 'Peter Morris' [John Gibson Lockhart], *Peter's Letters to his Kinsfolk*, 2nd edn, 3 vols, Edinburgh: William Blackwood, 1819, vol. 2, p. 143.
11 Wordsworth attacked Jeffrey in the *Essay, Supplementary to the Preface* (1815), and *A Letter to a Friend of Robert Burns* (1816); see *PWW*, vol. 3, pp. 62, 126–9.
12 For Wordsworth's reputation in the 1820s see Gill, *Wordsworth: A Life*, Oxford: Clarendon Press, 1989, pp. 347–52. Gill deals with the 1830s and 1840s in *Wordsworth and the Victorians*, chapter 1.
13 For example, 'G. M.', 'On the Genius and Writings of Wordsworth', *Imperial Magazine*, July 1821, pp. 598–602; [John Scott], 'Living Authors No. II: Wordsworth', *LM*, March 1820, pp. 275–85; [Thomas Noon Talfourd], 'On the Genius and Writings of Wordsworth', *NMM*, November and December 1820, pp. 483–508, 648–55.
14 Alan Lang Strout, 'John Wilson, "Champion" of Wordsworth', *Modern Philology* 31, 1934, pp. 383–94.
15 Ibid., pp. 392–3.
16 J. H. Alexander, '*Blackwood's*: Magazine as Romantic Form', *Wordsworth Circle* 15, 1984, pp. 57–68 (p. 61).
17 [John Wilson], 'Noctes Ambrosianae. No XXI', *BEM*, September 1825, pp. 380–1.
18 Margaret Oliphant, *Annals of a Publishing House: William Blackwood and his Sons*, 3 vols, Edinburgh: William Blackwood, 1899, vol. 1, pp. 277–87. Three years later, Wilson published a lengthy attack on *The Excursion* for its lack of Christian doctrine: 'Sacred Poetry', *BEM*, December 1828, pp. 917–38.
19 'Essays on the Lake School of Poetry No. I: Wordsworth's *White Doe of Rhylstone*', July 1818, pp. 255–63; 'Essays on the Lake School of Poetry No. II: On the Habits of Thought, Inculcated by Wordsworth', December 1818, pp. 369–80; 'Letters from the Lakes', January and March 1819, pp. 396–404, 735–44. These articles were all by John Wilson, who also wrote a number of reviews of Wordsworth: *Peter Bell*, May 1819, pp. 130–6; *The Waggoner*, June 1819, pp. 332–4; *The River Duddon*, May 1820, pp. 206–13; *Ecclesiastical Sketches* and *Memorials of a Tour on the Continent*, August 1822, pp. 175–91. He also praised Wordsworth strongly in a review of Crabbe's *Tales of the Hall*, July 1819, pp. 469–83. Patmore's two 'Sonnets to Mr Wordsworth' appeared in February 1818, pp. 512–13. Moir published a sonnet on the poet in February 1821, p. 542. Lockhart praised Wordsworth in several passages in *Peter's Letters*: for example, vol. 1, pp. 121–3, 179; vol. 2, pp. 143–4; vol. 3, p. 130.
20 [John Wilson], 'Essays on the Lake School of Poetry No. I: Wordsworth's *White Doe of Rhylstone*', *BEM*, July 1818, p. 371.
21 [John Wilson], 'Wordsworth's Sonnets and Memorials', *BEM*, August 1822, p. 175.
22 Jeffrey N. Cox, 'Leigh Hunt's Cockney School: The Lakers' "Other"', *Romanticism on the Net* 14, 1999, paragraph 4. Online available http://www.erudit.org/revue/ron/1999/v/n14/005859ar.html (accessed 6 July 2004).
23 See 'Z.' [Lockhart], 'On the Cockney School of Poetry No. I', *BEM*, October 1817, p. 41, and 'On the Cockney School of Poetry No. IV', *BEM*, August 1818, p. 520.
24 For example, [John Wilson], 'An Hour's Tete-a-Tete [*sic*] with the Public', *BEM*, October 1820, p. 93.
25 [John Wilson and William Maginn], 'Preface', *BEM*, 1826, p. xxii.
26 I do not mean to suggest that *Blackwood's* literary criticism was straightforwardly 'Romantic', or that the *Edinburgh's* was consistently 'Augustan'. It is simply that *Blackwood's* represented its criticism as revolutionary and the *Edinburgh's* as reactionary.
27 [John Wilson], 'Observations on Coleridge's Biographia Literaria', *BEM*, October 1817, pp. 3–18.
28 See Nicholas Roe, *John Keats and the Culture of Dissent*, Oxford: Clarendon Press, 1997, pp. 272–3 and Alan Lang Strout, 'Samuel Taylor Coleridge and John Wilson of

Blackwood's Magazine'. PMLA 48, 1933, pp. 100–28 (pp. 108–10). Robert Morrison gives an account of Coleridge's association with *Blackwood's* in 'Opium-Eaters and Magazine Wars: De Quincey and Coleridge in 1821', *VPR* 30, 1997, pp. 27–40.

29 Quoted in Roe, *John Keats*, p. 273.

30 [John Wilson], 'On Literary Censorship', *BEM*, November 1818, p. 177.

31 For a detailed account of the relationship between Wilson and Wordsworth up to 1817, see Alan Lang Strout, 'William Wordsworth and John Wilson: A Review of their Relations between 1802 and 1817', *PMLA* 49, 1934, pp. 143–83. See also Mary Gordon, *Christopher North: A Memoir of John Wilson*, 2nd edn, Edinburgh: Thomas C. Jack, 1879, chapter 5 and Elsie Swann, *Christopher North*, Edinburgh: Oliver and Boyd, 1934, chapter 3.

32 *The Letters of William and Dorothy Wordsworth*, ed. Ernest de Selincourt, 2nd edn, rev. Mary Moorman and Alan G. Hill, 8 vols, Oxford: Clarendon Press, 1967–93, vol. 2, p. 260.

33 Robert Morrison, '*Blackwood's* Berserker: John Wilson and the Language of Extremity', *Romanticism on the Net* 20, 2000, paragraph 4. Online available http://www.erudit.org/revue/ron/2000/v/n20/005951ar.html (accessed 6 July 2004).

34 John Wilson, *The Isle of Palms and Other Poems*, Edinburgh: Ballantyne, 1812, p. 186.

35 Henry Crabb Robinson, *Henry Crabb Robinson on Books and their Writers*, ed. Edith Morley, 3 vols, London: J. M. Dent & Sons, 1938, vol. 1, p. 160.

36 'Letters from the Lakes', *BEM*, January 1819, p. 396.

37 Ibid., pp. 396–7. Compare 'Tintern Abbey': 'The still, sad music of humanity' (l. 91). There is another echo in the third letter; Kempferhausen writes that 'no wonder that these mountains, and glens, and groves, are becoming every day more dear to me . . . This beautiful country is dear to me for its own sake' – compare 'Tintern Abbey', ll. 157–9.

38 Ibid., p. 401.

39 Ibid., p. 404.

40 Swaab (ed.) *Lives of the Great Romantics*, vol. 3, p. 7.

41 [William Hazlitt], 'Character of Mr Wordsworth's New Poem, The Excursion', *The Examiner*, 21 August, 28 August and 2 October, pp. 541–2, 555–8, 636–8. It is reprinted in *CWH*, vol. 19, pp. 9–25. The review was also published, with changes which made it much more negative, in *The Round Table* (1817); see *CWH*, vol. 4, pp. 111–25.

42 [Francis Jeffrey], 'Wordsworth's Excursion', *ER*, November 1814, p. 3.

43 Ibid.

44 Ibid., pp. 3–4.

45 Raymond Williams, *Culture and Society*, London: The Hogarth Press, 1993, chapter 2.

46 'Philip Kempferhausen' [John Wilson], 'Letters from the Lakes: Written during the Summer of 1818. Letter III', *BEM*, March 1819, pp. 739–40. All further references to this article are within the text.

47 See 'Baron von Lauerwinkel' [Lockhart], 'Remarks on the Periodical Criticism of England', *BEM*, March 1818, pp. 670–9. Also [Wilson], 'On Literary Censorship', pp. 176–8.

48 See Mary Moorman, *William Wordsworth: A Biography*, 2 vols, Oxford: Clarendon Press, 1957–65, vol. 2, p. 409.

49 *Letters of William and Dorothy Wordsworth*, vol. 3, pp. 522–4.

50 Moorman, *William Wordsworth*, vol. 2, p. 409.

51 *PWW*, vol. 3, p. 122.

52 Ibid.

53 'Modern Periodical Literature', *NMM*, September 1820, pp. 309–10.

54 *PWW*, vol. 3, p. 80.

5 William Hazlitt and the degradation of genius

1 *CWH*, vol. 11, pp. 63–4. Further references to *CWH* are within the text in the form (vol. number, page number).

2 See Uttara Natarajan, *Hazlitt and the Reach of Sense*, Oxford: Clarendon Press, 1998, p. 109 for a survey of the 'established view of the Keats–Hazlitt relationship'. There is also a useful

chapter on Hazlitt and Keats in Jonathan Bate, *Shakespeare and the English Romantic Imagination*, Oxford: Clarendon Press, 1986, chapter 8.

3 W. P. Albrecht, *Hazlitt and the Creative Imagination*, Laurence: The University of Kansas Press, 1965, p. 78.

4 Natarajan, *Hazlitt*, pp. 107–10. She does not mention that Keats was certainly also influenced by Hazlitt's lecture 'On Shakespeare and Milton', delivered in January 1818, in which he further emphasises Shakespeare's sympathetic genius: 'He was the least of an egotist that it was possible to be . . . He was like the genius of humanity, changing places with all of us at his pleasure, and playing with our purposes as with his own' (*CWH*, vol. 5, p. 47). According to Stanley Jones, Keats would have attended this lecture; see *Hazlitt: A Life*, Oxford: Clarendon Press, 1989, p. 281.

5 Natarajan, *Hazlitt*, pp. 93–119.

6 Ibid., p. 96.

7 Gregory Dart, *Rousseau, Robespierre and English Romanticism*, Cambridge: Cambridge University Press, 1999, p. 241.

8 Natarajan, *Hazlitt*, p. 93.

9 Ibid., p. 99.

10 John Kinnaird, *William Hazlitt: Critic of Power*, New York: Columbia University Press, 1978, chapter 3. See also John Whale, *Imagination under Pressure, 1789–1832*, Cambridge: Cambridge University Press, 2000, chapter 4.

11 Kinnaird, *William Hazlitt*, p. 98.

12 Ibid., p. 101.

13 For example, in the *Letter to William Gifford* (1819), *CWH*, vol. 9, pp. 51–9.

14 There is a good summary of the postwar situation in Jones, *Hazlitt*, pp. 230–6.

15 Ibid., p. 227.

16 Ibid., pp. 158–60, 176–7.

17 Kinnaird has attributed the verses to Hazlitt (*William Hazlitt*, pp. 102–3, 392), but Jones has argued that they are more likely to have been written by Thomas Moore (*Hazlitt*, p. 92).

18 B. Bernard Cohen has given a detailed account of the political disagreement between Hazlitt and Wordsworth, and its influence on the revisions Hazlitt made to his 1814 review of the *Excursion* when it was reprinted in the *Round Table*; see 'William Hazlitt: Bonapartist Critic of "The Excursion" ', *MLQ* 10, 1949, pp. 158–67.

19 *CWH*, vol. 7, pp. 24–7 and vol. 19, pp. 115–17.

20 See Samuel Taylor Coleridge, *Essays on his Times in the 'Morning Post' and the 'Courier'*, ed. David Erdman, 3 vols, in *The Collected Works of Samuel Taylor Coleridge*, 3, ed. Kathleen Coburn, London: Routledge & Kegan Paul, 1978.

21 After Henry Pye's death in 1813, Hunt had suggested in the *Examiner* that the Laureateship should be abolished as a 'contemptible' office; see 'Office of Poet Laureate', 15 August, and 'The Laureateship', 29 August. He attacked Southey for accepting the post: 'The New Poet-Laureate', 26 September. For a detailed discussion of these articles, see Charles Mahoney, *Romantics and Renegades: The Poetics of Political Reaction*, Basingstoke: Palgrave Macmillan, 2003, chapter 1. In 1816, Hunt strongly criticized Wordsworth in an article entitled 'Heaven Made a Party to Earthly Disputes – Mr. Wordsworth's Sonnets on Waterloo', *Examiner*, 18 February 1816.

22 Robert Keith Lapp, *Contest for Cultural Authority: Hazlitt, Coleridge, and the Distresses of the Regency*, Detroit, MI: Wayne State University Press, 1999, p. 25.

23 The imminent publication of the book, then entitled 'The day of adversity', was announced in the *Times* and the *Courier* in the middle of the August, but the *Statesman's Manual* did not appear until December; see Lapp, *Contest*, p. 51.

24 The 'Scrutator' letter is attributed to Hazlitt by Stanley Jones in 'Three Additions to the Canon of Hazlitt's Political Writings', *Review of English Studies* n.s. 38, 1987, pp. 355–63.

25 Several critics have given detailed readings of this text; see, for example, Jonathan Bate, *Shakespearean Constitutions: Politics, Theatre, Criticism 1730–1830*, Oxford: Clarendon

Press, 1989, pp. 164–73; David Bromwich, *Hazlitt: The Mind of a Critic*, 2nd edn, New Haven, CT: Yale University Press, 1999, pp. 314–26; Mahoney, *Romantics and Renegades*, chapter 5.

26 My modern edition has 'jutty, frieze' for 'jutting frieze': *The Riverside Shakespeare*, ed. G. Blakemore Evans, 2nd edn, Boston, MA: Houghton Mifflin, 1997, p. 1365.

27 Natarajan, *Hazlitt*, p. 111.

28 'But thy most dreaded instrument,/ In working out a pure intent/ Is Man – arrayed for mutual slaughter,/ Yea, Carnage is thy daughter!'

29 'The Four Ages of Poetry', in *The Halliford Edition of the Works of Thomas Love Peacock*, ed. H. F. B. Smith and C. E. Jones, 10 vols, London: Constable, 1924–34; repr. New York: AMS Press, 1967, vol. 8, p. 4.

30 Shelley was in England when Hazlitt gave this lecture, but there is no evidence that he attended. However, he could easily have read accounts of it in the press, or later in the *Lectures on the English Poets* volume. Paul Dawson has shown that the *Essay on the Principles of Human Action* influenced Shelley, but does not mention 'On Poetry in General'; see *The Unacknowledged Legislator: Shelley and Politics*, Oxford: Clarendon Press, 1980, pp. 230–7.

31 Compare Hazlitt's argument in the *Round Table* essay 'On the Causes of Methodism' that poets have 'an original poverty of spirit and weakness of constitution', first published in the *Examiner*, 22 October 1815; *CWH*, vol. 4, p. 58.

32 See also *CWH*, vol. 7, pp. 151–2.

33 Jones, *Hazlitt*, p. 91.

34 Lapp, *Contest*, chapters 3 and 4.

35 Ibid., p. 88.

36 The pseudonym alludes 'to the opening line of Juvenal's *Satires*, "Semper ego auditor tantum?" – "Must I always be a listener only?" '; Ibid., p. 20.

37 See Edward Royle and James Walvin, *English Radicals and Reformers, 1760–1848*, Kentucky, KY: The University Press of Kentucky, 1982, chapter 5. Hazlitt may be referring to Napoleon's successes in Italy in 1796 and 1797. In the *Life of Napoleon Buonaparte* (1828–30), he describes the Italian campaign as 'that dawn of a brighter day, that spring-time of hope' (*CWH*, vol. 13, p. 318).

38 M. H. Abrams describes this poetic form in his famous essay, 'Structure and Style in the Greater Romantic Lyric', in *Romanticism and Consciousness*, ed. Harold Bloom, New York: Norton, 1970, pp. 201–29.

39 Samuel Taylor Coleridge, *Lay Sermons*, ed. R. J. White, p. 33 in *The Collected Works of Samuel Taylor Coleridge*, 6, ed. Kathleen Coburn, London: Routledge & Kegan Paul, 1972.

40 Lapp, *Contest*, p. 17.

41 More in-depth accounts of the term 'liberal' in the early nineteenth century can be found in Elie Halévy, *The Liberal Awakening: 1815–1830*, trans. E. I. Watkin, 2nd edn, London: Ernest Benn, 1949, pp. 81–2; Peter L. Thorslev, Jr, 'Post-Waterloo Liberalism: The Second Generation', *Studies in Romanticism* 28, 1989, pp. 437–61 (pp. 444–6); Raymond Williams, *Keywords*, 2nd edn, London: Fontana Press, 1983, pp. 179–81.

42 Leigh Hunt, 'Preface', *Liberal*, October 1822, p. vii.

43 Ibid., p. ix.

44 A full account can be found in William H. Marshall, *Byron, Shelley, Hunt, and 'The Liberal'*, Philadelphia, PA: University of Pennsylvania Press, 1960. See also W. Paul Elledge, 'The Liberal', in *BLM*, pp. 220–7.

45 *CWS*, vol. 10, p. 34.

46 Marshall, *Byron, Shelley, Hunt*, p. 24.

47 *CWS*, vol. 10, p. 318.

48 *Byron's Letters and Journals*, ed. Leslie A. Marchand, 12 vols, London: John Murray, 1973–82, vol. 10, p. 13.

49 Hunt, 'Preface', p. xii. For an interesting discussion of the relationship between *belles-lettres* and politics in Hunt's journalism, see Kevin Gilmartin, *Print Politics: The Press and*

Radical Opposition in Early Nineteenth-Century England, Cambridge: Cambridge University Press, 1996, chapter 5.

50 John Wilson, 'On the Scotch Character – By a Flunky', *BEM*, March 1823, p. 365.

51 Peter L. Thorslev discusses Hazlitt's doctrine of 'disinterestedness' in his account of 'post-Waterloo liberalism', but, remarkably, does not mention any of Hazlitt's actual contributions to the *Liberal*; Thorslev, 'Post-Waterloo Liberalism', pp. 454–6.

52 It is unclear why it did not appear; see Marshall, *Byron, Shelley, Hunt*, pp. 140–2.

53 *CWS*, vol. 7, p. 118.

54 This is a tricky question, but Malcolm Kelsall has given a good account of Byron's position within a Whiggish tradition of resistance to the Crown, rather than republicanism; see *Byron's Politics*, Sussex: The Harvester Press, 1987.

55 'R. S.' [J. Gillon or John Wilson], 'The Candid No. II', *BEM*, March 1823, p. 209.

56 Leigh Hunt, *Lord Byron and Some of his Contemporaries*, London: Henry Colburn, 1828, p. 63.

57 See Stanley Jones, 'First Flight: Image and Theme in a Hazlitt Essay', *Prose Studies* 8, 1985, pp. 35–47; James Mulvihill, 'Visions and Revisions: William Hazlitt and "My First Acquaintance with Poets" ', *Charles Lamb Bulletin* 109, 2000, pp. 11–14; Jeffrey C. Robinson, 'Hazlitt's "My First Acquaintance with Poets": The Autobiography of a Cultural Critic', *Romanticism* 6, 2000, pp. 178–84; Bill Ruddick, 'Recollecting Coleridge: The Internalization of Radical Energies in Hazlitt's Political Prose', *Yearbook of English Studies* 19, 1989, pp. 243–55.

58 Lapp, *Contest*, p. 167.

59 Hazlitt is quoting here from *PL*, II, ll. 964–5. Further references to *PL* are in the text.

60 Tom Paulin, *The Day-Star of Liberty: William Hazlitt's Radical Style*, London: Faber and Faber, 1998, pp. 133–4. Although Paulin does not offer a sustained reading of 'My First Acquaintance with Poets', his book contains many insights on Miltonic allusion in Hazlitt's writings, and I have found his account of the essay 'A Landscape of Nicholas Poussin' (chapter 9) particularly stimulating.

61 Lucy Newlyn, *Reading, Writing, and Romanticism: The Anxiety of Reception*, Oxford: Oxford University Press, 2000, pp. 366–7.

62 Ibid., p. 370.

63 There is a similar passage in Hazlitt's *Life of Thomas Holcroft* (1816); see *CWH*, vol. 3, pp. 156–7.

64 A. C. Grayling, *The Quarrel of the Age*, London: Weidenfield & Nicholson, 2000, p. 296.

65 Newlyn, *Paradise Lost and the Romantic Reader*, Oxford: Oxford University Press, 1993, p. 7.

66 Newlyn, *Paradise Lost and the Romantic Reader*, p. 97.

67 Hunt, 'Preface', p. viii.

68 The essay also ends hopefully, as Hazlitt describes his first meeting with Charles Lamb at Godwin's house, 'the beginning of a friendship between us, which I believe still continues' (*CWH*, vol. 17, p. 122). Perhaps Lamb's touching defence of his old friend a few months later, in the 'Letter of Elia to Robert Southey Esquire' (*LM*, October 1823, p. 405), showed Hazlitt that the sympathetic ideal of the 1790s was not entirely an empty dream.

69 P. G. Patmore, *My Friends and Acquaintance*, 3 vols, London: Saunders and Otley, 1854, vol. 3, p. 136.

70 Hazlitt and Hunt had clearly discussed the events surrounding the demise of the *Liberal* when they met in Florence early in 1825 and had arrived at virtually the same account. In *Lord Byron and Some of his Contemporaries*, Hunt describes the reaction of Byron's friends in a similar semi-comic manner, and quotes liberally from 'On Jealousy and Spleen of Party'; see Hunt, *Lord Byron*, p. 48.

71 Pierre Bourdieu, *The Rules of Art*, trans. Susan Emanuel, Cambridge: Polity Press, 1992, p. 130.

6 'The Quack Artist': Benjamin Robert Haydon and the dangers of publicity

1 *The Diary of Benjamin Robert Haydon*, ed. Willard Bissell Pope, 5 vols, Cambridge, MA: Harvard University Press, 1960–3, vol. 3, p. 376. All further references to the *Diary* are in the text in the form (vol. number, page number).

2 For general accounts of Haydon's art, see David Blayney Brown, ' "Fire and Clay" – Benjamin Robert Haydon, Historical Painter', in David Blayney Brown, Robert Woof and Stephen Hebron, *Benjamin Robert Haydon: 1786–1846*, Kendal: The Wordsworth Trust, 1996 and A. C. Sewter, 'A Revaluation of Haydon', *Art Quarterly* 5, 1942, pp. 323–37. For individual paintings, see John Barrell, 'Benjamin Robert Haydon: The Curtius of the Khyber Pass', in John Barrell (ed.) *Painting and the Politics of Culture*, Oxford: Oxford University Press, 1992, pp. 254–89; Frederick Cummings, 'Nature and the Antique in B. R. Haydon's *Assassination of Dentatus*', *Journal of the Warburg and Courtauld Institutes* 23, 1962, pp. 147–57 and, also by Cummings, 'Poussin, Haydon, and "The Judgement of Solomon" ', *Burlington Magazine* 104, 1962, pp. 146–52.

3 There are two modern biographies: Eric George's *The Life and Death of Benjamin Robert Haydon*, 2nd edn, Oxford: Clarendon Press, 1967, and Clarke Olney's *Benjamin Robert Haydon: Historical Painter*, Athens, GA: The University of Georgia Press, 1952. Haydon is the central figure in Alethea Hayter's *A Sultry Month: Scenes of London Literary Life in 1846*, London: Faber & Faber, 1965 and Penelope Hughes-Hallett's *The Immortal Dinner*, London: Viking, 2000.

4 The hierarchy of genres was highly contested during the period due to its incompatibility with the realities of the art market: see Andrew Hemingway, *Landscape Imagery and Urban Culture in Early Nineteenth-Century Britain*, Cambridge: Cambridge University Press, 1992, especially chapter 6; also Kay Dian Kriz, *The Idea of the English Landscape Painter*, New Haven, CT: Yale University Press, 1997.

5 Richard Altick, *The Shows of London*, Cambridge, MA: Harvard University Press, 1978, p. 413. For the tension between 'showmanship' and 'academic art' in the period, see Matthew Craske, *Art in Europe: 1700–1830*, Oxford: Oxford University Press, 1997, pp. 210–17.

6 Colbert Kearney gives an invaluable bibliography of Haydon's work in 'The Writings of Benjamin Robert Haydon', unpublished doctoral thesis, University of Cambridge, 1972, pp. 265–87.

7 Sir Joshua Reynolds, *Discourses*, ed. Pat Rogers, Harmondsworth: Penguin, 1992, p. 99.

8 B. R. Haydon, *Lectures on Painting and Design*, 2 vols, London: Longman, 1844–6, vol. 1, p. 3.

9 Samuel Johnson, *Lives of the English Poets*, ed. George Birkbeck Hill, 3 vols, Oxford: Clarendon Press, 1905, vol. 1, p. 2.

10 Haydon, *Lectures*, vol. 1, p. 4.

11 Ibid., vol. 2, p. 111.

12 *CWS*, vol. 1, p. 101.

13 Barrell, 'The Curtius of the Khyber Pass', p. 263.

14 John Barrell, *The Political Theory of Painting from Reynolds to Hazlitt*, New Haven, CT: Yale University Press, 1986, p. 309.

15 'An English Student' [Haydon], 'To the Critic of Barry's Works in the *Edinburgh Review*, Aug. 1810', *Examiner*, 2 February 1812, p. 76.

16 Barrell, *Political Theory of Painting*, p. 313.

17 See, for example, *Diary*, vol. 2, p. 459. His claim that painting historical works was in itself perceived as 'radical' is expressed most strongly in his pamphlet *On Academies of Art, (More Particularly the Royal Academy), and their Pernicious Effect on the Genius of Europe*, London: Henry Hooper, 1839, pp. 31–2.

18 For most of his life he believed genius to be independent of heredity only *within* particular racial types: *between* types, he thought, there were considerable intellectual

differences. See my article 'Art, Genius, and Racial Theory in the Early Nineteenth Century: Benjamin Robert Haydon', *History Workshop Journal* 58, 2004, pp. 17–40.

19   For a detailed account of the Cartoon Competition of 1843, see T. S. R. Boase, 'The Decoration of the New Palace at Westminster, 1841–1863', *Journal of the Warburg and Courtauld Institutes* 17, 1954, pp. 319–58 (pp. 320–30).

20   Craske, *Art in Europe*, pp. 58–9.

21   'Haydon's Judgment of Solomon', *Examiner*, 1 May 1814, pp. 286–7.

22   'Fine Arts', *NMM*, July 1814, p. 560.

23   [John Scott], 'Exhibition of Painters in Oil and Water Colours', *Champion*, 1 May 1814, p. 141; 'Fine Arts', *Champion*, 18 June 1815, p. 197.

24   Colbert Kearney, 'B. R. Haydon and *The Examiner*', *Keats–Shelley Journal* 27, 1978, pp. 108–32 (p. 121).

25   'To the Critic of Barry's Works in the *Edinburgh Review*, Aug. 1810', *Examiner*, 25 January, pp. 61–4; 2 February, pp. 76–8; 9 February, pp. 92–6.

26   See George Allan Cate, 'Annals of the Fine Arts', in *BLM*, pp. 7–12; Ian Jack, *Keats and the Mirror of Art*, Oxford: Clarendon Press, 1967, chapter 3; Paul Magnuson, *Reading Public Romanticism*, Princeton, NJ: Princeton University Press, 1998, chapter 6.

27   Magnuson, *Reading Public Romanticism*, p. 168.

28   Hemingway, *Landscape Imagery and Urban Culture*, p. 139.

29   [James Elmes], *AFA*, vol. 1, p. 98. All other references to *AFA* are in the text.

30   Haydon's *The Assassination of Dentatus* was finished and exhibited in 1809, when the painter was twenty-three.

31   Haydon also published a similar fantasy by 'Somnabulus' entitled 'Old St. Paul's: a Vision of Futurity'; *AFA*, vol. 5, p. 326.

32   Carey, William, *Desultory Exposition of an Anti-British System of Incendiary Publication, & c.*, London: the author, 1819, p. 204. At the end of 1812, Haydon was still referring to the subject of his attacks as 'the Edingburgh [*sic*] reviewer'; *Diary*, vol. 1, p. 259.

33   *Blackwood's*, the *NMM*, the *John Bull* newspaper and *FM*.

34   'Z.' [John Gibson Lockhart], 'The Cockney School of Poetry No. I', *BEM*, October 1817, p. 40; 'On the Cockney School of Poetry No. IV', *BEM*, August 1818, p. 320; 'On the Cockney School of Poetry No. V', *BEM*, April 1819, p. 97; 'On the Cockney School of Poetry No. VI', *BEM*, October 1819, p. 72.

35   'Mr Haydon's Picture', *BEM*, November 1820, p. 219.

36   [J. J. Halls?], 'A Letter Concerning Haydon's Paintings', *BEM*, December 1821, p. 681.

37   'Fine Arts', *NMM*, August 1818, p. 70.

38   Carey, *Desultory Exposition*, pp. 74–5.

39   Ibid., pp. 61–2.

40   Carey deploys 'unitarian' to mean that the *Annals* set Haydon up as the only contemporary artist who deserved praise, but of course it also had political connotations. Carey, *Desultory Exposition*, p. 186.

41   Ibid., p. 186.

42   'W. C.' [William Carey], 'Fine Arts', *NMM*, February 1819, p. 52.

43   'W. C.' [William Carey], 'Observations on the "Annals of the Fine Arts"', *NMM*, March 1819, pp. 135–9; 'Historical Observations on Anti-British and Anti-Contemporarian Prejudices', *NMM*, April 1819, pp. 258–63; 'Defence of the British Institution', *NMM*, November 1819, pp. 466–9; 'Defence of the British Institution (concluded)', *NMM*, December 1819, pp. 557–64.

44   'Preface', *NMM*, 1819.

45   Haydon's association with the *Examiner* contributed to this, especially as the Hunts tended to link artistic and political reform to a greater extent than did the painter; Hemingway, *Landscape Imagery and Urban Culture*, p. 121.

46   'Fine Arts', *NMM*, July 1820, p. 77.

47   'Memoir of Benjamin Robert Haydon, esq.', *NMM*, December 1820, p. 605.

48 See, for example, 'Haydon's Picture', *Repository of Arts*, May 1820, p. 308; 'Fine Arts', *Literary Gazette*, 1 April 1820, p. 220.

49 [Robert Hunt], 'Mr. Haydon's Picture', *Examiner*, 7 May 1820, p. 300.

50 [John Scott], 'Notices of the Fine Arts No. V', *LM*, May 1820, p. 583.

51 Ibid., p. 584.

52 Ibid., pp. 584–5.

53 J. Landseer, 'To the Author of a Critique of Mr. Haydon's Picture', *Examiner*, 14 May 1820, pp. 317–18; 28 May, pp. 346–7; 4 June, p. 365.

54 [John Scott], 'The Lion's Head', *LM*, July 1820, p. 3; [John Scott] and B. R. Haydon, 'Mr. Haydon's Address to the Public', *LM*, August 1820, pp. 206–9.

55 Ibid., pp. 208–9.

56 'Farington's Life of Sir Joshua Reynolds', *CWH*, vol. 16, p. 209. First published in August 1820.

57 Haydon did influence Hazlitt for a short time; this is apparent in the latter's review of 'The Catalogue Raisonné of the British Institution', *Examiner*, 3 November 1816 (*CWH*, vol. 18, pp. 104–11).

58 'Lady Morgan's Life of Salvator', *CWH*, vol. 16, p. 288. First published in the *ER* in July 1824.

59 'On the Qualifications Necessary to Success in Life', *CWH*, vol. 12, p. 205.

60 'Haydon's "Christ's Agony in the Garden"', *CWH*, vol. 18, pp. 141–2. The review was first published in May 1821.

61 Ibid., p. 142.

62 Ibid., pp. 142–3.

63 *CWH*, vol. 11, p. 252.

64 *CWH*, vol. 20, pp. 391–2.

65 After the demise of the *Annals*, James Elmes moved back to his old employer, the *Monthly Magazine*, and continued to praise Haydon. He seems to have left the *Monthly* late in 1821.

66 [John Britton?], 'Haydon's Gallery', *Magazine of the Fine Arts*, 1821, p. 53; 'Remarks on Cotemporary [*sic*] Criticism', p. 164.

67 'Society of British Artists', *John Bull*, 15 May 1825, p. 158.

68 'Fine Arts', *Literary Gazette*, 15 December 1827, p. 811.

69 'Mr. Haydon's Pictures', *Gentleman's Magazine*, April 1832, p. 440.

70 [Probably William Maginn], 'Haydon's Reform Banquet', *FM*, June 1834, p. 702. This article is unassigned in the *Wellesley Index to Victorian Periodicals*, but the style is Maginnian, and the echoes of *Blackwood's* and the *John Bull* make his authorship seem likely.

71 As well as the two discussed above, see also 'Memoir of Mr. Haydon', *European Magazine*, November 1824, pp. 383–9.

72 [Probably Maginn], 'Haydon's Reform Banquet', p. 702.

73 For example, see his portrayal as the artist 'Daubson' in John Poole's 'Extract From a Journal Kept During a Residence in Little Pedlington', *NMM*, October 1835, pp. 177–81. Later published in *Little Pedlington and the Pedlingtonians*, 2 vols, London: Colburn, 1839, vol. 1, chapter 6.

74 George, *Life and Death*, chapter 20.

75 Brown, Woof and Hebron, *Benjamin Robert Haydon*, p. 172; William Feaver, '"At it Again": Aspects of Cruikshank's Later Work', in Robert L. Patten (ed.) *George Cruikshank: A Revaluation*, Princeton, NJ: Princeton University Press, 1974, pp. 249–58 (p. 251); Robert L. Patten, *George Cruikshank's Life, Times, and Art*, 2 vols, Cambridge, MA: The Luttoch Press, 1992–6, vol. 2, p. 196.

76 In his diary for 8 June 1843, Haydon wrote, 'one man brought a Cartoon 16 feet – a villainous thing. Eastlake said it could not be admitted as it exceeded by a foot in length. He, the Artist, immediately ordered the Carpenter to saw off a Foot! which he did! – & perhaps improved it' (*Diary*, vol. 5, p. 283).

77 Brown, Woof and Hebron, *Benjamin Robert Haydon*, p. 172.

78 [George Cruikshank], 'The Unexhibited Cartoon of Guy Fawkes', *Comic Almanack*, 1844, p. 31.

79 *CWH*, vol. 18, pp. 142–3; 'Michael Angelo Titmarsh' [William Thackeray], 'Picture Gossip', *FM*, June 1845, p. 715.

80 Cruikshank would emphasize the ridiculous elements of this giganticism a few months later when discussing the Cartoon Competition, suggesting that 'the fact that there was many a Cartoon which would have gone in, but that there was no getting it through the door' revealed an 'awful enlargement of the imagination' among artists, 'a species of Elephantiasis, inducing the idea that one's self and one's subject are much more vast than they are in reality'. [George Cruikshank], 'Critical Essay on the Prize Cartoons', *Comic Almanack*, 1844, p. 56.

81 [Cruikshank], 'The Unexhibited Cartoon', p. 32. Cruikshank is punning on three meanings of 'guy': to refer to Guy Fawkes; to describe 'a person of grotesque appearance'; and the verb meaning 'to make an object of ridicule' (although the *OED* gives the earliest use of this latter meaning as 1853).

82 Brown, Woof and Hebron, *Benjamin Robert Haydon*, p. 172.

83 Patten, *George Cruikshank*, vol. 2, p. 196. The two caricatures are also discussed briefly in Feaver, 'At It Again', pp. 251–2.

84 'Jupiter and the Mother: An Idyll', *Comic Almanack*, 1847, pp. 28–9.

85 *The Miscellaneous Works of Oliver Goldsmith*, ed. James Prior, 4 vols, London: John Murray, 1834, vol. 2, p. 181.

Conclusion

1 *The Diary of Benjamin Robert Haydon*, ed. Willard Bissell Pope, 5 vols, Cambridge, MA: Harvard University Press, 1960–3, vol. 5, p. 558.

2 Ibid., p. 265.

3 Ibid., vol. 4, p. 588.

4 Charles Dickens, *Bleak House*, ed. Stephen Gill, Oxford: Oxford University Press, 1998, p. 864. Alethea Hayter links Haydon and Skimpole in *A Sultry Month: Scenes of London Literary Life in 1846*, London: Faber and Faber, 1965, p. 171.

5 In thinking about this reaction I have found two books particularly useful: J. H. Buckley, *The Victorian Temper*, London: Frank Cass, 1966, and Philip Davis, *The Victorians*, Oxford: Oxford University Press, 2002.

6 John Stuart Mill, *On Liberty*, ed. Gertrude Himmelfarb, Harmondsworth: Penguin, 1985, p. 73. For a clear account of Mill and Comte, see Basil Willey, *Nineteenth-Century Studies*, Harmondsworth: Penguin, 1964, chapters 6 and 7.

7 Willey, *Nineteenth-Century Studies*, p. 167.

8 For the degeneration controversy, see especially Daniel Pick, *Faces of Degeneration: A European Disorder, c. 1848–c. 1918*, Cambridge: Cambridge University Press, 1989.

9 Friedrich Nietzsche, *Twilight of the Idols*, trans. Duncan Large, Oxford: Oxford University Press, 1998, p. 69.

10 Ibid.

11 See John Carey, *The Intellectuals and the Masses: Pride and Prejudice among the Literary Intelligentsia, 1880–1939*, London: Faber and Faber, 1992.

Bibliography

Primary sources: periodicals consulted

The Album
Annals of the Fine Arts
The Athenaeum
Bentley's Miscellany
Blackwood's Edinburgh Magazine
British Lady's Magazine
The Champion
Comic Almanack
Dublin Review
Edinburgh Review
European Magazine
The Examiner
Fraser's Magazine
Gazette of Fashion and Magazine of the Fine Arts and Belle Lettres
Gentleman's Magazine
Imperial Magazine
The John Bull
John Bull Magazine and Literary Recorder
The Literary Gazette
London Magazine (Baldwin's)
London Magazine (Gold's)
Metropolitan Quarterly Magazine
Monthly Magazine
Monthly Repository
New Monthly Magazine
Philomathic Journal and Literary Review
Quarterly Review
Repository of Arts
Spirit and Manners of the Age
Tait's Edinburgh Magazine
The Times
Westminster Review

Primary sources: books cited

Austen, Jane, *The Works of Jane Austen*, ed. R. W. Chapman, 6 vols, London: Oxford University Press, 1923–54.

Brydges, Sir Samuel Egerton, *An Impartial Portrait of Lord Byron, as a Poet and a Man*, Paris: Galignani, 1825.

—— *The Autobiography, Times, Opinions, and Contemporaries of Sir Samuel Egerton Brydges*, 2 vols, London: Cochrane and M'Crone, 1834.

Bulwer, Edward Lytton, *England and the English*, 2 vols, London: Richard Bentley, 1833.

—— *Paul Clifford*, London: George Routledge, 1896.

Burns, Robert, *The Poems and Songs of Robert Burns*, ed. James Kinsley, 3 vols, Oxford: Clarendon Press, 1968.

Byron, Lord George Gordon, *Byron's Letters and Journals*, ed. Leslie A. Marchand, 12 vols, London: John Murray, 1973–82.

—— and Moore, Thomas, *The Works of Lord Byron: With his Letters and Journals and his Life*, 17 vols, London: John Murray, 1833.

Carey, William, *Desultory Exposition of an Anti-British System of Incendiary Publication, & c.*, London: the author, 1819.

Carlyle, Thomas, *The Works of Thomas Carlyle*, ed. H. D. Traill, 30 vols, London: Chapman and Hall, 1896–9.

Coleridge, Samuel Taylor, *Collected Letters*, ed. Earl Leslie Grigg, 6 vols, Oxford: Clarendon Press, 1956–71.

—— *The Friend*, ed. Barbara E. Rooke, 2 vols, in *The Collected Works of Samuel Taylor Coleridge*, 4, ed. Kathleen Coburn, London: Routledge & Kegan Paul, 1969.

—— *Lay Sermons*, ed. R. J. White, in *The Collected Works of Samuel Taylor Coleridge*, 6, ed. Kathleen Coburn, London: Routledge & Kegan Paul, 1972.

—— *Essays on his Times in the 'Morning Post' and the 'Courier'*, ed. David Erdman, 3 vols, in *The Collected Works of Samuel Taylor Coleridge*, 3, ed. Kathleen Coburn, London: Routledge & Kegan Paul, 1978.

—— *Biographia Literaria*, ed. James Engell and Walter Jackson Bate, 2 vols, in *The Collected Works of Samuel Taylor Coleridge*, 7, ed. Kathleen Coburn, London: Routledge & Kegan Paul, 1983.

Cunningham, Allan, *Biographical and Critical History of the British Literature of the Last Fifty Years*, Paris: Baudry's Foreign Library, 1834.

De Quincey, Thomas, *The Works of Thomas De Quincey*, ed. Grevel Lindop, 21 vols, London: Pickering & Chatto, 2000–3.

Dickens, Charles, *Bleak House*, ed. Stephen Gill, Oxford: Oxford University Press, 1998.

D'Israeli, Isaac, *An Essay on the Manners and Genius of the Literary Character*, London: Cadell and Davies, 1795.

—— *Calamities of Authors*, 2 vols, London: John Murray, 1812.

—— *The Literary Character, Illustrated by the History of Men of Genius, Drawn from their own Feelings and Confessions*, London: John Murray, 1818.

—— *The Literary Character, Illustrated by the History of Men of Genius, Drawn from their own Feelings and Confessions*, London: John Murray, 1822.

Duff, William, *An Essay on Original Genius*, London: Edward and Charles Dilly, 1767.

Gerard, Alexander, *An Essay on Genius*, London: W. Strahan, 1774; repr. Munich: Wilhelm Fink, 1966.

Gilfillan, George, *A Gallery of Literary Portraits*, Edinburgh: William Tait, 1845.

Gillies, Richard Pearse, *Recollections of Sir Walter Scott, Bart.*, London: James Fraser, 1837.

Goldsmith, Oliver, *The Miscellaneous Works of Oliver Goldsmith*, ed. James Prior, 4 vols, London: John Murray, 1834.

Haydon, Benjamin Robert, *On Academies of Art, (More Particularly the Royal Academy), and their Pernicious Effect on the Genius of Europe*, London: Henry Hooper, 1839.

—— *Lectures on Painting and Design*, 2 vols, London: Longman, 1844–6.

—— *Correspondence and Table-Talk with a Memoir by his Son, Frederick Wordsworth Haydon*, 2 vols, London: Chatto & Windus, 1876.

—— *The Autobiography and Memoirs of Benjamin Robert Haydon*, ed. Aldous Huxley, 3 vols, London: Peter Davies, 1926.

—— *The Diary of Benjamin Robert Haydon*, ed. Willard Bissell Pope, 5 vols, Cambridge, MA: Harvard University Press, 1960–3.

Hazlitt, William, *The Complete Works of William Hazlitt*, ed. P. P. Howe, 21 vols, London: J. M. Dent & Sons, 1930–3.

Heraud, John Abraham, *Substance of a Lecture on Poetic Genius as a Moral Power*, London: James Fraser, 1837.

Hofland, Barbara, *The Son of a Genius: A Tale for the Use of Youth*, London: J. Harris, 1812.

—— *The Daughter of a Genius*, London: John Harris, 1823.

Hogg, Thomas Jefferson, *The Life of Percy Bysshe Shelley*, 2 vols, London: Edward Moxon, 1858.

[Horne, Richard Henry], *Exposition of the False Medium and Barriers Excluding Men of Genius from the Public*, London: Effingham Wilson, 1833.

—— (ed.) *A New Spirit of the Age*, London: Smith, Elder and Co., 1844.

Hunt, Leigh, *Lord Byron and Some of his Contemporaries*, London: Henry Colburn, 1828.

Ireland, W. H., *Neglected Genius*, London: George Cowie, 1812.

Johnson, Samuel, *Lives of the English Poets*, ed. George Birkbeck Hill, 3 vols, Oxford: Clarendon Press, 1905.

—— *The Yale Edition of the Complete Works of Samuel Johnson*, ed. Walter Jackson Bate and Albrecht B. Strauss, 16 vols, New Haven, CT: Yale University Press, 1969–89.

Low, Donald A. (ed.) *Robert Burns: The Critical Heritage*, London: Routledge & Kegan Paul, 1974.

Madden, R. R., *The Infirmities of Genius*, 2 vols, London: Saunders and Otley, 1833.

Mill, John Stuart, *Collected Works of John Stuart Mill*, ed. John M. Robson, 33 vols, Toronto: University of Toronto Press, 1981–91.

—— *On Liberty*, ed. Gertrude Himmelfarb, Harmondsworth: Penguin, 1985.

Milton, John, *Paradise Lost*, ed. Christopher Ricks, Harmondsworth: Penguin, 1989.

Morris, Peter [Lockhart, John Gibson], *Peter's Letters to his Kinsfolk*, 2nd edn, 3 vols, Edinburgh: William Blackwood, 1819.

Mullan, John, Hart, Chris and Swaab, Peter (eds) *Lives of the Great Romantics by their Contemporaries I*, 3 vols, London: Pickering and Chatto, 1996.

—— Wallace, Jennifer, Pite, Ralph and Robertson, Fiona (eds) *Lives of the Great Romantics by their Contemporaries II*, 3 vols, London: Pickering and Chatto, 1997.

[Napier, Macvey?], *Hypocrisy Unveiled and Calumny Detected in a Review of Blackwood's Magazine*, Edinburgh: Francis Pillans, 1818.

Nietzsche, Friedrich, *Twilight of the Idols*, trans. Duncan Large, Oxford: Oxford University Press, 1998.

Patmore, P. G., *My Friends and Acquaintance*, 3 vols, London: Saunders and Otley, 1854.

Peacock, Thomas Love, *The Halliford Edition of the Works of Thomas Love Peacock*, ed. H. F. B. Smith and C. E. Jones, 10 vols, London: Constable, 1924–34; repr. New York: AMS Press, 1967.

Poole, John, *Little Pedlington and the Pedlingtonians*, 2 vols, London: Henry Colburn, 1839.

Reynolds, Sir Joshua, *Discourses*, ed. Pat Rogers, Harmondsworth: Penguin, 1992.

Robinson, Henry Crabb, *Henry Crabb Robinson on Books and their Writers*, ed. Edith J. Morley, 3 vols, London: J. M. Dent & Sons, 1938.

Schiller, Friedrich, *The Robbers*, trans. Alexander Tytler, London: G. G. J. & J. Robinson, 1792; repr. Oxford: Woodstock Books, 1992.

Scott, Walter, *Ivanhoe*, ed. Graham Tulloch, Edinburgh: Edinburgh University Press, 1998.

Shakespeare, William, *The Riverside Shakespeare*, ed. G. Blakemore Evans, 2nd edn, Boston, MA: Houghton Mifflin, 1997.

Shelley, Percy Bysshe, *The Complete Works of Percy Bysshe Shelley*, ed. Roger Ingpen and Walter E. Peck, 10 vols, London: Ernest Benn, 1965.

—— *The Manuscripts of the Younger Romantics: Percy Bysshe Shelley*, ed. Donald H. Reiman, 3 vols, New York: Garland, 1985, vol. 2: *The Mask of Anarchy*.

—— *Poems and Prose*, ed. Timothy Webb, London: J. M. Dent, 1995.

Stones, Graeme and Strachan, John (eds) *Parodies of the Romantic Age*, 5 vols, London: Pickering and Chatto, 1998.

'Sylvaticus' [J. F. Pennie], *The Tale of a Modern Genius; or, the Miseries of Parnassus*, 3 vols, London: J. Andrews, 1827.

Thackeray, William Makepeace, *The History of Pendennis*, ed. John Sutherland, Oxford: Oxford University Press, 1999.

Willis, Nathaniel, *Pencillings by the Way*, London: T. Werner Laurie, 1942.

Wilson, John, *The Isle of Palms and Other Poems*, Edinburgh: Ballantyne, 1812.

Wordsworth, William, *Prose Works*, ed. W. J. B. Owen and Jane Worthington Smyser, 3 vols, Oxford: Clarendon Press, 1974.

—— and Wordsworth, Dorothy, *The Letters of William and Dorothy Wordsworth*, ed. Ernest de Selincourt, 2nd edn, rev. Mary Moorman and Alan G. Hill, 8 vols, Oxford: Clarendon Press, 1967–93.

Young, Edward, *Conjectures on Original Composition in a Letter to the Author of Sir Charles Grandison*, London: A. Miller, 1759.

Secondary sources: books and articles cited

Abrams, M. H., *The Mirror and the Lamp*, London: Oxford University Press, 1953.

—— 'Structure and Style in the Greater Romantic Lyric', in Harold Bloom (ed.) *Romanticism and Consciousness*, New York: Norton, 1970, pp. 201–29.

Albrecht, W. P., *Hazlitt and the Creative Imagination*, Laurence: The University of Kansas Press, 1965.

Alexander, J. H., '*Blackwood's*: Magazine as Romantic Form', *Wordsworth Circle* 15, 1984, pp. 57–68.

Allen, Peter, *The Cambridge Apostles: The Early Years*, Cambridge: Cambridge University Press, 1978.

Altick, Richard D., *The English Common Reader*, Chicago, IL: University of Chicago Press, 1963.

—— *Lives and Letters: A History of Literary Biography in England and America*, New York: Alfred A. Knopf, 1965.

—— *The Shows of London*, Cambridge, MA: Harvard University Press, 1978.

Armstrong, Isobel, *Victorian Poetry: Poetry, Poetics and Politics*, London: Routledge, 1993.

Ashton, Rosemary, *The German Idea: Four English Writers and the Reception of German Thought 1800–1860*, Cambridge: Cambridge University Press, 1980.

Bainbridge, Simon, *Napoleon and English Romanticism*, Cambridge: Cambridge University Press, 1995.

Barrell, John, *English Literature in History 1730–80: An Equal, Wide Survey*, London: Hutchinson, 1983.

—— *The Political Theory of Painting from Reynolds to Hazlitt*, New Haven, CT: Yale University Press, 1986.

—— 'Benjamin Robert Haydon: The Curtius of the Khyber Pass', in John Barrell (ed.) *Painting and the Politics of Culture*, Oxford: Oxford University Press, 1992, pp. 254–89.

Bate, Jonathan, *Shakespeare and the English Romantic Imagination*, Oxford: Clarendon Press, 1986.

—— *Shakespearean Constitutions: Politics, Theatre, Criticism 1730–1830*, Oxford: Clarendon Press, 1989.

—— *The Genius of Shakespeare*, London: Macmillan, 1997.

Bate, Walter Jackson, *John Keats*, Cambridge, MA: Harvard University Press, 1963.

Battersby, Christine, *Gender and Genius*, London: The Women's Press, 1989.

Becker, George, *The Mad Genius Controversy*, Beverly Hills, CA: Sage Publications, 1978.

Bénichou, Paul, *The Consecration of the Writer, 1750–1830*, trans. Mark K. Jensen, Lincoln, NE: University of Nebraska Press, 1999.

Bennett, Andrew, *Romantic Poets and the Culture of Posterity*, Cambridge: Cambridge University Press, 1999.

Blainey, Ann, *The Farthing Poet*, London: Longman, 1968.

Bloom, Harold (ed.) *Romanticism and Consciousness*, New York: Norton, 1970.

Boase, T. S. R., 'The Decoration of the New Palace at Westminster, 1841–1863', *Journal of the Warburg and Courtauld Institutes* 17, 1954, pp. 319–58.

Bourdieu, Pierre, 'Intellectual Field and Creative Project', trans. Sian France, in M. F. D. Young (ed.) *Knowledge and Control*, London: Collier-Macmillan, 1971, pp. 161–88.

—— *Distinction: A Social Critique of the Judgement of Taste*, trans. Richard Nice, Cambridge, MA: Harvard University Press, 1984.

—— *The Rules of Art*, trans. Susan Emanuel, Cambridge: Polity Press, 1992.

—— *The Field of Cultural Production*, ed. Randal Johnson, Cambridge: Polity Press, 1993.

Bradley, Arthur and Rawes, Alan (eds) *Romantic Biography*, Aldershot: Ashgate, 2003.

Braudy, Leo, *The Frenzy of Renown: Fame and its History*, New York: Vintage, 1997.

Bromwich, David, *Hazlitt: The Mind of a Critic*, 2nd edn, New Haven, CT: Yale University Press, 1999.

Brown, David Blayney, Woof, Robert and Hebron, Stephen, *Benjamin Robert Haydon: 1786–1846*, Kendal: The Wordsworth Trust, 1996.

Buckley, J. H., *The Victorian Temper*, London: Frank Cass, 1966.

Butler, Marilyn, 'Culture's medium: the role of the review', in Stuart Curran (ed.) *The Cambridge Companion to British Romanticism*, Cambridge: Cambridge University Press, 1993, pp. 124–47.

Cafarelli, Annette Wheeler, *Prose in the Age of Poets*, Philadelphia, PA: University of Philadelphia Press, 1990.

Camlot, Jason Evan, 'Character of the Periodical Press: John Stuart Mill and Junius Redivivus', *VPR* 32, 1999, pp. 166–76.

Carey, John, *The Intellectuals and the Masses: Pride and Prejudice among the Literary Intelligentsia, 1880–1939*, London: Faber and Faber, 1992.

Cate, George Allan, 'Annals of the Fine Arts', in Alvin Sullivan (ed.) *British Literary Magazines: The Romantic Age, 1789–1836*, Westport, CT: Greenwood Press, 1983, pp. 7–12.

Chew, Samuel, *Byron in England*, London: John Murray, 1924.

Chittick, Kathryn, *Dickens and the 1830s*, Cambridge: Cambridge University Press, 1990.

Clark, Timothy, *The Theory of Inspiration*, Manchester: Manchester University Press, 1997.

Clive, John, *Scotch Reviewers: The 'Edinburgh Review', 1802–1815*, London: Faber & Faber, 1957.

Cohen, B. Bernard, 'William Hazlitt: Bonapartist Critic of "The Excursion"', *MLQ* 10, 1949, pp. 158–67.

Connell, Philip, 'Bibliomania: Book Collecting, Cultural Politics, and the Rise of Literary Heritage in Romantic Britain', *Representations* 71, 2000, pp. 24–47.

—— *Romanticism, Economics and the Question of 'Culture'*, Oxford: Oxford University Press, 2001.

Cox, Jeffrey N., *Poetry and Politics in the Cockney School*, Cambridge: Cambridge University Press, 1998.

—— 'Leigh Hunt's Cockney School: The Lakers' "Other" ', *Romanticism on the Net* 14, 1999. Online available http://www.erudit.org/revue/ron/1999/v/n14/005859ar.html (accessed 6 July 2004).

Craske, Matthew, *Art in Europe: 1700–1830*, Oxford: Oxford University Press, 1997.

Crawford, Robert (ed.) *Robert Burns and Cultural Authority*, Edinburgh: Polygon, 1999.

Cronin, Richard, 'Shelley, Tennyson, and the Apostles, 1828–1832', *Keats–Shelley Review* 5, 1990, pp. 14–40.

—— *Romantic Victorians: English Literature, 1824–1840*, Basingstoke: Palgrave, 2002.

Cross, Ashley J., 'From Lyrical Ballads to Lyrical Tales: Mary Robinson's Reputation and the Problem of Literary Debt', *Studies in Romanticism* 40, 2001, pp. 571–605.

Cross, Nigel, *The Common Writer*, Cambridge: Cambridge University Press, 1985.

Cummings, Frederick, 'Nature and the Antique in B. R. Haydon's *Assassination of Dentatus*', *Journal of the Warburg and Courtauld Institutes* 23, 1962, pp. 147–57.

—— 'Poussin, Haydon, and "The Judgement of Solomon" ', *Burlington Magazine* 104, 1962, pp. 146–52.

Cunningham, Andrew and Jardine, Nicholas (eds) *Romanticism and the Sciences*, Cambridge: Cambridge University Press, 1990.

Currie, Robert, *Genius: An Ideology in Literature*, London: Chatto & Windus, 1974.

Dart, Gregory, *Rousseau, Robespierre and English Romanticism*, Cambridge: Cambridge University Press, 1999.

—— 'Hazlitt and Biography', *Cambridge Quarterly* 29, 2000, pp. 338–48.

Davidoff, Leonore and Hall, Catherine, *Family Fortunes: Men and Women of the English Middle Class, 1780–1850*, London: Routledge, 1992.

Davis, Philip, *The Victorians*, Oxford: Oxford University Press, 2002.

Dawson, Paul, *The Unacknowledged Legislator: Shelley and Politics*, Oxford: Clarendon Press, 1980.

De Groot, H. B., 'The Status of the Poet in the Age of Brass: Isaac D'Israeli, Peacock, W. J. Fox and Others', *Victorian Periodicals Newsletter* 10, 1977, pp. 106–22.

Demata, Massimiliano and Wu, Duncan (eds) *British Romanticism and the Edinburgh Review: Bicentenary Essays*, Basingstoke: Palgrave, 2002.

DeNora, Tia, *Beethoven and the Construction of Genius*, Berkeley, CA: University of California Press, 1995.

—— and Mehan, Hugh, 'Genius: A Social Construction: The Case of Beethoven's Initial Recognition', in Theodore Sarbin and John I. Kitsuse (eds) *Constructing the Social*, London: Sage Publications, 1994, pp. 157–73.

Dieckmann, Herbert, 'Diderot's Conception of Genius', *Journal of the History of Ideas* 2, 1941, pp. 151–82.

Duerksen, Roland A., *Shelleyan Ideas in Victorian Literature*, The Hague: Mouton, 1966.

Eagleton, Terry, *The Function of Criticism: From 'The Spectator' to Post-Structuralism*, London: Verso, 1984.

Elfenbein, Andrew, *Byron and the Victorians*, Cambridge: Cambridge University Press, 1995.

—— *Romantic Genius: The Prehistory of a Homosexual Role*, New York: Columbia University Press, 1999.

Elledge, W. Paul, 'The Liberal', in Alvin Sullivan (ed.) *British Literary Magazines: The Romantic Age, 1789–1836*, Westport, CT: Greenwood Press, 1983, pp. 220–7.

Elwin, Malcolm, *Victorian Wallflowers*, London: Jonathan Cape, 1934.

Engelberg, Karsten Klejs, *The Making of the Shelley Myth*, London: Mansell Publishing, 1988.

Engell, James, *The Creative Imagination*, Cambridge, MA: Harvard University Press, 1985.

Erickson, Lee, *The Economy of Literary Form: English Literature and the Industrialization of Publishing, 1800–1850*, Baltimore, MD: The John Hopkins University Press, 1996.

Everest, Kelvin (ed.) *Shelley Revalued: Essays from the Gregynog Conference*, Leicester: Leicester University Press, 1983.

Feaver, William, ' "At it Again": Aspects of Cruikshank's Later Work', in Robert L. Patten (ed.) *George Cruikshank: A Revaluation*, Princeton, NJ: Princeton University Press, 1974.

Ferris, Ina, *The Achievement of Literary Authority*, Ithaca, NY: Cornell University Press, 1991.

Fielding, K. J., 'Thackeray and the "Dignity of Literature" ', *Times Literary Supplement*, 19 September 1958, p. 536 and 26 September 1958, p. 552.

Fontana, Biancamaria, *Rethinking the Politics of Commercial Society: The 'Edinburgh Review' 1802–1832*, Cambridge: Cambridge University Press, 1985.

Forgan, Sophie (ed.) *Science and the Sons of Genius: Studies on Humphry Davy*, London: Science Reviews, 1980.

Fraistat, Neil, 'Illegitimate Shelley: Radical Piracy and the Textual Edition as Cultural Performance', *PMLA* 10, 1994, pp. 409–23.

George, Eric, *The Life and Death of Benjamin Robert Haydon*, 2nd edn, Oxford: Clarendon Press, 1967.

Gill, Stephen, *Wordsworth: A Life*, Oxford: Clarendon Press, 1989.

—— *Wordsworth and the Victorians*, Oxford: Clarendon Press, 1998.

Gilmartin, Kevin, *Print Politics: The Press and Radical Opposition in Early Nineteenth-Century England*, Cambridge: Cambridge University Press, 1996.

Golinski, Jan, *Science as Public Culture: Chemistry and Enlightenment in Britain, 1760–1820*, Cambridge: Cambridge University Press, 1992.

Gordon, Mary, *Christopher North: A Memoir of John Wilson*, 2nd edn, Edinburgh: Thomas C. Jack, 1879.

Grayling, A. C., *The Quarrel of the Age*, London: Weidenfield & Nicholson, 2000.

Gross, John, *The Rise and Fall of the Man of Letters*, Harmondsworth: Penguin, 1969.

Gross, Jonathan, 'Byron and *The Liberal*: Periodical as Political Posture', *Philological Quarterly* 72, 1993, pp. 471–85.

Habermas, Jurgen, *The Structural Transformation of the Public Sphere*, trans Thomas Burger, Cambridge: Polity Press, 1989.

Halévy, Elie, *The Liberal Awakening: 1815–1830*, trans. E. I. Watkin, 2nd edn, London: Ernest Benn, 1949.

Halkett, Samuel and Laing, John, *Dictionary of Anonymous and Pseudonymous English Literature*, new edn by James Kennedy, W. A. Smith and A. F. Johnson, 9 vols, Edinburgh: Oliver and Boyd, 1928.

Hall, Samuel Carter, *Retrospect of a Long Life: From 1815 to 1883*, 2 vols, London: Richard Bentley, 1883.

Hart, Francis R., *Lockhart as Romantic Biographer*, Edinburgh: Edinburgh University Press, 1971.

Hayden, John O., *The Romantic Reviewers 1802–1824*, London: Routledge & Kegan Paul, 1969.

Hayter, Alethea, *A Sultry Month: Scenes of London Literary Life in 1846*, London: Faber & Faber, 1965.

Hemingway, Andrew, 'Genius, Gender and Progress: Benthamism and the Arts in the 1820s', *Art History* 16, 1992, pp. 619–46.

—— *Landscape Imagery and Urban Culture in Early Nineteenth-Century Britain*, Cambridge: Cambridge University Press, 1992.

Heyck, T. W., *The Transformation of Intellectual Life in Victorian England*, London: Croom Helm, 1982.

Higgins, David, 'Art, Genius, and Racial Theory in the Early Nineteenth Century: Benjamin Robert Haydon', *History Workshop Journal* 58, 2004, pp. 17–40.

Hofkosh, Sonia, *Sexual Politics and the Romantic Author*, Cambridge: Cambridge University Press, 1998.

Hogsette, David S., 'Coleridge as Victorian Heirloom: Nostalgic Rhetoric in the Early Victorian Reviews of Poetical Works', *Studies in Romanticism* 37, 1998, pp. 63–75.

Holmes, Richard, *Shelley: The Pursuit*, Harmondsworth: Penguin, 1987.

Houghton, Walter E. (ed.) *The Wellesley Index to Victorian Periodicals, 1824–1900*, 5 vols, Toronto: University of Toronto Press, 1966–89.

Howe, Michael, *Genius Explained*, Cambridge: Cambridge University Press, 1999.

Howe, P. P., *The Life of William Hazlitt*, Harmondsworth: Penguin, 1949.

Hughes-Hallett, Penelope, *The Immortal Dinner*, London: Viking, 2000.

Jack, Ian, *Keats and the Mirror of Art*, Oxford: Clarendon Press, 1967.

Johnston, Kenneth R. and Ruoff, Gene W. (eds) *The Age of William Wordsworth*, New Brunswick, NJ: Rutgers University Press, 1987.

Jones, Stanley, 'First Flight: Image and Theme in a Hazlitt Essay', *Prose Studies* 8, 1985, pp. 35–47.

—— 'Three Additions to the Canon of Hazlitt's Political Writings', *Review of English Studies* n.s. 38, 1987, pp. 355–63.

——*Hazlitt: A Life*, Oxford: Clarendon Press, 1989.

Jordan, John E., *De Quincey to Wordsworth: A Biography of a Relationship*, Berkeley, CA: University of California Press, 1962.

Kearney, Colbert, 'The Writings of Benjamin Robert Haydon', unpublished doctoral thesis, University of Cambridge, 1972.

—— 'B. R. Haydon and the Examiner', *Keats–Shelley Journal* 27, 1978, pp. 108–32.

Kelsall, Malcolm, *Byron's Politics*, Sussex: The Harvester Press, 1987.

Kinnaird, John, *William Hazlitt: Critic of Power*, New York: Columbia University Press, 1978.

Klancher, Jon P., *The Making of English Reading Audiences, 1790–1832*, Madison, WI: The University of Wisconsin Press, 1987.

Kriz, Kay Dian, *The Idea of the English Landscape Painter*, New Haven, CT: Yale University Press, 1997.

Kucich, Greg, 'Gendering the Canons of Romanticism: Past and Present', *Wordsworth Circle* 27, 1996, pp. 95–102.

Lapp, Robert Keith, *Contest for Cultural Authority: Hazlitt, Coleridge, and the Distresses of the Regency*, Detroit, MI: Wayne State University Press, 1999.

—— 'Romanticism Repackaged: The New Faces of "Old Man" Coleridge in *Fraser's Magazine*, 1830–35', *European Romantic Review* 11, 2000, pp. 235–47.

Latané, David E., 'The Birth of the Author in the Victorian Archive', *VPR* 22, 1989, pp. 109–17.

Leary, Patrick, '*Fraser's Magazine* and the Literary Life 1830–1847', *VPR* 27, 1994, pp. 105–26.

Leighton, Angela, *Victorian Women Poets: Writing Against the Heart*, Hemel Hempstead: Harvester Wheatsheaf, 1992.

Levere, Trevor H., 'Humphry Davy, "The Sons of Genius", and the Idea of Glory', in Sophie Forgan (ed.) *Science and the Sons of Genius: Studies on Humphry Davy*, London: Science Reviews, 1980.

Lindop, Grevel, *The Opium Eater: A Life of Thomas De Quincey*, Oxford: Oxford University Press, 1985.

Lund, Michael, *Reading Thackeray*, Detroit, MI: Wayne State University Press, 1988.

McCalman, Iain (ed.) *An Oxford Companion to the Romantic Age*, Oxford: Oxford University Press, 1999.

McGann, Jerome J., *The Romantic Ideology: A Critical Investigation*, Chicago, IL: The University of Chicago Press, 1983.

Magnuson, Paul, *Reading Public Romanticism*, Princeton, NJ: Princeton University Press, 1998.

Mahoney, Charles, *Romantics and Renegades: The Poetics of Political Reaction*, Basingstoke: Palgrave Macmillan, 2003.

Mahoney, John L., *Wordsworth and the Critics*, Rochester, NY: Camden House, 2001.

Mandell, Laura, *Romantic Canons: A Bibliography and an Argument*, 1998. Online available http://www.orgs.muohio.edu/anthologies/canon.htm (accessed 6 July 2004).

Marchand, Leslie A., *Byron: A Biography*, 3 vols, New York: Alfred A. Knopf, 1957.

—— *The Athenaeum: A Mirror of Victorian Culture*, New York: Octagon Books, 1971.

Marshall, William H., *Byron, Shelley, Hunt, and 'The Liberal'*, Philadelphia, PA: University of Pennsylvania Press, 1960.

Mellor, Anne K., *Romanticism and Gender*, London: Routledge, 1993.

Mineka, Francis E., *The Dissidence of Dissent*, New York: Octagon Books, 1972.

Moi, Toril, 'The Challenge of the Particular Case: Bourdieu's Sociology of Culture and Literary Criticism', *MLQ* 58, 1997, pp. 497–508.

Moorman, Mary, *William Wordsworth: A Biography*, 2 vols, Oxford: Clarendon Press, 1957–65.

Morgan, Peter F., *Literary Critics and Reviewers in Early Nineteenth-Century Britain*, London: Croom Helm, 1983.

Morrison, Robert, 'De Quincey, Champion of Shelley', *Keats–Shelley Journal* 41, 1992, pp. 36–41.

—— 'Opium-Eaters and Magazine Wars: De Quincey and Coleridge in 1821', *VPR* 30, 1997, pp. 27–40.

—— 'Red De Quincey', *Wordsworth Circle* 29, 1998, pp. 131–6.

—— 'John Wilson and the Editorship of *Blackwood's Magazine*', *Notes and Queries* n.s. 46, 1999, pp. 48–50.

—— '*Blackwood's* Berserker: John Wilson and the Language of Extremity', *Romanticism on the Net* 20, 2000. Online available http://www.erudit.org/revue/ron/2000/v/n20/005951ar.html (accessed 6 July 2004).

—— ' "Abuse Wickedness, but Acknowledge Wit": *Blackwood's* and the Shelley Circle', *VPR* 34, 2001, pp. 147–64.

Mulvihill, James, 'Character and Culture in Hazlitt's *Spirit of the Age*', *Nineteenth-Century Literature* 45, 1990, pp. 281–99.

—— 'Visions and Revisions: William Hazlitt and "My First Acquaintance with Poets"', *Charles Lamb Bulletin* 109, 2000, pp. 11–14.

Murphy, Peter T., 'Impersonation and Authorship in Romantic Britain', *English Literary History* 59, 1992, pp. 625–49.

Murray, Penelope (ed.) *Genius: The History of an Idea*, Oxford: Basil Blackwell, 1989.

Natarajan, Uttara, *Hazlitt and the Reach of Sense*, Oxford: Clarendon Press, 1998.

Newlyn, Lucy, *Paradise Lost and the Romantic Reader*, Oxford: Oxford University Press, 1993.

—— *Reading, Writing, and Romanticism: The Anxiety of Reception*, Oxford: Oxford University Press, 2000.

Newman, Rebecca Edwards, ' "Prosecuting the Onus Criminus": Early Criticism of the Novel in *Fraser's Magazine*', *VPR* 35, 2002, pp. 401–19.

North, Julian, 'Self-Possession and Gender in Romantic Biography', in Arthur Bradley and Alan Rawes (eds) *Romantic Biography*, Aldershot: Ashgate, 2003, pp. 109–38.

Ogden, James, *Isaac D'Israeli*, Oxford: Clarendon Press, 1969.

O'Leary, Patrick, *Regency Editor: The Life of John Scott*, Aberdeen: Aberdeen University Press, 1983.

Oliphant, Margaret, *Annals of a Publishing House: William Blackwood and his Sons*, 3 vols, Edinburgh: William Blackwood, 1899.

Olney, Clarke, *Benjamin Robert Haydon: Historical Painter*, Athens, GA: The University of Georgia Press, 1952.

Owen, W. J. B., 'Costs, Sales, and Profits of Longman's Editions of Wordsworth', *The Library* n.s. 12, 1956, pp. 93–107.

Parker, Mark, *Literary Magazines and British Romanticism*, Cambridge: Cambridge University Press, 2000.

Pascal, Roy, *The German Sturm und Drang*, Manchester: Manchester University Press, 1953.

Patten, Robert L. (ed.) *George Cruikshank: A Revaluation*, Princeton, NJ: Princeton University Press, 1974.

——*George Cruikshank's Life, Times, and Art*, 2 vols, Cambridge, MA: The Luttoch Press, 1992–6.

Paulin, Tom, *The Day-Star of Liberty: William Hazlitt's Radical Style*, London: Faber & Faber, 1998.

Pfau, Thomas, *Wordsworth's Profession*, Stanford, CA: Stanford University Press, 1997.

Prickett, Stephen, *Romanticism and Religion: The Tradition of Wordsworth and Coleridge in the Victorian Church*, Cambridge: Cambridge University Press, 1976.

Ray, Gordon N., *Thackeray: The Age of Wisdom: 1847–1863*, London: Oxford University Press, 1958.

Raysor, Thomas M., 'The Establishment of Wordsworth's Reputation', *Journal of English and German Philology* 54, 1955, pp. 61–71.

Reed, Joseph, *English Biography in the Early Nineteenth Century: 1801–1838*, New Haven, CT: Yale University Press, 1966.

Robinson, Charles E., 'Percy Bysshe Shelley, Charles Ollier, and William Blackwood: The Contexts of Early Nineteenth-Century Publishing', in Kelvin Everest (ed.) *Shelley Revalued: Essays from the Gregynog Conference*, Leicester: Leicester University Press, 1983, pp. 183–226.

Robinson, Jeffrey C., 'Hazlitt's "My First Acquaintance with Poets": The Autobiography of a Cultural Critic', *Romanticism* 6, 2000, pp. 178–84.

Roe, Nicholas, *John Keats and the Culture of Dissent*, Oxford: Clarendon Press, 1997.

Roper, Derek, *Reviewing Before the 'Edinburgh': 1788–1802*, London: Metheun, 1978.

Rose, Mark, *Authors and Owners: The Invention of Copyright*, Cambridge, MA: Harvard University Press, 1993.

Ross, Marlon B., *The Contours of Masculine Desire: Romanticism and the Rise of Women's Poetry*, New York: Oxford University Press, 1989.

Royle, Edward and Walvin, James, *English Radicals and Reformers, 1760–1848*, Kentucky, KY: The University Press of Kentucky, 1982.

Ruddick, Bill, 'Recollecting Coleridge: The Internalization of Radical Energies in Hazlitt's Political Prose', *Yearbook of English Studies* 19, 1989, pp. 243–55.

Russett, Margaret, *De Quincey's Romanticism*, Cambridge: Cambridge University Press, 1997.

Ryan, Robert M., *The Romantic Reformation: Religious Politics in English Literature, 1789–1824*, Cambridge: Cambridge University Press, 1997.

Sadleir, Michael, *Bulwer and His Wife: A Panorama*, London: Constable, 1931.

——*Blessington-D'Orsay: A Masquerade*, London: Constable, 1933.

Sarbin, Theodore and Kitsuse, John I. (eds) *Constructing the Social*, London: Sage Publications, 1994.

Schacterle, Lance, 'The British Magazine', in Alvin Sullivan (ed.) *British Literary Magazines: The Romantic Age, 1789–1836*, Westport, CT: Greenwood Press, 1983, pp. 66–8.

Schaffer, Simon, 'Genius in Romantic Natural Philosophy', in Andrew Cunningham and Nicholas Jardine (eds) *Romanticism and the Sciences*, Cambridge: Cambridge University Press, 1990, pp. 82–98.

Schoenfield, Mark, *The Professional Wordsworth*, Athens, GA: University of Georgia Press, 1996.

Sewter, A. C., 'A Revaluation of Haydon', *Art Quarterly* 5, 1942, pp. 323–37.

Shaaban, Bouthaina, 'Shelley in the Chartist Press', *Keats–Shelley Memorial Bulletin* 34, 1983, pp. 41–60.

Shattock, Joanne, *Politics and Reviewers: The 'Edinburgh' and the 'Quarterly' in the Early Victorian Age*, London: Leicester University Press, 1989.

Shine, Hill and Shine, Helen, *The Quarterly Review under Gifford*, Chapel Hill, NC: The University of North Carolina Press, 1949.

Siegel, Jonah, *Desire and Excess: The Nineteenth-Century Culture of Art*, Princeton, NJ: Princeton University Press, 2000.

Smiles, Samuel, *A Publisher and his Friends: Memoirs and Correspondence of the Late John Murray*, 2 vols, London: John Murray, 1891.

Spurgeon, Dickie A., 'The Edinburgh Review', in Alvin Sullivan (ed.) *British Literary Magazines: The Romantic Age. 1789–1836*, Westport, CT: Greenwood Press, 1983, pp. 139–44.

Stephenson, Glennis, *Letitia Landon: The Woman Behind L.E.L.*, Manchester: Manchester University Press, 1995.

Story, Patrick, 'Hazlitt's Definition of the Spirit of the Age', *Wordsworth Circle* 6, 1975, pp. 97–108.

—— 'Emblems of Infirmity: Contemporary Portraits in Hazlitt's *The Spirit of the Age*', *Wordsworth Circle* 10, 1979, pp. 81–90.

Strout, Alan Lang, '*Maga*, Champion of Shelley', *Studies in Philology* 29, 1932, pp. 95–119.

—— 'Samuel Taylor Coleridge and John Wilson of *Blackwood's Magazine*', *PMLA* 48, 1933, pp. 100–28.

—— 'John Wilson, "Champion" of Wordsworth', *Modern Philology* 31, 1934, pp. 383–94.

—— 'William Wordsworth and John Wilson: A Review of their Relations between 1802 and 1817', *PMLA* 49, 1934, pp. 143–83.

—— 'Hunt, Hazlitt, and *Maga*', *ELH* 4, 1937, pp. 151–9.

—— 'Lockhart, Champion of Shelley', *Times Literary Supplement*, 12 August 1955, p. 468.

—— *A Bibliography of Articles in 'Blackwood's Magazine'*, Lubbock: The Texas Tech Press, 1959.

Sullivan, Alvin (ed.) *British Literary Magazines: The Romantic Age, 1789–1836*, Westport, CT: Greenwood Press, 1983.

Swann, Elsie, *Christopher North*, Edinburgh: Oliver and Boyd, 1934.

Sweet, Nanora, 'The *New Monthly Magazine* and the Liberalism of the 1820's', *Prose Studies* 25, 2002, pp. 147–62.

Symonds, Barry, '"Do not suppose that I am underwriting myself": The Labyrinth of De Quincey's Manuscripts', *Wordsworth Circle* 29, 1998, pp. 137–40.

Tenger, Zeynep and Trolander, Paul, 'Genius versus Capital: Eighteenth-Century Theories of Genius and Adam Smith's *Wealth of Nations*', *MLQ* 55, 1994, pp. 169–89.

Thorslev, Peter L., 'Post-Waterloo Liberalism: The Second Generation', *Studies in Romanticism* 28, 1989, pp. 437–61.

Thrall, Miriam J., *Rebellious Fraser's*, New York: Columbia University Press, 1934.

Tonelli, Giorgio, 'Genius from the Renaissance to 1770', in Philip P. Wiener (ed.) *The Dictionary of the History of Ideas*, New York: Charles Scribner's Sons, 1973, pp. 293–7.

Tuite, Clara, 'Domesticity', in Iain McCalman (ed.) *An Oxford Companion to the Romantic Age*, Oxford: Oxford University Press, 1999, pp. 125–33.

Van Dann, J., 'Fraser's Magazine', in Alvin Sullivan (ed.) *British Literary Magazines: The Romantic Age, 1789–1836*, Westport, CT: Greenwood Press, 1983, pp. 171–5.

Wallins, Roger P., 'The Quarterly Review', in Alvin Sullivan (ed.) *British Literary Magazines: The Romantic Age, 1789–1836*, Westport, CT: Greenwood Press, 1983, pp. 359–67.

Ward, William S., 'Wordsworth, the "Lake" Poets, and their Contemporary Magazine Critics, 1798–1820', *Studies in Philology* 42, 1945, pp. 87–113.

Weinstein, Mark A., 'Tait's Edinburgh Magazine', in Alvin Sullivan (ed.) *British Literary Magazines: The Romantic Age, 1789–1836*, Westport, CT: Greenwood Press, 1983, pp. 401–5.

Whale, John, *Imagination under Pressure, 1789–1832*, Cambridge: Cambridge University Press, 2000.

Wheatley, Kim, 'The *Blackwood's* Attacks on Leigh Hunt', *Nineteenth-Century Literature* 47, 1992, pp. 1–37.

——*Shelley and his Readers: Beyond Paranoid Politics*, Columbia, MO: University of Missouri Press, 1999.

Wiener, Philip P. (ed.) *The Dictionary of the History of Ideas*, New York: Charles Scribner's Sons, 1973.

Willey, Basil, *Nineteenth-Century Studies*, Harmondsworth: Penguin, 1964.

Williams, Raymond, *Keywords*, 2nd edn, London: Fontana Press, 1983.

——*Culture and Society*, London: The Hogarth Press, 1993.

Wittkower, Rudolf, 'Genius: Individualism in Art and Artists', in Philip P. Wiener (ed.) *The Dictionary of the History of Ideas*, New York: Charles Scribner's Sons, 1973, pp. 297–312.

Woodmansee, Martha, 'The Genius and the Copyright: Economic and Legal Conditions of the Emergence of the Author', *Eighteenth-Century Studies* 17, 1984, pp. 425–48.

Woodring, Carl, 'Wordsworth and the Victorians', in Kenneth R. Johnston and Gene W. Ruoff (eds) *The Age of William Wordworth*, New Brunswick, NJ: Rutgers University Press, 1987, pp. 261–75.

Young, M. F. D. (ed.) *Knowledge and Control*, London: Collier-Macmillan, 1971.

Index